Ethical Issues Relating to Life and Death

Ethical Issues Relating to Life and Death

Edited by JOHN LADD

Professor of Philosophy   Brown University

New York • Oxford
OXFORD UNIVERSITY PRESS
1979

Copyright © 1979 by Oxford University Press, Inc.

Library of Congress Cataloging in Publication Data

Main entry under title:
Ethical issues relating to life and death.

   Bibliography: p.
   Includes index.
   1. Euthanasia.   2. Right to die.
3. Life and death, Power over.
I. Ladd, John, 1917-
R726.E775   174'.24   79-726
ISBN 0-19-502543-1   ISBN 0-19-502544-X pbk.

Printed in the United States of America

Preface

The purpose of this book is to provide a theoretical discussion of ethical issues connected with euthanasia. The papers that form the core of the book were presented at a small conference held at Brown University in February, 1974. All the authors, except Foot and Rachels, were participants at the conference, which was designed to explore some of the philosophical problems raised by recent advances in medical science and technology.

The original papers have been extensively revised and a few other chapters have been added, including the essays by Foot and Rachels; the chapter by Rachels is the original, longer essay of which the well-known article in the *New England Journal of Medicine* is an abridgment. With the exception of the chapter by Philippa Foot, all the chapters in this book are new and original.

As might be expected from philosophers, the essays in this collection represent a variety of different points of view and approaches. The common assumption underlying all of them, however, is that the issues, however complicated and controversial they may be, are susceptible to rational investigation and are not to be decided on the basis of blind faith or emotion. In this vein, it is hoped that the book as a whole will make a contribution to a better understanding of the many complex ethical problems that our society faces in making decisions about life and death in the medical context.

I wish to thank the Committee on Biomedical Ethics of Brown University, which sponsored the original conference, and the Ittleson Foundation, which provided financial support for the conference, for the impetus that gave rise to this book. I also want to thank the authors for their contributions to it.

I am especially grateful to Jeffrey House of the Oxford University Press for his help in preparing the manuscript. The book is much more readable than it would have been without his detailed editorial advice and assistance.

J. L.

Brown University
January 1979

Contents

Contributors

John Ladd is professor of philosophy, Brown University. He is author of *The Structure of a Moral Code* (1957), translator and editor of Kant's *Metaphysical Elements of Justice* (1965), and editor of *Ethical Relativism* (1973). He is chairman of the Committee on Philosophy and Medicine of the American Philosophical Association and President of the American Society for Political and Legal Philosophy.

Philippa Foot is professor in residence in the Department of Philosophy, University of California, Los Angeles, and Senior Research Fellow, Somerville College, Oxford. She is author of *Virtues and Vices and Other Essays in Moral Philosophy* (1979) and editor of *Theories of Ethics* (1967).

Peter Singer is professor of philosophy, Monash University, Australia. He was visiting professor at New York University, 1972–73, and Radcliffe lecturer in philosophy, University College, Oxford, 1971–73. He is author of *Democracy and Disobedience* (1974), *Animal Liberation* (1975), and editor, with Tom Regan, of *Animal Rights and Human Obligations* (1976). He has articles in philosophical journals, the *New York Times Magazine,* and the *New York Review of Books.*

Michael Tooley is Social Science Research Fellow at the Australian National University, Canberra, Australia. Before going to Australia, he was assistant professor of philosophy, Stanford University. Among his writings, his article "Abortion and Infanticide" has been widely read and discussed.

Dan W. Brock is associate professor of philosophy, Brown University. He has written articles in ethics and political philosophy. He is chairman of the Committee on Bio-Medical Ethics, Brown University.

James Rachels is professor of philosophy, University of Alabama at Birmingham. He is editor of *Moral Problems: A Collection of Philosophical Essays,* 3rd ed. (1979); *Understanding Philosophy* (1976), and with Frank Tillman, *Philosophical Issues* (1972).

Raymond S. Duff, M.D., is professor of pediatrics, Yale Medical School. He is coauthor with August B. Hollingshead of *Sickness and Society* (1968). His article, coauthored with A.G.M. Campbell on "Moral and ethical dilemmas in the special care nursery," published in the *New England Journal of Medicine* (1973) has provoked widespread discussion.

Ethical Issues Relating to Life and Death

1 Introduction

JOHN LADD

The subject of this book might, in a broad sense, be called "euthanasia." In the popular mind, euthanasia is something that one must be either for or against. But as soon as we ask, What is euthanasia? we encounter a welter of confusing and conflicting answers and discover that euthanasia is a very complicated as well as controversial ethical subject. The purpose of this book is to explore some of these complications and to try to identify the pertinent ethical issues relating to euthanasia. Perhaps the easiest way to begin is with a brief review of various meanings of the word.

The original meaning of "euthanasia" derived from the Greek *eu,* meaning "good," and *thanasia,* meaning "death." Early uses of the word in English contrast euthanasia, meaning a good, quiet and gentle death, with a death that is violent or tortured.[1] More recently, it has come to mean "the action of inducing a gentle and easy death,"[2] which in turn has been taken by many to mean "mercy killing" or some other kind of act, usually of doctors, that hastens a person's death. Nowadays, more often than not the term "euthanasia" is used pejoratively, to designate acts of a kind that are usually thought to be impermissible, e.g. immoral or illegal homicide.[3]

The shift in meaning is instructive. Originally, "euthanasia" referred to the manner of *dying* rather than to the action of another party aimed at bringing about or permitting a person's death. In contrast to verbs like "to kill," "to die" is intransitive and therefore strictly speaking has as its grammatical subject only the person who dies and does not have a grammatical object at all. The term's original meaning, therefore, did not include the notion of committing an act of euthanasia on another person.

Why, one might ask, did the intransitive notion of dying gently develop into the transitive notion of one person's acting on another by killing or letting him die? And why did the word change from meaning something unquestionably good to meaning something bad or at least something whose moral status is a matter of dispute? It is interesting to speculate about possible reasons for this metamorphosis.

To begin with, the Western notion of dying, what it means and how it is done, has obviously undergone a radical transformation since the eighteenth century, when "euthanasia" was still used in its original meaning. Present-day notions of death are the result of revolutionary changes in medicine as well as in life-style; for example, the common causes of death are now quite different from what they were two hundred years ago. Today, accidents, homicide and suicide are the principal causes of death among young people, and chronic diseases are the principal causes of death among the old. Furthermore, it is now highly probable that when a person dies, his death will be either sudden and unexpected, as in an accident, or else long and drawn out, with pain and mental or physical deterioration. In the latter case, more than likely it will be in a hospital bed rather than at home.[4] An eighteenth century death, on the other hand, was likely to be caused by an infectious disease and so by comparison was not as unexpected or drawn out. It was more often possible then to die "gently" and "quietly" in one's own bed, surrounded by family and friends.[5]

What was once considered to be a good death is now a highly improbable occurrence. Hence, it is no wonder that when asked about what kind of death they would prefer, most people nowadays say that they want to die without any prior warning—as in an accident; what they fear most is dying alone in a strange hospital hooked up by tubes to machines and other devices. What I am suggesting, therefore, is that according to present conceptions or misconceptions, the only way left for a person to die in euthanasia is to be killed somehow. Consequently, we have developed a new notion of euthanasia, one that is obviously quite at variance with the original concept.

It is a great mistake, however, to assume that the only alternatives are dying through being killed (directly or indirectly) or dying through a long terminal illness involving suffering, debilitation and loss of human dignity. To do so inevitably puts the problem of euthanasia in the wrong light; it makes it merely a matter of killing. Accordingly, we lose sight of the basic ethical problem: What should we do about dying in our society? How can we make dying more gentle and humane, less violent and catastrophic?

In order to focus our attention on this more basic problem, perhaps it would be better to dispense with the word *euthanasia* and use in its stead the opposite, *cacothanasia,* an ugly, violent and tortured death. What we should be concerned with, I suggest, is how to avoid cacothanasia.[6] If we think of our problem in this light, as a problem of cacothanasia rather than of euthanasia, we may be able to put the discussion of the ethics of life and death back on the track, for it is the threat and reality of cacothanasia that is clearly uppermost in people's minds.

The problem of cacothanasia has particular urgency for present-day society because medical technology has perfected the means of prolonging biological life far beyond what was thought possible even a short while ago. At the same time, it has not been able to find cures for many of the chronic diseases that would quickly lead to death were it not for this life-prolonging technology. To make matters worse, our society and its health care system have failed to provide a satisfactory and humane way of caring for the incurable.[7]

All these developments have placed modern medicine in a bind: the availability of new technology makes using it to prolong life almost irresistible. Not only does the prolongation of life appear to accord with the traditional ethos of the physician, but external pressures, such as those exerted by hospital administrations and other kinds of bureaucracies, make it difficult if not impossible for individual physicians and others making the decisions to refrain from using this technology, even when they think it wrong to do so.[8] Furthermore, hovering over any decision not to employ life-prolonging technology is what Justice Hughes aptly called "the brooding presence of medical liability."[9] All these social and legal factors encourage and reinforce the frequently ill-advised and indiscriminate use of life-saving equipment such as respirators to keep people alive. Perhaps an even more critical factor in delaying death has been the development of drugs to control infectious diseases. As a result of this development, pneumonia, which used to be nature's way of bringing a quick death to persons dying slowly of other diseases and was therefore called "the old man's friend," can no longer play that role. For example, hospital regulations require that any patient in an intensive care unit who contracts pneumonia must be automatically treated for it; persons who are in comas or who are otherwise chronically ill are watched carefully and treated immediately for any infection they contract. In sum, what Dr. William Osler said about death at the beginning of this century no longer obtains:

There is truth in the paradoxical statement that persons rarely die of the disease with which they suffer. Secondary terminal infections carry off m⁻ ny patients with incurable disease.[10]

What has happened is that modern medicine has eliminated a traditional way of dying and has nothing to offer in its stead. As a result, our society is now confronted with a number of comparatively new moral predicaments involving severe chronic disease and death that urgently call for reflective discussion and critical analysis by moral philosophers and physicians. By a "predicament" I mean "an unpleasant, trying or dangerous situation,"[11] in this case a situation in which the termination of life-prolonging treatment or even the termination of life must be taken seriously as a "genuine option" (to use William James's term).[12] There are at least four different kinds of situation that present ethical predicaments in this sense:

Predicament 1: Coma cases like the Quinlan case, where the definition of death in terms of total brain death does not apply, but there is an irreversible coma and no prospect of recovering any higher brain functions; cases like these often include dependence on a respirator and other equipment for survival. Elderly persons suffering from extreme senile brain disease might also be included under this category. The obvious question is, How much effort, if any, should be made to keep these bodies alive and why should one try? In this connection, it should be observed that there are different kinds and amounts of brain damage which, in the view of some, result in essentially different moral implications for action.

Predicament 2: Chronically ill patients suffering, say, from terminal cancer. Unlike predicament 1, however, a person in this situation is unquestionably mentally competent—by lay standards, at least. The chief factors are suffering, progressive deterioration, physical incapacity, and a terminal illness. Does such a person have a right to die, if he so chooses? Should we allow him to die "in dignity"?

Predicament 3: Accident victims who have lost almost all capacity to function independently, including those who are completely paralyzed or entirely dependent on machines for survival. Again, unlike predicament 1, persons in this category are mentally competent but unlike predicament 2, their cases are not terminal.[13] If they want to die, should they be allowed to do so? Why? and How?

Predicament 4: New-born infants with incurable and uncorrectable genetic defects of great severity; many of these cases are terminal in the sense that the infants in question are unlikely to survive more than a year or two. In the meantime, they are doomed to a life of hopeless suffering and incapacity.[14] We may not wish to include here children afflicted with Down's syndrome (mongolism), since the life of a retarded person is usually not one of "hopeless suffering and incapacity." At least, they represent borderline cases. It might not be right, therefore, to include under category 4 a case like the Johns Hopkins case, the case in which an infant with Down's syndrome who also had an operable duodenal atresia was allowed to die without being operated on. (This case is discussed in other chapters of this book. It is the subject of the Kennedy Foundation film *Who Should Survive?*)

It should be obvious from this list of predicaments that the issues surrounding the termination or prolongation of life are not only complicated and novel, but they arise in a large variety of situations. Moral answers to each of these predicaments hinge on quite different kinds of moral consideration and consequently call for quite different lines of inquiry. The fourfold descriptive categorization that I have presented is itself crude and artificial; most cases that demand our attention involve a tangle of different factors that, when considered all together, make each individual case unique and peculiarly tragic. The ethically relevant factors are so diverse that a simple theory of euthanasia, a "philosopher's stone," for solving every ethical problem in which death is an option is utterly out of the question. One cannot say, for example, that an effort ought always to be made to prolong a person's life or, on the other hand, that if a person's life has lost its quality it is right to terminate it. Each predicament must be dealt with in terms of its own particular context.

The complexity of these issues is recognized in some commonly accepted distinctions between types of "euthanasia." Because these distinctions are so frequently cited in discussions of euthanasia, it may be worthwhile to discuss them briefly here. However, I should point out that the distinctions are by no means universally accepted; indeed, they are repudiated by many philosophers.

The first distinction is between *voluntary* and *involuntary* euthanasia. Euthanasia, in the sense of bringing on a person's death, is voluntary if the person himself requests it or in some other way indicates his assent. It is obvious that in order to consent to his death the person in question must be conscious and mentally competent. When applied to persons who are in a coma or who are mentally incompetent in some other way, euthanasia is said, in contrast, to be involuntary. To call it *in*voluntary is misleading, however, since the word may mean either *against* a person's will or *without* a person's will. Following Aristotle, philosophers are accustomed to distinguish between these two meanings, reserving the term "involuntary" for the former and using the term "nonvoluntary" for the latter. In this sense of "involuntary," a person must be conscious and competent if something done to him is to be considered involuntary; rape is something that is involuntary in this sense.

Several chapters in this book refer to the distinction between voluntary and involuntary euthanasia. It is not uncommon to find moralists arguing that voluntary, in contrast to involuntary (nonvoluntary), euthanasia is permissible on the grounds that a person cannot be injured by something to which he consents (*volenti non fit iniuria*). Just how and when a person must consent to euthanasia to make it justifiable raises other questions, e.g. questions about the validity of so-called "Living Wills." It is obvious that questions about the morality of voluntary euthanasia are, in important respects, similar to questions about the morality of suicide. If you believe that a person has the right to commit suicide then you will have little difficulty in admitting the rightness of voluntary euthanasia; on the other hand, anyone who believes that suicide is always wrong is bound to condemn voluntary euthanasia. In this connection, it is interesting to note that Roman

Stoics like Cicero called suicide "voluntary death" (*mors voluntaria*), which links it with the concept of dying rather than of killing.[15] Following this lead, we might sidestep the issue of killing and call voluntary euthanasia "voluntary death."

A second distinction that is frequently cited in discussions of euthanasia is between *active* and *passive* euthanasia. Active euthanasia is said to involve a positive act of some kind to bring about a person's death. It is often called "mercy killing." Passive euthanasia, on the other hand, consists in refraining from further treatment and "letting the patient die." Again, for reasons that are given in Chapters 7 and 8, the distinction is a questionable one. The terms "active" and "passive" are misnomers, for a physician usually cannot let a patient die without being active in some way, e.g. he has to make a decision and leave instructions on how to carry it out. Furthermore, it hardly seems correct to say that the physician is passive in the sense of being acted upon by an external force. The chief sense in which he could be said to be "passive" is psychological; he has given up and has decided to let "nature," i.e. the disease, take its course. "Passive" simply means not active in a certain regard.

A third distinction is often drawn between *direct* and *indirect* euthanasia. Direct euthanasia is the use of some means or other directly to cause the person's death. Indirect euthanasia is the treatment of a patient for one purpose, e.g. giving a drug to reduce his suffering, with the full knowledge that a "side-effect" of that treatment will be the hastening of the patient's death. Again, we have a distinction that is questionable philosophically because it is based on an abstruse distinction between the intended, and the foreseen but unintended consequences of an act.[16]

These three distinctions raise more issues than they settle, particularly as far as philosophers are concerned, for philosophers are often skeptical of distinctions that are taken for granted by others. The philosophical approach to ethical problems relating to life and death, including euthanasia, is quite different from other approaches to these problems, e.g. those of moral theologians (religious ethicists) and lawyers.

Perhaps the most important difference is that philosophers rarely conceive their aim to be to set up authoritative rules of conduct and to offer authoritative answers to difficult ethical questions. Accordingly, they are not primarily concerned with establishing the kind of consensus that might be used as a basis for political or legal action. Philosophers tend to accept the issues themselves as controversial, over which intelligent, well-informed people of goodwill may disagree. As the essays in this book will attest, there is no unanimity among philosophers on the ethical issues relating to decisions concerning life and death.

Traditionally, philosophers have conceived of their role as that of a gadfly. Like Socrates, they feel that it is their job to reexamine and challenge commonly accepted notions that seem to them to be based on confusions of one sort or another. In pursuit of this aim, philosophers use what is called the method of *conceptual analysis;* its purpose is to clarify concepts by means of logical analysis and argumentation. It is easy to see, then, why philosophers eschew appeals to authority; that is, appeals to the authority of a text, of an institution, or of a person. For practical purposes, as of law and politics, authorities of this kind may be necessary; but for philosophical purposes they are not. Indeed, the appeal to authority in matters that concern us here is inconsistent with the integrity of philosophical inquiry itself, which demands the pursuit of truth without regard to what others believe or to what is generally accepted as true.

Bearing in mind that the chief aim of philosophy is the logical clarification of concepts, let us review some of the issues of concern to the philosophers whose essays appear in this book.

To begin with, philosophers look for a clarification of the concepts of life and death. What is meant by these terms? What is the scope of the concept of life? What are the criteria of life and death? Are the concepts value concepts? If so, how do they relate to other kinds of value concepts, such as ethical concepts?

What is the place of life and death in ethics in general? We might begin, as Philippa Foot does in her essay, by discussing the question of whether life is intrinsically good. If life is intrinsically good, does it also have sanctity? If so, why doesn't the life of animals have as much sanctity as that of human beings?

These questions lead us to ask whether there are important ethical differences between kinds of things that are alive, e.g. bacteria, plants, animals, fetuses, newborn infants, children, adults, senile persons and persons in irreversible coma; and if so, what these differences are. On what grounds can we say that it is all right to do certain things to some of them and not to others; say, to kill them? If there are important differences, what are they?

Peter Singer, who approaches these questions about life from the point of view of hedonistic utilitarianism, takes the ethically crucial aspect of life to be the ability to suffer. Since animals share this ability with human beings, why are we justified in treating them differently in regard to the termination of life?

One traditional answer to the question about crucial ethical differences between human beings and other living things is to say that only human beings have souls. That naturally raises the question, What do we mean by "soul" and what are the criteria for possessing a soul? Contemporary philosophers prefer to use the term "person" instead of "soul" because of the latter's religious connotations. We might say, then, that it is by virtue of their being persons that we are justified in treating human beings differently from animals. What then do we mean by "person," and how do we know when a human body is also a person? These questions are discussed by Tooley.

It has often been held to be definitive of a person that he is a possessor of rights (and duties). Hence, the discussion of personhood leads to questions about rights. Can animals have rights? And, if not, how can we say that fetuses, newborn infants, persons in coma, or even dead persons have rights? If the ability to exercise or to waive a right is essential to having a right, then it would follow that only competent adults have rights in the full-blown sense.

For these and other obvious reasons, the concept of rights is a central one in this book. We must answer a number of questions about rights in general before we can ask what kinds of rights persons have as persons, or more particular questions about the right to life or the right to die. The philosophical background for these rights is discussed in some detail in the essays by Tooley, Brock and Ladd. It should be noted, however, that some doubts might be raised about the usefulness of the concept of rights in discussions of euthanasia. As Foot points out in her essay, perhaps euthanasia calls for charity rather than justice (i.e. rights); it might be a matter of humanitarianism rather than rights.

Finally, a number of philosophical issues are discussed in connection with distinctions like those between active and passive euthanasia and between direct and indirect euthanasia. The issues involved here call for a clarification of the concept of action: How is an act related to its consequences and to its intention? Philosophy of action has been the subject of lively debate in philosophical circles in recent years. One aspect of the debate has been an emphasis on questions concerning the connection between act and responsibility, a matter that is of particular relevance to euthanasia.

Philosophical issues relating to the concept of responsibility lead us to more questions, namely, to questions concerning the doctor's responsibility, the patient's responsibility, parental and familial responsibility, hospital responsibility and the responsibility of society in general vis-à-vis what I have called cacothanasia. Whose duty is it to prevent or mitigate cacothanasia? Or, indeed, is it anyone's duty? And, regarding the matter retrospectively, Who, if anyone, is responsible for the ugly, tormented death of a particular person? If responsibility is analyzed, as it is by some philosophers, in terms of preventability, who could have prevented such a death of a person? And how could it have been prevented?

At the end of the book, we return to a consideration of more concrete aspects of medical decisions relating to life and death. Duff and Campbell explain how new developments in medical technology and the rise of a new kind of medical professionalism have aggravated the moral dilemmas involved in such decisions. They show how the concomitant institutionalization of medical care has affected the physician-patient relationship, in particular as regards providing care for the dying and making choices about death. As practicing physicians, they offer some concrete suggestions for handling the particular problems that the rest have discussed at a more abstract level.

Notes

1. "Give me but gentle death: Euthanasia, euthanasia, that is all." See *Oxford English Dictionary* (1933), vol. III, p. 325 for further references.
2. Ibid.
3. In order to offset this pejorative meaning, one author has invented the odd-sounding term "beneficent euthanasia." See Marvin Kohl, *Beneficent Euthanasia,* (Buffalo: Prometheus Press, 1975). This book contains a useful collection of articles on euthanasia.
4. See Melvin Krant, *Dying and Dignity: The Meaning and Control of a Personal Death,* (Springfield, Ill.: Charles C. Thomas, 1974).

5. See Philippe Aries, *Western Attitudes toward Death*, (Baltimore: Johns Hopkins Press, 1974).

6. "Cacothanasia" is suggested as a name for the opposite of "euthanasia" on the etymological analogy of the opposites "cacophony" and "euphony."

7. The most notable exception, of course, is the hospice movement, which has been reported on widely. See, for example, Leonard Pearson, ed., *Death and Dying: Current Issues in the Treatment of the Dying Person*, (Cleveland: Case Western Reserve Press, 1969). (This book contains many bibliographical references.)

8. For detailed descriptions of some of the problems faced by sick, and particularly indigent, patients when they come up against hospital bureaucracies, see Raymond S. Duff and August B. Hollingshead, *Sickness and Society*, (New York: Harper and Row, 1968). For a general account of the morality of bureaucracies, see John Ladd, "Morality and the Ideal of Rationality in Formal Organizations," *Monist* 54 (October 1970).

9. See "In the Matter of Karen Quinlan, an Alleged Incompetent," Supreme Court of New Jersey, A116, September term, 1975. For a reportorial account of the Quinlan case and other similar cases, see B. D. Colen, *Karen Ann Quinlan: Dying in an Age of Eternal Life*, (New York: Nash Publishing Co., 1976).

10. W. O. Osler, *The Principles and Practice of Medicine*, 12th ed, revised by T. McCrae, (New York: D. Appleton-Century, 1935). Quoted in Ernest M. Gruenberg, "The Failures of Success," *Health and Society*, (Winter 1977). Gruenberg presents statistical evidence of the dramatic changes in morality rates among persons afflicted with mongolism, senile brain disease, and other chronic diseases such as arteriosclerosis, diabetes and spina bifida who a short time ago would have died of secondary infections.

11. *The Shorter Oxford English Dictionary.*

12. James describes a "genuine option" as one that is forced (i.e. unavoidable), living (i.e. it has some appeal, however small), and momentous (i.e. fraught with consequences). See *The Will to Believe*, (New York: Longmans, Green, 1919), p. 3.

13. See, for example, an interesting videotape entitled *Please Let Me Die!*, which presents a real life situation of this type. It is produced by the Medical Branch of the University of Texas, Galveston.

14. See Raymond S. Duff and A.G.M. Campbell, "Moral and Ethical Dilemmas in the Special Care Nursery," and Anthony Shaw, "Dilemmas of 'Informed Consent' in Children." *New England Journal of Medicine* 289 (25 October 1973): 885–890; 890–894.

15. See David Daube, "The Linguistics of Suicide," *Philosophy and Public Affairs* (Summer 1974).

16. The theory in question includes the so-called Law of Double Effect, discussed in several places in this book.

2 Euthanasia

PHILIPPA FOOT

The widely used *Shorter Oxford English Dictionary* gives three meanings for the word "euthanasia": the first, "a quiet and easy death"; the second, "the means of procuring this"; and the third, "the action of inducing a quiet and easy death." It is a curious fact that no one of the three gives an adequate definition of the word as it is usually understood. For "euthanasia" means much more than a quiet and easy death, or the means of procuring it, or the action of inducing it. The definition specifies only the manner of the death, and if this were all that was implied a murderer, careful to drug his victim, could claim that his act was an act of euthanasia. We find this ridiculous because we take it for granted that in euthanasia it is death itself, not just the manner of death, that must be kind to the one who dies.

To see how important it is that "euthanasia" should not be used as the dictionary definition allows it to be used, merely to signify that a death was quiet and easy, one has only to remember that Hitler's "euthanasia" program traded on this ambiguity. Under this program, planned before the War but brought into full operation by a decree of

Philippa Foot, "Euthanasia," *Philosophy & Public Affairs* 6, no. 2 (Winter 1977). Copyright © 1977 by Philippa Foot. Reprinted by permission of the author and Princeton University Press.

I would like to thank Derek Parfit and the editors of *Philosophy & Public Affairs* for their very helpful comments.

1 September 1939, some 275,000 people were gassed in centers which were to be a model for those in which Jews were later exterminated. Anyone in a state institution could be sent to the gas chambers if it was considered that he could not be "rehabilitated" for useful work. As Dr. Leo Alexander reports, relying on the testimony of a neuropathologist who received 500 brains from one of the killing centers,

In Germany the exterminations included the mentally defective, psychotics (particularly schizophrenics), epileptics and patients suffering from infirmities of old age and from various organic neurological disorders such as infantile paralysis, Parkinsonism, multiple sclerosis and brain tumors. . . . In truth, all those unable to work and consider nonrehabilitable were killed.[1]

These people were killed because they were "useless" and "a burden on society"; only the manner of their deaths could be thought of as relatively easy and quiet.

Let us insist, then, that when we talk about euthanasia we are talking about a death understood as a good or happy event for the one who dies. This stipulation follows etymology, but is itself not exactly in line with current usage, which would be captured by the condition that the death should *not* be an evil rather than that it *should* be a good. That this is how people talk is shown by the fact that the case of Karen Ann Quinlan and others in a state of permanent coma is often discussed under the heading of "euthanasia." Perhaps it is not too late to object to the use of the word "euthanasia" in this sense. Apart from the break with the Greek origins of the word, there are other unfortunate aspects of this extension of the term. For if we say that the death must be supposed to be a good to the subject, we can also specify that it shall be for his sake that an act of euthanasia is performed. If we say merely that death shall not be an evil to him, we cannot stipulate that benefiting him shall be the motive where euthanasia is in question. Given the importance of the question, For whose sake are we acting? it is good to have a definition of euthanasia which brings under this heading only cases of opting for death for the sake of the one who dies. Perhaps what is most important is to say either that euthanasia is to be for the good of the subject or at least that death is to be no evil to him, thus refusing to talk Hitler's language. However, in this paper it is the first condition that will be understood, with the additional proviso that by an act of euthanasia we mean one of inducing or otherwise opting for death for the sake of the one who is to die.

A few lesser points need to be cleared up. In the first place it must be said that the word "act" is not to be taken to exclude omission: we shall speak of an act of euthanasia when someone is deliberately allowed to die, for his own good, and not only when positive measures are taken to see that he does. The very general idea we want is that of a choice of action or inaction directed at another man's death and causally effective in the sense that, in conjunction with actual circumstances, it is a sufficient condition of death. Of complications such as overdetermination, it will not be necessary to speak.

A second, and definitely minor, point about the definition of an act of euthanasia concerns the question of fact versus belief. It has already been implied that one who performs an act of euthanasia thinks that death will be merciful for the subject since we have said that it is on account of this thought that the act is done. But is it enough that he acts with this thought, or must things actually be as he thinks them to be? If one man kills another, or allows him to die, thinking that he is in the last stages of a terrible disease though in fact he could have been cured—is this an act of euthanasia or not? Nothing much seems to hang on our decision about this. The same condition has got to enter into the definition whether as an element in reality or only as an element in the agent's belief. And however we define an act of euthanasia culpability or justifiability will be the same: if a man acts through ignorance his ignorance may be culpable or it may not.[2]

These are relatively easy problems to solve, but one that is dauntingly difficult has been passed over in this discussion of the definition and must now be faced. It is easy to say, as if this raised no problems, that an act of euthanasia is by definition one aiming at the *good* of the one whose death is in question, and that it is *for his sake* that his death is desired. But how is this to be explained? Presumably we are thinking of some evil already with him or to come on him if he continues to live, and death is thought of as a release from this evil. But this cannot be enough. Most people's lives contain evils such as grief or pain, but we do not therefore think that death would be a blessing to them. On the contrary life is generally supposed to be a good even for someone who is unusually unhappy or frustrated. How is it that one can ever wish for death for the sake of the one who is to die? This difficult question is central to the discussion of euthanasia, and we shall literally not know what we are talking about if we ask whether acts of euthanasia defined as we have defined them are ever morally permissible without first understanding better the reason for saying that life is a good, and the possibility that it is not always so.

If a man should save my life he would be my benefactor. In normal circumstances this is plainly true; but does one always benefit another in saving his life? It seems certain that he does not. Suppose, for instance, that a man were being tortured to death and was given a drug that lengthened his sufferings; this would not be a benefit but the reverse. Or suppose that in a ghetto in Nazi Germany a doctor saved the life of someone threatened by disease, but that the man once cured was transported to an extermination camp; the doctor might wish for the sake of the patient that he had died of the disease. Nor would a longer stretch of life always be a benefit to the person who was given it. Comparing Hitler's camps with those of Stalin, Dmitri Panin observes that in the latter the method of extermination was made worse by agonies that could stretch out over months.

Death from a bullet would have been bliss compared with what many millions had to endure while dying of hunger. The kind of death to which they were condemned has nothing to equal it in treachery and sadism.[3]

These examples show that to save or prolong a man's life is not always to do him a service: it may be better for him if he dies earlier rather than later. It must therefore be agreed that while life is normally a benefit to the one who has it, this is not always so.

The judgment is often fairly easy to make—that life is or is not a good to someone—but the basis for it is very hard to find. When life is said to be a benefit or a good, on what grounds is the assertion made?

The difficulty is underestimated if it is supposed that the problem arises from the fact that one who is dead has nothing, so that the good someone gets from being alive cannot be compared with the amount he would otherwise have had. For why should this particular comparison be necessary? Surely it would be enough if one could say whether or not someone whose life was prolonged had more good than evil in the extra stretch of time. Such estimates are not always possible, but frequently they are; we say, for example, "He was very happy in those last years," or, "He had little but unhappiness then." If the balance of good and evil determined whether life was a good to someone we would expect to find a correlation in the judgments. In fact, of course, we find nothing of the kind. First, a man who has no doubt that existence is a good to him may have no idea about the balance of happiness and unhappiness in his life, or of any other positive and negative factors that my be suggested. So the supposed criteria are not always operating where the judgment is made. And secondly the application of the criteria gives an answer that is often wrong. Many people have more evil than good in their lives; we do not, however, conclude that we would do these people no service by rescuing them from death.

To get around this last difficulty, Thomas Nagel has suggested that experience itself is a good which must be brought in to balance accounts.

> . . . life is worth living even when the bad elements of experience are plentiful, and the good ones too meager to outweigh the bad ones on their own. The additional positive weight is supplied by experience itself, rather than by any of its contents.[4]

This seems implausible because if experience itself is a good it must be so even when what we experience is wholly bad, as in being tortured to death. How should one decide how much to count for this experiencing; and why count anything at all?

Others have tried to solve the problem by arguing that it is a man's desire for life that makes us call life a good: if he wants to live then anyone who prolongs his life does him a benefit. Yet someone may cling to life where we would say confidently that it would be better for him if he died, and he may admit it too. Speaking of those same conditions in which, as he said, a bullet would have been merciful, Panin writes.

> I should like to pass on my observations concerning the absence of suicides under the extremely severe conditions of our concentration camps. The more that life became desperate, the more a prisoner seemed determined to hold onto it.[5]

One might try to explain this by saying that hope was the ground of this wish to survive for further days and months in the camp. But there is nothing unintelligible in the idea that a man might cling to life though he knew those facts about his future which would make any charitable man wish that he might die.

The problem remains, and it is hard to know where to look for a solution. Is there a conceptual connection between *life* and *good?* Because life is not always a good we are apt to reject this idea and to think that it must be a contingent fact that life is usually a good, as it is a contingent matter that legacies are usually a benefit, if they are. Yet it seems not to be a contingent matter that to save someone's life is ordinarily to benefit him. The problem is to find where the conceptual connection lies.

It may be good tactics to forget for a time that it is euthanasia we are discussing and to see how *life* and *good* are connected in the case of living beings other than men. Even plants have things done to them that are harmful or beneficial, and what does them good must be related in some way to their living and dying. Let us therefore consider plants and animals, and then come back to human beings. At least we shall get away from the temptation to think that the connection between life and benefit must everywhere be a matter of happiness and unhappiness or of pleasure and pain; the idea being absurd in the case of animals and impossible even to formulate for plants.

In case anyone thinks that the concept of the beneficial applies only in a secondary or analogical way to plants, he should be reminded that we speak quite straightforwardly in saying, for instance, that a certain amount of sunlight is beneficial to most plants. What is in question here is the habitat in which plants of particular species flourish, but we can also talk, in a slightly different way, of what does them good, where there is some suggestion of improvement or remedy. What has the beneficial to do with sustaining life? It is tempting to answer, "everything," thinking that a healthy condition just is the one apt to secure survival. In fact, however, what is beneficial to a plant may have to do with reproduction rather than the survival of the individual member of the species. Nevertheless there is a plain connection between the beneficial and the life-sustaining even for the individual plant; if something makes it better able to survive in conditions normal for that species, it is ipso facto good for it. We need go no further, and could go no further, in explaining why a certain environment or treatment is good for a plant than to show how it helps this plant to survive.[6]

This connection between the life-sustaining and the beneficial is reasonably unproblematic, and there is nothing fanciful or zoomorphic in speaking of benefiting or doing good to plants. A connection with its survival can make something beneficial to a plant. But this is not, of course, to say that we count life as a good to a plant. We may save its life by giving it what is beneficial; we do not benefit it by saving its life.

A more ramified concept of benefit is used in speaking of animal life. New things can be said, such as that an animal is better or worse off for something that happened, or that it was a good or bad thing for it that it did happen. And new things count as benefit. In the first place, there is comfort, which often is, but need not be, related to health. When loosening a collar which is too tight for a dog we can say, "That will be better for it." So we see that the words "better for it" have two different meanings which we mark when necessary by a difference of emphasis, saying "better *for* it" when health is involved. And secondly an animal can be benefited by having its life saved. "Could you do anything for it?" can be answered by, "Yes, I managed to save its life." Sometimes we may understand this, just as we would for a plant, to mean that we had checked some disease. But we can also do something for an animal by scaring away its predator. If we do this, it is a good thing for the animal that we did, unless of course it immediately meets a more unpleasant end by some other means. Similarly, on the bad side, an animal may be worse off for our intervention, and this not because it pines or suffers but simply because it gets killed.

The problem that vexes us when we think about euthanasia comes on the scene at this point. For if we can do something for an animal—can benefit it—by relieving its suffering but also by savings its life, where does the greater benefit come when only death will end pain? It seemed that life was a good in its own right; yet pain seemed to be an evil with equal status and could therefore make life not a good after all. Is it only life without pain that is a good when animals are concerned? This does not seem a crazy suggestion when we are thinking of animals, since unlike human beings they do not have suffering as part of their normal life. But it is perhaps the idea of ordinary life that matters here. We would not say that we had done anything for an animal if we had merely kept it alive, either in an unconscious state or in a condition where, though conscious, it was unable to operate in an ordinary way; and the fact is that animals in severe and continuous pain simply do not operate normally. So we do not, on the whole, have the option of doing the animal good by saving its life though the life would be a life of pain. No doubt there are borderline cases, but that is no problem.

We are not trying to make new judgments possible, but rather to find the principle of the ones we do make.

When we reach human life the problems seem even more troublesome. For now we must take quite new things into account, such as the subject's own view of his life. It is arguable that this places extra constraints on the solution: might it not be counted as a necessary condition of life's being a good to a man that he should see it as such? Is there not some difficulty about the idea that a benefit might be done to him by the saving or prolonging of his life even though he himself wished for death? Of course he might have a quite mistaken view of his own prospects, but let us ignore this and think only of cases where it is life as he knows it that is in question. Can we think that the prolonging of this life would be a benefit to him even though he would rather have it end than continue? It seems that this cannot be ruled out. That there is no simple incompatibility between life as a good and the wish for death is shown by the possibility that a man should wish himself dead, not for his own sake, but for the sake of someone else. And if we try to amend the thesis to say that life cannot be a good to one who wishes *for his own sake* that he should die, we find the crucial concept slipping through our fingers. As Bishop Butler pointed out long ago not all ends are either benevolent or self-interested. Does a man wish for death for his own sake in the relevant sense if, for instance, he wishes to revenge himself on another by his death. Or what if he is proud and refuses to stomach dependence or incapacity even though there are many good things left in life for him? The truth seems to be that the wish for death is sometimes compatible with life's being a good and sometimes not, which is possible because the description "wishing for death" is one covering diverse states of mind from that of the determined suicide, pathologically depressed, so that of one who is surprised to find that the thought of a fatal accident is viewed with relief. On the one hand, a man may see his life as a burden but go about his business in a more or less ordinary way; on the other hand, the wish for death may take the form of a rejection of everything that is in life, as it does in severe depression. It seems reasonable to say that life is not a good to one permanently in the latter state, and we must return to this topic later on.

When are we to say that life is a good or a benefit to a man? The dilemma that faces us is this. If we say that life as such is a good we find ourselves refuted by the examples given at the beginning of this discussion. We therefore incline to think that it is as bringing good things that life is a good, where it is a good. But if life is a good only because it is the condition of good things why is it not equally an evil when it brings bad things? And how can it be a good even when it brings more evil than good?

It should be noted that the problem has here been formulated in terms of the balance of good and evil, not that of happiness and unhappiness, and that it is not to be solved by the denial (which may be reasonable enough) that unhappiness is the only evil or happiness the only good. In this paper no view has been expressed about the nature of goods other than life itself. The point is that on any view of the goods and evils that life can contain, it seems that a life with more evil than good could still itself be a good.

It may be useful to review the judgments with which our theory must square. Do we think that life can be a good to one who suffers a lot of pain? Clearly we do. What about severely handicapped people; can life be a good to them? Clearly it can be, for even if someone is almost completely paralyzed, perhaps living in an iron lung, perhaps able to move things only by means of a tube held between his lips, we do not rule him out of order if he says that some benefactor saved his life. Nor is it different with mental handicap. There are many fairly severely handicapped people—such as those with Down's syndrome (mongolism)—for whom a simple affectionate life is possible. What about senility? Does this break the normal connection between life and good? Here we must surely distinguish between forms of senility. Some forms leave a life which we count someone as better off having than not having, so that a doctor who prolonged it would benefit the person concerned. With some kinds of senility this is however no longer true. There are some in geriatric wards who are barely conscious, though they can move a little and swallow food put into their mouths. To prolong such a state, whether in the old or in the very severely mentally handicapped is not to do them a service or confer a benefit. But of course it need not be the reverse: only if there is suffering would one wish for the sake of the patient that he should die.

It seems, therefore, that merely being alive even without suffering is not a good, and that we must make a distinction similar to that which we made when animals were our topic. But how is the line to be drawn in the case of men? What is to count as ordinary human life in the relevant sense? If it were only the very senile or very ill who were to be said not to have this life it might seem right to describe it in terms of *operation*. But it will be hard to find the sense in which the men described by Panin were not operating, given that they dragged themselves out to the forest to work. What is it about the life that the prisoners were living that makes us put it on the other side of the dividing line from that of some severely ill or suffering patients, and from most of the physically or mentally handicapped? It is not that they were in captivity, for life in captivity can certainly be a good. Nor is it merely the unusual nature of their life. In some ways the prisoners were living more as other men do than the patient in an iron lung.

The suggested solution to the problem is, then, that there is a certain conceptual connection between *life* and *good* in the case of human beings as in that of animals and even plants. Here, as there, however, it is not the mere state of being alive that can determine, or itself count as, a good, but rather life coming up to some standard of normality. It was argued that it is as part of ordinary life that the elements of good that a man may have are relevant to the question of whether saving his life counts as benefiting him. Ordinary human lives, even very hard lives, contain a minimum of basic goods, but when these are absent the idea of life is no longer linked to that of good. And since it is in this way that the elements of good contained in a man's life are relevant to the question of whether he is benefited if his life is preserved, there is no reason why it should be the balance of good and evil that counts.

It should be added that evils are relevant in one way when, as in the examples discussed above, they destroy the possibility of ordinary goods, but in a different way when they invade a life from which the goods are already absent for a different reason. So, for instance, the connection between *life* and *good* may be broken because consciousness has sunk to a very low level, as in extreme senility or severe brain damage. In itself this kind of life seems to be neither good nor evil, but if suffering sets in one would hope for a speedy end.

The idea we need seems to be that of life which is ordinary human life in the following respect—that it contains a minimum of basic human goods. What is ordinary in human life—even in very hard lives—is that a man is not driven to work far beyond his capacity; that he has the support of a family or community; that he can more or less satisfy his hunger; that he has hopes for the future; that he can lie down to rest at night. Such things were denied to the men in the Vyatlag camps described by Panin; not even rest at night was allowed them when they were tormented by bed-bugs, by noise and stench, and by routines such as body-searches and bath-parades—arranged for the night time so that work norms would not be reduced. Disease too can so take over a man's life that the normal human goods disappear. When a patient is so overwhelmed by pain or nausea that he cannot eat with pleasure, if he can eat at all, and is out of the reach of even the most loving voice, he no longer has ordinary human life in the sense in which the words are used here. And we may now pick up a thread from an earlier part of the discussion by remarking that crippling depression can destroy the enjoyment of ordinary goods as effectively as external circumstances can remove them.

This, admittedly inadequate, discussion of the sense in which life is normally a good, and of the reasons why it may not be so in some particular case, completes the account of what euthanasia is here taken to be. An act of euthanasia, whether literally act or rather omission, is attributed to an agent who opts for the death of another because in his case life seems to be an evil rather than a good. The question now to be asked is whether acts of euthanasia are ever justifiable. But there are two topics here rather than one. For it is one thing to say that some acts of euthanasia considered only in themselves and their results are morally unobjectionable, and another to say that it would be all right to legalize them. Perhaps the practice of euthanasia would allow too many abuses, and perhaps there would be too many mistakes. Moreover the practice might have very important and highly undesirable side effects, because it is unlikely that we could change our principles about the treatment of the old and the ill without changing fundamental emotional attitudes and social relations. The topics must, therefore, be treated separately. In the next part of the discussion, nothing will be said about the social consequences and possible abuses of the practice of euthanasia, but only about acts of euthanasia considered in themselves.

What we want to know is whether acts of euthanasia, defined as we have defined them, are ever morally permissible. To be more accurate, we want to know whether it is ever sufficient justification of the choice of death for another that death can be counted a benefit rather than harm, and that this is why the choice is made.

It will be impossible to get a clear view of the area to which this topic belongs without first marking the distinct grounds on which objection may lie when one man opts for the death of another. There are two different virtues whose requirements are, in general, contrary to such actions. An unjustified act of killing, or allowing to die, is contrary to justice or to charity, or to both virtues, and the moral failings are distinct. Justice has to do with what men *owe* each other in the way of noninterference and positive service. When used in this wide sense, which has its history in the doctrine of the cardinal virtues, justice is not especially connected with, for instance, law courts, but with the whole area of rights, and duties corresponding to rights. Thus murder is one form of injustice, dishonesty another, and wrongful failure to keep contracts a third; chicanery in a law court or defrauding someone of his inheritance are simply other cases of injustice. Justice as such is not directly linked to the good of another, and may require that something be rendered to him even where it will do him harm, as Hume pointed out when he remarked that a debt must be paid even to a profligate debauchee who "would rather receive harm than benefit from large possessions."[7] Charity, on the other hand, is the virtue which attaches us to the good of others. An act of charity is in question only where something is not demanded by justice, but a lack of charity and of justice can be shown where a man is denied something which he both needs and has a right to; both charity and justice demand that widows and orphans are not defrauded, and the man who cheats them is neither charitable nor just.

It is easy to see that the two grounds of objection to inducing death are distinct. A murder is an act of injustice. A culpable failure to come to the aid of someone whose life is threatened is normally contrary, not to justice, but to charity. But where one man is under contract, explicit or implicit, to come to the aid of another, injustice too will be shown. Thus injustice may be involved either in an act or an omission, and the same is true of a lack of charity; charity may demand that someone be aided, but also that an unkind word not be spoken.

The distinction between charity and justice will turn out to be of the first importance when voluntary and nonvoluntary euthanasia are distinguished later on. This is because of the connection between justice and rights, and something should now be said about this. I believe it is true to say that wherever a man acts unjustly he has infringed a right, since justice has to do with whatever a man is owed, and whatever he is owed is his as a matter of right. Something should therefore be said about the different kinds of rights. The distinction commonly made is between having a right in the sense of having a liberty, and having a "claim-right" or "right of recipience."[8] The best way to understand such a distinction seems to be as follows. To say that a man has a right in the sense of a liberty is to say that no one can demand that he do not do the thing which he has a right to do. The fact that he has a right to do it consists in the fact that a certain kind of objection does not lie against his doing it. Thus a man has a right in this sense to walk down a public street or park his car in a public parking space. It does not follow that no one else may prevent him from doing so. If for some reason I want a certain man not to park in a certain place I may lawfully park there myself or get my friends to do so, thus preventing him from doing what he has a right (in the sense of a liberty) to do. It is different, however, with a claim-right. This is the kind of right which I have in addition to a liberty when, for example, I have a private parking space; now others have duties in the way of noninterference, as in this case, or of service, as in the case where my claim-right is to goods or services promised to me. Sometimes one of these rights gives other people the duty of securing to me that to which I have a right, but at other times their duty is merely to refrain from interference. If a fall of snow blocks my private parking space there is normally no obligation for anyone else to clear it away. Claim rights generate duties; sometimes these duties are duties of noninterference; sometimes they are duties of service. If your right gives me the duty not to interfere with you, I have "no right" to do it; similarly, if your right gives me the duty to provide something for you, I have "no right" to refuse to do it. What *I* lack is the right which is a liberty; I am not "at liberty" to interfere with you or to refuse the service.

Where in this picture does the right to life belong? No doubt people have the right to live in the sense of a liberty, but what is important is the cluster of claim-rights brought together under the title of the right to life. The chief of these is, of course, the right to be free from interferences that threaten life. If other people aim their guns at us or try to pour poison into our drink we can, to put it mildly, demand that they desist. And then there are the services we can claim from doctors, health officers, bodyguards, and firemen; the rights that depend on contract or public arrangement. Perhaps there is no particular point in saying that the duties these people owe us belong to the right to life; we might as well say that all the services owed to anyone by tailors, dressmakers, and couturiers belong to a right called the right to be elegant. But contracts such as those understood in the patient-doctor relationship come in an important way when we are discussing the rights and wrongs of euthanasia, and are therefore mentioned here.

Do people have the right to what they need in order to survive, apart from the right conferred by special contracts into which other people have entered for the supplying of these necessities? Do people in the underdeveloped countries in which starvation is rife have the right to the food they so evidently lack? Joel Feinberg, discussing this question, suggests that they should be said to have "a claim," distinguishing this from a "valid claim," which gives a claim-right.

The manifesto writers on the other side who seem to identify needs, or at least basic needs, with what they call "human rights," are more properly described, I think, as urging upon the world community the moral principle that *all* basic human needs ought to be recognized as *claims* (in the customary *prima facie* sense) worthy of sympathy and serious consideration right now, even though, in many cases, they cannot yet plausibly be treated as *valid* claims, that is, as gounds of any other people's duties. This way of talking avoids the anomaly of ascribing to all human beings now, even those in pre-industrial societies, such "economic and social rights" as "periodic holidays with pay."[9]

This seems reasonable, though we notice that there are some actual rights to service which are not based on anything like a contract, as for instance the right that children have to support from their parents and parents to support from their children in old age, though both sets of rights are to some extent dependent on existing social arrangements.

Let us now ask how the right to life affects the morality of acts of euthanasia. Are such acts sometimes or always ruled out by the right to life? This is certainly a possibility; for although an act of euthanasia is, by our definition, a matter of opting for death for the good of the one who is to die, there is, as we noted earlier, no direct connection between that to which a man has a right and that which is for his good. It is true that men have the right only to the kind of thing that is, in general, a good: we do not think that people have the right to garbage or polluted air. Nevertheless, a man may have the right to something which he himself would be better off without: where rights exist it is a man's will that counts not his or anyone else's estimate of benefit or harm. So the duties complementary to the right to life—the general duty of noninterference and the duty of service incurred by certain persons—are not affected by the quality of a man's life or by his prospects. Even if it is true that he would be, as we say, "better off dead," so long as he wants to live this does not justify us in killing him and may not justify us in deliberately allowing him to die. All of us have the duty of noninterference, and some of us may have the duty to sustain his life. Suppose, for example, that a retreating army has to leave behind wounded or exhausted soldiers in the wastes of an arid or snowbound land where the only prospect is death by starvation or at the hands of an enemy notoriously cruel. It has often been the practice to accord a merciful bullet to men in such desperate straits. But suppose that one of them demands that he should be left alive? It seems clear that his comrades have no right to kill him, though it is a quite different question as to whether they should give him a life-prolonging drug. The right to life can sometimes give a duty of positive service, but does not do so here. What it does give is the right to be left alone.

Interestingly enough, we have arrived by way of a consideration of the right to life at the distinction normally labeled "active" versus "passive" euthanasia, and often thought to be irrelevant to the moral issue.[10] Once it is seen that the right to life is a distinct ground of objection to certain acts of euthanasia, and that this right creates a duty of noninterference more widespread than the duties of care, there can be no doubt about the relevance of the distinction between passive and active euthanasia. Where everyone may have the duty to leave someone alone, it may be that no one has the duty to maintain his life, or that only some people do.

Where then do the boundaries of the "active" and "passive" lie? In some ways the words are themselves misleading, because they suggest the difference between act and omission which is not quite what we want. Certainly the act of shooting someone is the kind of thing we were talking about under the heading of "interference," and omitting to give him a drug a case of refusing care. But the act of turning off a respirator should surely be thought of as no different from the decision not to start it; if doctors had decided that a patient should be allowed to die, either course of action might follow, and both should be counted as passive rather than active euthanasia if euthanasia were in question. The point seems to be that interference in a course of treatment is not the same as other interference in a man's life, and particularly if the same body of people are responsible for the treatment and for its discontinuance. In such a case we could speak of the disconnecting of the apparatus as killing the man, or of the hospital as allowing him to die. By and large, it is the act of killing that is ruled out under the heading of noninterference, but not in every case.

Doctors commonly recognize this distinction, and the grounds on which some philosophers have denied it seem untenable. James Rachels, for instance, believes that if the difference between active and passive is relevant anywhere, it should be relevant everywhere, and he has pointed to an example in which it seems to make no difference which is done. If someone saw a child drowning in a bath it would seem just as bad to let it drown as to push its head under water.[11] If "it makes no difference" means that one act would be as iniquitous as the other, this is true. It is not that killing is *worse* than allowing to die, but that the two are contrary to distinct virtues, which gives the possibility that in some circumstances one is impermissible and the other permissible. In the circumstances invented by Rachels, both are wicked: it is contrary to justice to push the child's head under the water—something one has no right to do. To leave it to drown is not contrary to justice, but it is a particularly glaring example of lack of charity. Here it makes no practical difference because the requirements of justice and charity coincide; but in the case of the retreating army they did not: charity would have required that the wounded soldier be killed had not justice required that he be left alive.[12] In such a case it makes all the difference whether a man opts for the death of another in a positive action, or whether he allows him to die. An analogy with the right to property will make the point clear. If a man owns something, he has the right to it even when its possession does him harm, and we have no right to take it from him. But if one day it should blow away, maybe nothing requires us to get it back for him; we could not deprive him of it, but we may allow it to go. This is not to deny that it will often be an unfriendly act or one based on an arrogant judgment when we refuse to do what he wants. Nevertheless, we would be within our rights, and it might be that no moral objection of any kind would lie against our refusal.

It is important to emphasize that a man's rights may stand between us and the action we would dearly like to take for his sake. They may, of course, also prevent action which we would like to take for the sake of others, as when it might be tempting to kill one man to save several. But it is interesting that the limits of allowable interference, however uncertain, seem stricter in the first case than the second. Perhaps there are no cases in which it would be all right to kill a man against his will *for his own sake* unless they could equally well be described as cases of allowing him to die, as in the example of turning off the respirator. However, there are circumstances, even if these are very rare, in which one man's life would justifiably be sacrificed to save others, and "killing" would be the only description of what was being done. For instance, a vehicle which had gone out of control might be steered from a path on which it would kill more than one man to a path on which it would kill one.[13] But it would not be permissible to steer a vehicle towards someone in order to kill him, against his will, for his own good. An analogy with property rights illustrates the point. One may not destroy a man's property against his will on the grounds that he would be better off without it; there are however circumstances in which it could be destroyed for the sake of others. If his house is liable to fall and kill him that is his affair; it might, however, without injustice be destroyed to stop the spread of a fire.

We see then that the distinction between active and passive, important as it is elsewhere, has a special importance in the area of euthanasia. It should also be clear why James Rachels's other argument, that it is often "more humane" to kill than to allow to die, does not show that the distinction between active and passive euthanasia is morally irrelevant. It might be "more humane" in this sense to deprive a man of the property that brings evils on him, or to refuse to pay what is owed to Hume's profligate debauchee; but if we say this, we must admit that an act which is "more humane" than its alternative may be morally objectionable because it infringes rights.

So far we have said very little about the right to service as opposed to the right to noninterference, though it was agreed that both might be brought under the heading of "the right to life." What about the duty to preserve life that may belong to special classes of persons such as bodyguards, firemen, or doctors? Unlike the general public they are not within their rights if they merely refrain from interfering and do not try to sustain life. The subject's claim-rights are two-fold as far as they are concerned and passive as well as active euthanasia may be ruled out here if it is against his will. This is not to say that he has the right to any and every service needed to save or prolong his life; the rights of other people set limits to what may be demanded, both because they have the right not to be interfered with and because they may have a competing right to services. Furthermore one must enquire just what the contract or implicit agreement amounts to in each case. Firemen and bodyguards presumably have a duty which is simply to preserve life, within the limits of justice to others and of reasonableness to themselves. With doctors it may however be different, since their duty relates not only to preserving life but also to the relief of suffering. It is not clear what a doctor's duties are to his patient if life can be prolonged only at the cost of suffering or suffering relieved only by measures that shorten life. George Fletcher has argued that what the doctor is under contract to do depends on what is generally done, because this is what a patient will reasonably expect.[14] This seems right. If procedures are part of normal medical practice then it seems that the patient can demand them however much it may be against his interest to do so. Once again it is not a matter of what is "most humane."

That the patient's right to life may set limits to permissible acts of euthanasia seems undeniable. If he does not want to die no one has the right to practice active euthanasia on him, and passive euthanasia may also be ruled out where he has a right to the services of doctors or others.

Perhaps few will deny what has so far been said about the impermissibility of acts of euthanasia simply because we have so far spoken about the case of one who positively wants to live, and about his rights; whereas those who advocate euthanasia are usually thinking either about those who wish to die or about those whose wishes cannot be ascertained either because they cannot properly be said to have wishes or because, for one reason or another, we are unable to form a reliable estimate of what they are. The question that must now be asked is whether the latter type of case, where euthanasia though not involuntary would again be nonvoluntary, is different from the one discussed so far. Would we have the right to kill someone for his own good so long as we had no idea that he positively wished to live? And what about the life-prolonging duties of doctors in the same circumstances? This is a very difficult problem. On the one hand, it seems ridiculous to suppose that a man's right to life is something which generates duties only where he has signaled that he wants to live; as a borrower does indeed have a duty to return something lent on indefinite loan only if the lender indicates that he wants it back. On the other hand, it might be argued that there is something illogical about the idea that a right has been infringed if someone incapable of saying whether he wants it or not is deprived of something that is doing him harm rather than good. Yet on the analogy of property we would say that a right has been infringed. Only if someone had earlier told us that in such circumstances he would not want to keep the thing could we think that his right had been waived. Perhaps if we could make confident judgments about what anyone in such circumstances would wish, or what he would have wished beforehand had he considered the matter, we could agree to consider the right to life as "dormant," needing to be asserted if the normal duties were to remain. But as things are we cannot make any such assumption; we simply do not know what most people would want, or would have wanted, us to do unless they tell us. This is certainly the case so far as active measures to end life are concerned. Possibly it is different, or will become different, in the matter of being kept alive, so general is the feeling against using sophisticated procedures on moribund patients, and so much is this dreaded by people who are old or terminally ill. Once again the distinction between active and passive euthanasia has come on the scene, but this time because most people's attitudes to the two are so different. It is just possible that we might presume, in the absence of specific evidence, that someone would not wish, beyond a certain point, to be kept alive; it is certainly not possible to assume that he would wish to be killed.

In the last paragraph we have begun to broach the topic of voluntary euthanasia, and this we must now discuss. What is to be said about the case in which there is no doubt about someone's wish to die: either he has told us beforehand that he would wish it in circumstances such as he is now in, and has shown no sign of a change of mind, or else he tells us now, being in possession of his faculties and of a steady mind. We should surely say that the objections previously urged against acts of euthanasia, which it must be remembered were all on the ground of rights, had disappeared. It does not seem that one would infringe someone's right to life in killing him with his permission and in fact at his request. Why should someone not be able to waive his right to life, or rather, as would be more likely to happen, to cancel some of the duties of noninterference that this right entails? (He is more likely to say that he should be killed by this man at this time in this manner, than to say that anyone may kill him at any time and in any way.) Similarly someone may give permission for the destruction of his property, and request it. The important thing is that he gives a critical permission, and it seems that this is enough to cancel the duty normally associated with the right. If someone gives you permission to destroy his property it can no longer be said that you have no right to do so, and I do not see why it should not be the case with taking a man's life. An objection might be made on the ground that only God has the right to take life, but in this paper religious as opposed to moral arguments are being left aside. Religion apart, there seems to be no case to be made out for an infringement of rights if a man who wishes to die is allowed to die or even killed. But of course it does not follow that there is no moral objection to it. Even with property, which is after all a relatively small matter, one might be wrong to destroy what one had the right to destroy. For, apart from its value to other people, it might be valuable to the man who wanted it destroyed, and charity might require us to hold our hand where justice did not.

Let us review the conclusion of this part of the argument, which has been about euthanasia and the right to life. It has been argued that from this side come stringent restrictions on the acts of euthanasia that could be morally permissible. Active nonvoluntary euthanasia is ruled out by that part of the right to life which creates the duty of non-interference though passive nonvoluntary euthanasia is not ruled out, except where the right to life-preserving action has been created by some special condition such as a contract between a man and his doctor, and it is not always certain just what such a contract involves. Voluntary euthanasia is another matter: as the preceding paragraph suggested, no right is infringed if a man is allowed to die or even killed at his own request.

Turning now to the other objection that normally holds against inducing the death of another, that it is against charity, or benevolence, we must tell a very different story. Charity is the virtue that gives attachment to the good of others, and because life is normally a good, charity normally demands that it should be saved or prolonged. But as we so defined an act of euthanasia that it seeks a man's death for his own sake—for his good—charity will normally speak in favor of it. This is not, of course, to say that charity can require an act of euthanasia which justice forbids, but if an act of euthanasia is not contrary to justice—that is, it does not infringe rights—charity will rather be in its favor than against.

Once more the distinction between nonvoluntary and voluntary euthanasia must be considered. Could it ever be compatible with charity to seek a man's death although he wanted to live, or at least had not let us know that he wanted to die? It has been argued that in such circumstances active euthanasia would infringe his right to life, but passive euthanasia would not do so, unless he had some special right to life-preserving service from the one who allowed him to die. What would charity dictate? Obviously when a man wants to live there is a presumption that he will be benefited if his life is prolonged, and if it is so the question of euthanasia does not arise. But it is, on the other hand, possible that he wants to live where it would be better for him to die: perhaps he does not realize the desperate situation he is in, or perhaps he is afraid of dying. So, in spite of a very proper resistance to refusing to go along with a man's own wishes in the matter of life and death, someone might justifiably refuse to prolong the life even of someone who asked him to prolong it, as in the case of refusing to give the wounded soldier a drug that would keep him alive to meet a terrible end. And it is even more obvious that charity does not always dictate that life should be prolonged where a man's own wishes, hypothetical or actual, are not known.

So much for the relation of charity to nonvoluntary passive euthanasia, which was not, like nonvoluntary active euthanasia, ruled out by the right to life. Let us now ask what charity has to say about voluntary euthanasia both active and passive. It was suggested in the discussion of justice that if of sound mind and steady desire, a man might give others the *right* to allow him to die or even to kill him, where otherwise this would be ruled out. But it was pointed out that this would not settle the question of whether the act was morally permissible, and it is this that we must now consider. Could not charity speak against what justice allowed? Indeed it might do so. For while the fact that a man wants to die suggests that his life is wretched, and while his rejection of life may itself tend to take the good out of the things he might have enjoyed, nevertheless his wish to die might here be opposed for his own sake just as it might be if suicide were in question. Perhaps there is hope that his mental condition will improve. Perhaps he is mistaken in thinking his disease incurable. Perhaps he wants to die for the sake of someone else on whom he feels he is a burden, and we are not ready to accept this sacrifice whether for ourselves or others. In such cases, and there will surely be many of them, it could not be for his own sake that we kill him or allow him to die, and therefore euthanasia as defined in this paper would not be in question. But this is not to deny that there could be acts of voluntary euthanasia both passive and active against which neither justice nor charity would speak.

We have now considered the morality of euthanasia both voluntary and nonvoluntary, and active and passive. The conclusion has been that nonvoluntary active euthanasia (roughly, killing a man against his will or without his consent) is never justified; that is to say, that a man's being killed for his own good never justifies the act unless he himself has consented to it. A man's rights are infringed by such an action, and it is therefore contrary to justice. However, all the other combinations, nonvoluntary passive euthanasia, voluntary active euthanasia, and voluntary passive euthanasia are sometimes compatible with both justice and charity. But the strong condition carried in the definition of euthanasia adopted in this paper must not be forgotten; an act of euthanasia as here understood is one whose purpose is to benefit the one who dies.

In the light of this discussion let us look at our present practices. Are they good or are they bad? And what changes might be made, thinking now not only of the morality of particular acts of euthanasia but also of the indirect effects of instituting different practices, of the abuses to which they might be subject and of the changes that might come about if euthanasia became a recognized part of the social scene.

The first thing to notice is that it is wrong to ask whether we should introduce the practice of euthanasia as if it were not something we already had. In fact we do have it. For instance it is common, where the medical prognosis is very bad, for doctors to recommend against

measures to prolong life, and particularly where a process of degenera-
tion producing one medical emergency after another has already set in.
If these doctors are not certainly within their legal rights, this is
something that is apt to come as a surprise to them as to the general
public. It is also obvious that euthanasia is often practiced where old
people are concerned. If someone very old and soon to die is attacked
by a disease that makes his life wretched, doctors do not always come
in with life-prolonging drugs. Perhaps poor patients are more fortu-
nate in this respect than rich patients, being more often left to die in
peace; but it is in any case a well recognized piece of medical practice,
which is a form of euthanasia.

No doubt the case of infants with mental or physical defects will be
suggested as another example of the practice of euthanasia as we
already have it, since such infants are sometimes deliberately allowed
to die. That they are deliberately allowed to die is certain; children with
severe spina bifida malformations are not always operated on even
where it is thought that without the operation they will die; and even in
the case of children with Down's syndrome who have intestinal obstructions, the relatively simple operation that would make it possible
to feed them is sometimes not performed.[15] Whether this is euthanasia
in our sense or only as the Nazis understood it is another matter. We
must ask the crucial question, "Is it for the sake of the child himself
that the doctors and parents choose his death?" In some cases the
answer may really be yes, and what is more important it may really be
true that the kind of life which is a good is not possible or likely for this
child, and that there is little but suffering and frustration in store for
him.[16] But this must presuppose that the medical prognosis is wretchedly bad, as it may be for some spina bifida children. With children
who are born with Down's syndrome it is, however, quite different.
Most of these are able to live on for quite a time in a reasonably
contented way, remaining like children all their lives, but capable of
affectionate relationships and able to play games and perform simple
tasks. The fact is, of course, that the doctors who recommend against
life-saving procedures for handicapped infants are usually thinking not
of them but rather of their parents and of other children in the family
or of the "burden on society" if the children survive. So it is not for
their sake but to avoid trouble to others that they are allowed to die.
When brought out into the open this seems unacceptable: at least we

do not easily accept the principle that adults who need special care should be counted too burdensome to be kept alive. It must in any case be insisted that if children with Down's syndrome are deliberately allowed to die this is not a matter of euthanasia except in Hitler's sense. And for our children, since we scruple to gas them, not even the manner of their death is "quiet and easy"; when not treated for an intestinal obstruction a baby simply starves to death. Perhaps some will take this as an argument for allowing active euthanasia, in which case they will be in the company of an S.S. man stationed in the Warthgenau who sent Eichmann a memorandum telling him that "Jews in the coming winter could no longer be fed" and submitting for his consideration a proposal as to whether "it would not be the most humane solution to kill those Jews who were incapable of work through some quicker means."[17] If we say we are *unable* to look after children with handicaps we are no more telling the truth than was the S.S. man who said that the Jews could not be fed.

Nevertheless if it is ever right to allow deformed children to die because life will be a misery to them, or not to take measures to prolong for a little the life of a newborn baby whose life cannot extend beyond a few months of intense medical intervention, there is a genuine problem about active as opposed to passive euthanasia. There are well-known cases in which the medical staff has looked on wretchedly while an infant died slowly from starvation and dehydration because they did not feel able to give a lethal injection. According to the principles discussed in the earlier part of this paper, they would indeed have had no right to give it, since an infant cannot ask that it should be done. The only possible solution—supposing that voluntary active euthanasia were to be legalized—would be to appoint guardians to act on the infant's behalf. In a different climate of opinion this might not be dangerous, but at present, when people so readily assume that the life of a handicapped baby is of no value, one would be loath to support it.

Finally, on the subject of handicapped children, another word should be said about those with severe mental defects. For them too it might sometimes be right to say that one would wish for death for their sake. But not even severe mental handicap automatically brings a child within the scope even of a possible act of euthanasia. If the level of consciousness is low enough it could not be said that life is a good to them, any more than in the case of those suffering from extreme senility. Nevertheless if they do not suffer it will not be an act of euthanasia by which someone opts for their death. Perhaps charity does not demand that strenuous measures are taken to keep people in this state alive, but euthanasia does not come into the matter, any more than it does when someone is, like Karen Ann Quinlan, in a state of permanent coma. Much could be said about this last case. It might even be suggested that in the case of unconsciousness this "life" is not the life to which "the right to life" refers. But that is not our topic here.

What we must consider, even if only briefly, is the possibility that euthanasia, genuine euthanasia, and not contrary to the requirements of justice or charity, should be legalized over a wider area. Here we are up against the really serious problem of abuse. Many people want, and want very badly, to be rid of their elderly relatives and even of their ailing husbands or wives. Would any safeguards ever be able to stop them describing as euthanasia what was really for their own benefit? And would it be possible to prevent the occurrence of acts which were genuinely acts of euthanasia but morally impermissible because infringing the rights of a patient who wished to live?

Perhaps the furthest we should go is to encourage patients to make their own contracts with a doctor by making it known whether they wish him to prolong their life in case of painful terminal illness or of incapacity. A document such as the Living Will seems eminently sensible, and should surely be allowed to give a doctor following the previously expressed wishes of the patient immunity from legal proceedings by relatives.[18] Legalizing active euthanasia is, however, another matter. Apart from the special repugnance doctors feel towards the idea of a lethal injection, it may be of the very greatest importance to keep a psychological barrier up against killing. Moreover it is active euthanasia which is the most liable to abuse. Hitler would not have been able to kill 275,000 people in his "euthanasia" program if he had had to wait for them to need life-saving treatment. But there are other objections to active euthanasia, even voluntary active euthanasia. In the first place it would be hard to devise procedures that would protect people from being persuaded into giving their consent. And secondly the possibility of active voluntary euthanasia might change the social scene in ways that would be very bad. As things are, people do, by and large, expect to be looked after if they are old or ill. This is one of the good things that we have, but we might lose it, and be much worse off without it. It might come to be expected that someone likely to need a lot of looking after should call for the doctor and demand his own death. Something comparable could be good in an extremely poverty-stricken community where the children genuinely suffered from lack of food; but in rich societies such as ours it would surely be a spiritual disaster. Such possibilities should make us very wary of supporting large measures of euthanasia, even where moral principle applied to the individual act does not rule it out.

Notes

1. Leo Alexander, "Medical Science under Dictatorship," *New England Journal of Medicine* (14 July 1949), p. 40.
2. For a discussion of culpable and nonculpable ignorance see Thomas Aquinas, *Summa Theologica,* first part of the second part, question 6, article 8, and question 19, articles 5 and 6.
3. Dmitri Panin, *The Notebooks of Sologdin* (London, 1976), pp. 66–67.
4. Thomas Nagel, "Death," in James Rachels, ed., *Moral Problems* (New York, 1971), p. 362.
5. Panin, *Sologdin,* p. 85.
6. Yet some detail needs to be filled in to explain why we should not say that a scarecrow is beneficial to the plants it protects. Perhaps what is beneficial must either be a feature of the plant itself, such as protective prickles, or else must work on the plant directly, such as a line of trees which give it shade.
7. David Hume, *Treatise,* Book III, part II, section 1.
8. See, for example D.D. Raphael, "Human Rights Old and New," in D.D. Raphael, ed., *Political Theory and the Rights of Man* (London, 1967), and Joel Feinberg, "The Nature and Value of Rights," *The Journal of Value Inquiry* 4, no. 4 (Winter 1970): 243–57. Reprinted in Samuel Gorovitz, ed., *Moral Problems in Medicine* (Englewood Cliffs, N.J., 1976).
9. Feinberg, "Human Rights," *Moral Problems in Medicine,* p. 465.
10. See, for example, James Rachels, "Active and Passive Euthanasia," *New England Journal of Medicine* 292, no. 2 (9 Jan. 1975): 78–80.
11. Ibid.
12. It is not, however, that justice and charity conflict. A man does not lack charity because he refrains from an act of injustice which would have been for someone's good.
13. For a discussion of such questions, see my article "The Problem of Abortion and the Doctrine of Double Effect," *Oxford Review,* no. 5 (1967); reprinted in Rachels, *Moral Problems,* and Gorovitz, *Moral Problems in Medicine.*

14. George Fletcher, "Legal Aspects of the Decision not to Prolong Life," *Journal of the American Medical Association* 203, no. 1 (1 Jan. 1968): 119–22. Reprinted in Gorovitz.

15. I have been told this by a pediatrician in a well-known medical center in the United States. It is confirmed by Anthony M. Shaw and Iris A. Shaw, "Dilemma of Informed Consent in Children," *The New England Journal of Medicine* 289, no. 17 (25 Oct. 1973): 885–90. Reprinted in Gorovitz.

16. It must be remembered, however, that many of the social miseries of spina bifida children could be avoided. Professor R. B. Zachary is surely right to insist on this. See, for example, "Ethical and Social Aspects of Spina Bifida," *The Lancet* (3 Aug. 1968), pp. 274–76. Reprinted in Gorovitz.

17. Quoted by Hannah Arendt, *Eichmann in Jerusalem* (London, 1963), p. 90.

18. Details of this document are to be found in J.A. Behnke and Sissela Bok, eds., *The Dilemmas of Euthanasia* (New York, 1975), and in A.B. Downing, ed., *Euthanasia and the Right to Life: The Case for Voluntary Euthanasia* (London, 1969).

3   Unsanctifying Human Life

PETER SINGER

As a preface to the substantive part of this chapter, I offer a comment on the nature of medical ethics which may clarify my approach.

The professional philosopher with an interest in ethics, and in particular what might be called "applied moral philosophy," may well discuss with his students and colleagues the moral problems that doctors encounter in the course of their practice. Since the professional philosopher is specially trained to think about these issues and has all the time he requires at his disposal to do so, one might think that the philosopher would be able to give considerable assistance to the doctor, whose training and time are devoted to medicine rather than moral philosophy. Yet with few exceptions, this is not the case. Doctors discuss their ethical dilemmas in the medical journals and philosophers keep to the philosophical journals; the footnotes in each case remain within the circle of the author's colleagues.

All this is not just a matter of the old academic failure to look at work outside one's own discipline. Anyone who reads both philosophical and medical journals containing discussions of problems in medical ethics can hardly avoid noticing that there is a more fundamental gap between the discussions than the fact that they appear in different kinds of journals. There is also a difference in the presuppositions employed and the problems discussed.

For example, in recent issues of philosophical journals we can find articles in which it is argued, quite seriously and on plausible grounds, that a normal, healthy human infant has no right to life and that it is, in this respect, in the same position as a fetus.[1] Doctors, on the other hand, are so far from even considering this position that they regard as serious ethical dilemmas such questions as, What should be done with a patient certain never to recover consciousness? or, Are parents to be given the option of deciding how far a doctor should go in using all available techniques to save the life of a hopelessly retarded infant with, in addition, a congenital heart defect?[2]

There are a number of reasons why the ethical concerns of philosophers and practicing physicians should be so far apart. One important reason is the different ways in which they are affected by the law. The busy doctor, who would rather be doing medicine than philosophy, turns to ethical questions only when they actually confront him. He tends not to raise questions which he would never face in practice, since he has enough problems without thinking up hypothetical ones. So if some course of action is straightforwardly illegal—for instance, the direct killing of a retarded infant—then most doctors are not even going to consider whether this course of action might be morally justifiable. When the law is clear, it resolves the doctor's ethical problem for him. So long as the doctor obeys the law, he can hardly be blamed for the outcome, because he can regard himself as purely a medical man, a technician whose business it is to carry out policy but not to set it; if he goes against the law, however, he risks criminal proceedings and disqualification from practice. No wonder that most medical ethics is concerned with cases on which the law fails to give any clear guide—cases like those involving the use of extraordinary means to save life.

The philosopher, of course, is in a quite different position. Untroubled by such mundane issues as what the law allows, he turns his attention to cases which invoke basic moral principles. If real cases do not serve this purpose, he is free to make up hypothetical ones. So he follows the argument wherever it leads him, and if it leads him to the view that infanticide is often justifiable, well, this conclusion is not likely to cause him, personally, any problems.

Now one can certainly sympathize with the doctor who confines his attention to those cases that he *has* to deal with, and regards the moral philosopher as an irresponsible theorizer. Nevertheless, the resulting limited scope of much of the work by medical people in medical ethics has had, I think, a harmful effect on the conclusions reached even within those areas that have received close attention. While we may agree that in general a doctor ought to obey the law, there has been a tendency to lose sight of the difference between this view and the idea that the law, and the conventional moral standards it embodies, is an indisputable starting point for further ethical debate. Because in practice a doctor can not challenge the law when it is clear and straightforward, the moral standards behind the law also do not often get challenged; if these conventional moral standards are in fact dubious, however, then conclusions which presuppose them are also likely to be dubious.

My purpose in what follows is to challenge one of these conventional moral doctrines: the doctrine of the sanctity of human life. I know that in taking this approach I run the risk of being regarded as yet another philosopher far removed from the world of real people. I shall try to guard against this danger by discussing some current, widely accepted medical practices. My strategy will be to bring together two distinct areas of medicine that are normally discussed only in quite separate moral contexts, and to show thereby that current attitudes in medical ethics are either plainly inconsistent or else guilty of a crude form of discrimination that is no more defensible than racial discrimination. In this way I want to force those involved in medicine to reconsider the foundations of the decisions they make. Foundations that give rise to the kind of inconsistency or discrimination that I am referring to are in urgent need of reconsideration; and the core of the problem, I believe, is the doctrine of the sanctity of human life.

People often say that life is sacred. They almost never mean what they say. They do not mean, as their words seem to imply, that *all* life is sacred. If they did, killing a pig or even pulling up a cabbage would be as contrary to their doctrine as infanticide. So when in the context of medical ethics people talk of the sanctity of life, it is the sanctity of *human* life that they really mean. It is this doctrine that I shall be discussing from now on.

In discussing the doctrine of the sanctity of human life, I shall not take the term "sanctity" in any specifically religious sense. Although I think that the doctrine does have a religious origin, and I shall say more about this shortly, it is now part of a broadly secular ethic, and it is as part of this secular ethic that it is most influential today. Not all those who talk about "the sanctity of life" are religious, and of those that are religious, in many cases their affirmation of the sanctity of life is independent of their religious views. In the secular context in which problems of medical ethics are usually discussed today, those who talk of the sanctity of human life are trying to say essentially that human life has some very special value; and a crucial implication of this assertion is the idea that there is a radical difference between the value of a human life and the value of the life of some other animal—a difference not merely of degree, but of quality or kind.

It is this idea, the idea that *human* life as such has unique value, that I shall criticize. Before I do so, however, I want to demonstrate how deep-seated and pervasive this idea of the unique value of human life is and how far this idea is sometimes taken in our own society and within the field of medicine. To demonstrate this, I offer two instances from different areas of medicine.

First, as an example of the value attributed to human life, a summary of a case history from Anthony Shaw's recent article, "Dilemmas of 'Informed Consent' in Children":

A baby was born with Down's syndrome (mongolism), intestinal obstruction, and a congenital heart condition. The mother, believing that the retarded infant would be impossible for her to care for adequately, refused to consent to surgery to remove the intestinal obstruction. Without surgery, of course, the baby would soon die. Thereupon a local child-welfare agency, invoking a state child-abuse statute, obtained a court order directing that surgery be performed. After a complicated course of surgery and thousands of dollars worth of medical care, the infant was returned to her mother. In addition to her mental retardation, the baby's physical growth and development remained markedly retarded because of her severe cardiac disease. A follow-up enquiry eighteen months after the baby's birth revealed that the mother felt more than ever that she had been done an injustice.[3]

This case shows how much some people are prepared to do in order to ensure that a human infant lives, irrespective of the actual or potential mental capacities of the infant, its physical condition, or the wishes of the mother.

While some doctors are struggling to preserve life in cases of this sort, others are using their medical training in another way: they design and carry out experiments on nonhuman animals. I will give an example of the kind of work that is quite frequently done because its nature is not as well known as it ought to be. This particular experiment was carried out at the University of Michigan Medical School and funded by the National Research Council and the U.S. Public Health Service. The description which follows is drawn from the researchers' own account, which they published in the journal *Psychopharmocologia:*

The researchers confined sixty-four monkeys in small cubicles. These monkeys were then given unlimited access to a variety of drugs through tubes implanted in their arms. They could control the intake by pressing a lever. In some cases, after the monkeys had become addicted, supplies were abruptly cut off. Of the monkeys that had become addicted to morphine, three were "observed to die in convulsions" while others found dead in the morning were "presumed to have died in convulsions." Monkeys that had taken large amounts of cocaine inflicted severe wounds upon themselves, including biting off their fingers and toes, before dying convulsive deaths. Amphetamines caused one monkey to "pluck all of the hair off his arms and abdomen." In general, the experimenters found that "The manifestations of toxicity . . . were similar to the well-known toxicities of these drugs in man." They noted that experiments on animals with addictive drugs had been going on in their laboratory for "the last 20 years."[4]

I know that it is not pleasant to think about experiments of this nature; but since they are a real part of medicine, they should not be ignored. In fact this experiment is by no means exceptional and is perhaps no worse than the routine testing of new drugs, foodstuffs, and cosmetics, which results in the poisoning of millions of animals annually in the United States.[5] Nor, for that matter, is the case of the mongoloid infant exceptional, apart from the fact that it was necessary to invoke the law; more commonly, the doctors would have obtained the mother's signature, though how often that signature implies genuine "informed consent" is another matter.

The question that arises from consideration of these two kinds of case is simply this: Can it be right to make great efforts to save the life of a mongoloid human infant when the mother does not want the infant to live, and at the same time can it not be wrong to kill, slowly and painfully, a number of monkeys?

One obvious defence of the addiction experiment that might be offered is that by means of such experiments, results are obtained which lead to the elimination of more suffering than is caused by the experiments themselves. Certainly in the experiment I described, no startling new discoveries were made, and any connection with the alleviation of suffering seems very tenuous. However, this defence is irrelevant to the comparison I am drawing between the way we treat humans and other animals. We would not forcibly addict mongoloid infants to drugs and then allow them to die in convulsions even if we did believe that useful knowledge could thus be obtained. Why do we think it wrong to treat members of our own species in the same way that we treat other species?

Can it ever be right to treat one kind of being in a way that we would not treat another kind? Of course it can, if the beings differ in relevant respects. Which respects are relevant will depend on the treatment in question. We could defend a decision to teach young members of our own species to read, without making the same effort on behalf of young dogs, on the grounds that the two kinds of being differ in their capacity to benefit from these efforts. This difference is obviously relevant to the particular proposal. On the other hand, anyone who proposed teaching some humans to read but not others, on the grounds that people whose racial origin is different from his own should not be encouraged to read, would be discriminating on an arbitrary basis since race as such has nothing to do with the extent to which a person can benefit from being able to read.

Now what is the position when we compare severely and irreparably retarded human infants with nonhuman animals like pigs and dogs, monkeys and apes? I think we are forced to conclude that in at least some cases the human infant does not possess any characteristics or capacities that are not also possessed, to an equal or higher degree, by many nonhuman animals. This is true of such capacities as the capacity to feel pain, to act intentionally, to solve problems, and to communicate with and relate to other beings; and it is also true of such characteristics as self-awareness, a sense of one's own existence over time, concern for other beings, and curiosity.[6] In all these respects adult members of the species I have mentioned equal or surpass many retarded infant members of our own species; moreover some of these nonhumans surpass anything that some human infants might eventually achieve even with intensive care and assistance. (In case anyone should be uncertain about this, it should be noted that chimpanzees have now been taught to communicate by means of American Sign

Language, the standard language used by deaf people in this country, and have mastered vocabularies of well over a hundred signs, including signs which indicate that they possess both self-awareness and the idea of time.[7]

So when we decide to treat one being—the severely and irreparably retarded infant—in one way, and the other being—the pig or monkey—in another way, there seems to be no difference between the two that we can appeal to in defence of our discrimination. There is, of course, the fact that one being is, biologically, a member of our own species, while the others are members of other species. This difference, however, cannot justify different treatment, except perhaps in very special circumstances; for it is precisely the kind of arbitrary difference that the most crude and overt kind of racist tries to use to justify racial discrimination. Just as a person's race is in itself nearly always irrelevant to the question of how that person should be treated, so a being's species is in itself nearly always irrelevant. If we are prepared to discriminate against a being simply because it is not a member of our own species, although it has capacities equal or superior to those of a member of our own species, how can we object to the racist discriminating against those who are not of his own race, although they have capacities equal or superior to those of members of his own race?

I said a moment ago that a difference of species cannot justify different treatment except perhaps in very special circumstances. It may be worth mentioning the circumstances I have in mind. If we discovered a new drug which we thought could be a very powerful aid in the treatment of serious diseases, we might feel that it should be tested in some way before being used on normal humans, in order to see if it had dangerous side-effects. Assuming that there was no reliable way of testing it except on a living, sentient creature, should we test it on a severely and irreparably retarded human infant, or on some other animal, like a monkey? Here, if the capacities of the beings are equal, I think we might be justified in saying that the biological species of the being was relevant. Since many drugs affect different species in unpredictably different ways, we would probably achieve our goal sooner by testing the drug on the retarded member of our own species than on the monkey; this would mean that we would have to use fewer subjects for our experiment and so inflict less suffering all told. This seems to be a reasonable ground for preferring to use the human infant, rather than the monkey, if we have already decided to test the drug on one or the other. So discrimination on the basis of species, in the rare cases in which it is justified, seems to go *against* our present practices rather than in favor of them. (Even here we would not really be discriminating on the basis of species *as such,* but rather using the species of the being as an indication of further possible unknown differences between them.)

The doctrine of the sanctity of human life, as it is normally understood, has at its core a discrimination on the basis of species and nothing else. Those who espouse the doctrine make no distinction, in their opposition to killing, between normal humans who have developed to a point at which they surpass anything that other animals can achieve, or humans in a condition of hopeless senility, or human fetuses, or infant humans, or severely brain damaged humans. Yet those who use the sanctity of life doctrine as a ground for opposition to killing any human beings show little or no concern over the vast amount of quite unnecessary killing of nonhuman animals that goes on in our society, despite the fact that many of these other animals equal or surpass humans (except for normal humans beyond the age of infancy) on any test that I can imagine to be relevant, in all the categories I have just mentioned. It is significant to note, too, that even if we allow the relevance of a being's potential (and I agree with Michael Tooley that there are serious objections to so doing),[8] there are still human beings—the hopelessly senile and the irreparably brain damaged—whose life is allegedly sacrosanct, who cannot be distinguished from other animals in respect of their potential.

A doctrine which went by the name of "the sanctity of human life" would not necessarily have to be a speciesist doctrine. The term "human" is not strictly a biological term and, as Tooley has pointed out, it is a mistake to assume that "human being" refers to precisely the same beings as are designated by the biological idea of "member of the species *homo sapiens.*" "Human," according to the *Oxford English Dictionary,* means "of, belonging to, or characteristic of man"; or in a slightly different sense, "having or showing the qualities or attributes proper to or distinctive of man." If the advocates of the "sanctity of human life" doctrine were to take this definition seriously, they would find their views radically transformed. According to the definition, whether we class a being as "human" will depend on what qualities or attributes we think characteristic of, proper to, or distinctive of man (and I assume that by "man," the dictionary here means men and women, mankind as a whole). So we would then have to try to draw up a list of these qualities or attributes—something which some writers in the field have already tried to do.[9] This list would probably include some or all of the capacities and characteristics that I mentioned earlier, when comparing retarded infants and monkeys, but to decide which properties were necessary and which sufficient would be difficult. Let us say, though, just to take an example, that we decide that what is characteristic or distinctive of men and women is a capacity of self-awareness or self-consciousness. Then we will not count severely retarded infants as human beings even though they are clearly members of *homo sapiens*; at the same time we might decide, after examining the abilities displayed by apes, dolphins and perhaps some other mammals, to count these beings as human beings.

In any case, if we follow the dictionary definition of "human," one point seems certain no matter what criteria we eventually select as distinctive of men and women: severely and irreparably retarded *homo sapiens* infants would be in the same category as a great many members of other species. This seems true, anyway, so long as we stay within the secular context that I have been assuming throughout this discussion. If we allow appeals to religious doctrines, based on special revelations, other conclusions might be possible—a point on which I shall say a little more later.

Is the only problem with the doctrine of the sanctity of human life, then, a misconception about the boundaries of "human"? Is it just that the advocates of this doctrine have got hold of a biological notion of what it is to be human instead of a notion that defines the term as the dictionary suggests it should be defined, with regard to characteristics distinctive of our species?

We could, perhaps, try to save the doctrine by modifying it in this way (and it would be no small modification). I chose my two contrasting examples of medical practice to show how far from this kind of position our present attitudes are. The suggested modification of the doctrine would place lethal experiments on the more developed non-human animals in the same category as experiments on severely retarded members of our own species. Similarly if, as Jonathan Swift once suggested, human infants, boiled, roasted or fricasseed, make a tasty dish, then we would have to choose between ceasing to rear animals like pigs and cattle for food, and admitting that there is no moral objection to fattening retarded infants for the table. Clearly, this is not a position that many present advocates of the sanctity of human life would be prepared to embrace. In fact, it is so far from what present advocates of the doctrine mean that it would be downright misleading to continue to use the same name for the doctrine. Whatever the proper or dictionary meaning of the word, "human" is now, in popular usage, too closely identified with "member of the species *homo sapiens*" for us to apply it to chimpanzees or deny it to retarded infants. I myself, in this paper, have used and for reasons of convenience shall continue to use the word in its popular, rather than dictionary, sense.

A further difficult question which conditions any attempt to redraw the boundaries of the "human" community is: where do we place normal embryonic or infant members of our species who have the potential, given normal development, to satisfy the criteria for membership but do not satisfy them at present? Judged by the characteristics they actually possess, and excluding for the moment such indirect factors as the concerns of parents or others, an infant *homo sapiens* aged six months would seem to be much less of a "human" than an adult chimpanzee; and if we consider a one-month-old infant, it compares unfavorably with those adult members of other species— pigs, cattle, sheep, rats, chickens and mice—that we destroy by the million in our slaughterhouses and laboratories. Does the potential of these infants make a difference to the wrongness of killing them?

It is impossible for me to discuss this question adequately here, so I will only point out that if we believe it is the potential of the infant that makes it wrong to kill it, we seem to be committed to the view that abortion, however soon after conception it may take place, is as seriously wrong as infanticide. Moreover, it is not easy to see on what grounds mere potential could give rise to a right to life, unless we valued what it was that the being had the potential to become—in this case a rational, self-conscious being. Now while we may think that a rational, self-conscious being has a right to life, relatively few of us, I think, value the existence of rational self-conscious beings in the sense that the more of them there are, the better we think it is. If we did value the existence of rational self-conscious beings in this way, we would be opposed to contraception, as well as abortion and infanticide, and even to abstinence or celibacy. But most of us think that there are enough rational, self-conscious beings around already—in which case I find it hard to see why we should place great moral weight on every potentially rational, self-conscious being realizing its potential. For further discussion of this important topic, though, I must refer you to the articles by Tooley and Warren that I have already mentioned.

Assuming that we can settle the criteria for being "human" in the strict sense, and can settle this problem about potentially "human" beings, would this mean that we had settled the question of which lives are sacred and which beings it is justifiable to kill for rather trivial reasons? Unfortunately, even then we would not have solved all our problems for there is no necessary connection between what is characteristic of, or distinctive of, mankind, and what it is that makes it wrong to kill a being. Proponents of the doctrine of the sanctity of human life, even after revising their definition of "human" so that it refers to characteristics distinctive of our species, need to *argue* for the view that the lives of all and only humans, so defined, are sacred. To believe that this connection was automatic and followed immediately without further argument would only be a slightly more sophisticated form of speciesism than the crude biological basis of discrimination discussed earlier. While we might, in the end, decide that all and only those beings whose lives were sacred were those that possessed the characteristics distinctive of mankind, this would be a moral decision that could not be deduced simply from the definition of "human." We might, on reflection, decide the other way—for instance, we might hold that no sentient being should be killed if the probability is that its life will contain a favorable balance of pleasure or happiness over pain and suffering.

Although I have been unable to make up my own mind about the necessary criteria for a right to life—and I leave this question open in the hope that others will be able to help me decide—it is clear that we shall have to change our attitudes about killing so as to obliterate the sharp distinction that we currently make between beings that are members of our own species and beings that are not. How shall we do this?

There are three possibilities:

1. While holding constant our attitudes to members of other species, we change our attitudes to members of our own species so that we

consider it legitimate to kill retarded human infants in painful ways for experimental purposes even when no immediately useful knowledge is likely to be derived from these experiments; and in addition we give up any moral objections we may have to rearing and killing these infants for food.

2. While holding constant our attitudes to members of our own species, we change our attitudes to members of other species so that we consider it wrong to kill them because we like the taste of their flesh or for experimental purposes even when the experiment would result in immediately useful knowledge; moreover we refuse to kill them even when they are suffering severe pain from some incurable disease and are a burden to those who must look after them.

3. We change our attitudes to both humans and nonhumans so that they come together at some point in between the present extremes.

None of these three positions makes an arbitrary discrimination on the basis of species, and all are consistent. So we cannot decide between them on these grounds; accordingly, while I am quite certain that our present attitudes are wrong, I am a little more tentative about which of these possibilities is right. Still, if we look at what each implies, I think we can see that the third possibility has much in its favor—not surprisingly, in view of its median position. Thus, I doubt that anyone could seriously advocate performing an experiment like that I described earlier on retarded infants of our own species; nor do I think that many of us could treat retarded infants as if they were purely means towards our gastronomic ends. I think that we can only carry on these practices with regard to other species because we have a huge prejudice in favor of the interests of our own species and a corresponding tendency to neglect the interests of other species. If I am right about this, we are not likely to transfer this prejudice to members of our own species. White racist slave-owners, if forced to stop discriminating, would be unlikely to start enslaving their fellow whites.

As for the second possibility, while I advocate a very radical change in our attitudes towards other species, I do not think this change should go so far as to imply that we should eliminate all mercy-killing or attempt to keep alive an animal which can only live in misery.

So we have to change our attitudes in both directions. We have to bring nonhumans within the sphere of our moral concern and cease to treat them purely as means to our ends. At the same time, once we realize that the fact that severely and irreparably retarded infants are members of the species *homo sapiens* is not in itself relevant to how we should treat them, we should be ready to reconsider current practices which cause suffering to all concerned and benefit nobody. As an example of such a practice, I shall consider, very briefly, the practice of allowing these infants to die by withholding treatment.

It quite often happens that a severely and irreparably retarded infant has, in addition to its retardation, a condition which unless treated will cause it to die in some foreseeable period—perhaps a day, perhaps a few months or a year. The condition may be one which doctors could, and in the case of a normal infant certainly would, cure; but sometimes, when the infant is severely and irreparably retarded, the doctor in charge will withhold this treatment and allow the infant to die. In general, we can only guess at how often this occurs but a recent investigation of the Yale-New Haven special care nursery showed that over a 2½ year period, 43 deaths, or 14% of all deaths in the nursery, were related to withholding treatment. The decision to withhold treatment at this nursery was in each case made by parents and physicians together on the basis that there was little or no chance for a meaningful life for the infant.[10] The investigators, Duff and Campbell, cautiously endorse this practice, and within the alternatives legally available to the doctors, it does seem to be the best that they can do; but if it is justifiable to withhold available forms of treatment knowing that this will result in the death of the infant, what possible grounds can there be for refusing to kill the infant painlessly?

The idea that there is a significant moral distinction between an act and an omission, between killing and letting die, has already been attacked by philosophers.[11] I accept their arguments and have nothing new to add to them, except for the reflection that we would never consider allowing a horse or dog to die in agony if it could be killed painlessly. Once we see that the case of a dying horse is really quite parallel to the case of a dying infant, we may be more ready to drop the distinction between killing and letting die in the case of the infant too.

This is by no means an academic issue. Enormous, and in my view utterly needless, suffering is caused by our present attitudes. Take, for example, the condition known as spina bifida, in which the infant is born with its spinal cord exposed. Three out of every thousand babies have this condition, which adds up to a large number of babies.

Although treatment is possible, with the more severe cases even immediate surgery and vigorous treatment will not result in successful rehabilitation. The children will grow up severely handicapped, both mentally and physically, and they will probably die in their teens. The
burden on the family can easily be imagined, and it is doubtful if the
child's life is a benefit for him. But what is the alternative to surgery,
under present medical ethics?

If surgery is not performed, the spina bifida baby will die—but not
immediately. Some of them, perhaps a third, will last more than three
months and a few will survive for several years. One writer has described their condition in the following terms:

Virtually all will be paralysed from the waist down, and incontinent because of
damage to their exposed nerves. Four out of five of these survivors will get
hydrocephalus; their heads will swell out, some until they are too heavy to hold
up. Severely retarded, often spastic and blind, they will spend their childhood
in institutions that most of us do not care to think about, let alone visit. By
adolescence virtually all will be dead.[12]

This kind of life is the alternative that parents must face if they hesitate
to consent to surgery. It is a horrible, immoral choice to offer anyone,
let alone parents immediately after the birth of their child. The obvious
alternative to trying to bring up a severely retarded and handicapped
child—a swift, painless death for the infant—is not available because
the law enforces the idea that the infant's life is sacred and cannot be
directly terminated.

This, then, is one way in which our treatment of severely and
irreparably retarded infants needs to be brought closer to our better
form of treatment of members of other species.

I said at the beginning of this paper that the moral philosopher and
the doctor with an interest in medical ethics have different concerns, at
least partly because of their different positions vis-à-vis the law. No
doubt this applies to the practice of allowing infants to die while
refusing to kill them. The law prohibits killing, but gives no clear
directive about letting die; so doctors do what they can to relieve
suffering within the boundaries of the law. For this, of course, they are
to be commended; but there are indications that a policy which should
be defended only in terms of making the best of a bad legal situation is
also being thought of as embodying a significant moral distinction.
Doctors can be heard sagely quoting Arthur Clough's lines: "Thou

shalt not kill, but needst not strive officiously to keep alive," as if these lines were a piece of ancient wisdom—they seem to be unaware that the lines were written to satirize the moral position in support of which they are being quoted.[13] More seriously, the House of Delegates of the American Medical Association recently adopted a policy statement condemning "the intentional termination of the life of one human being by another" as "contrary to that for which the medical profession stands," although the same statement went on to allow the "cessation of the employment of extraordinary means to preserve the life of the body."[14] But what is the cessation of any form of life-sustaining treatment if it is not the intentional termination of the life of one human being by another? And what exactly is it for which the medical profession stands that allows it to kill millions of sentient nonhuman beings while prohibiting it from releasing from suffering an infant *homo sapiens* with a lower potential for a meaningful life? While doctors may have to obey the law, they do not have to defend it.

I have suggested some ways in which, once we eliminate speciesist bias from our moral views, we might bring our attitudes to human and nonhuman animals closer together. I am well aware that I have not given any precise suggestions about when it is justifiable to kill either a retarded infant or a nonhuman animal. I have not made up my mind on this problem, but hope that others will offer suggestions.

In the remainder of this chapter, I shall look at the doctrine of the sanctity of human life from a perspective rather different from that which I have used up to now. Instead of producing arguments against the doctrine, I shall comment briefly on its historical origins. My motive for so doing is not, of course, the belief that normative consequences follow logically from historical facts. That belief is mistaken. To refute a doctrine it is necessary to produce sound arguments against it. Unfortunately, when a doctrine is very deeply embedded in people's moral institutions, it is sometimes necessary to do more than refute the doctrine in order to convince people that it is false. If one produces apparently valid objections to the doctrine but does no more, one is liable to be met by a reply rather like that which Moore used when he said that he was more certain of the existence of his hands than he could possibly be of the validity of any argument that purported to show that he could not know that his hands existed. In moral philosophy too people will say that they are more certain of the wrongness of killing human infants and the rightness of killing monkeys and pigs than they are of the validity of any arguments to the contrary. Instead of jettisoning their intuitions they will seek desperately for any foothold, however slender, from which they can support their intuitions. So the following historical excursion is intended to be a kind of softening-up operation on your intuitions, to persuade you that the doctrine of the sanctity of human life is a legacy of attitudes and beliefs that were once widespread, but which few people would now try to defend.

The doctrine of the sanctity of all human life, and the seriousness with which the killing of any member of our species is regarded, mark off the Christian ethical and cultural tradition from almost all others. Of course there have been cultures which regard all life, or at least all sentient life, as sacred and which prohibit the taking of the life of *homo sapiens;* and there have been other cultures which are as careless of the life of nonhuman animals as the Christian tradition, without being as scrupulous of the lives of all human beings; but the Christian tradition is distinctive for the sharpness of the line it draws between all beings that are members of our species and all other beings.

That very many different societies have seen no moral objection to abortion and infanticide is, I think, well-known. Even if we restrict our attention to infanticide, the list is almost endless. Westermarck's *Origin and Development of the Moral Ideas* has twenty pages chronicling the practice in societies which range geographically from the South Sea Islands over every continent to Greenland, and vary in habits and culture from nomadic Australian aborigines to the sophisticated city-dwellers of ancient Greece or mandarin China. In some of these cultures infanticide is not merely permitted, it is, in certain circumstances, morally obligatory. The use of either exposure or the direct killing of the new-born infant as a means of population control is not unusual, and in many societies the killing of deformed or sickly infants is obligatory. In other cultures where infanticide is not obligatory, it may still be performed without any sense of guilt or wrongdoing.[15]

It is, of course, possible to disregard accounts of the morals of so-called "primitive" societies by taking the line that we have advanced as far beyond these cultures in morals as we have in technology. Sometimes there is a certain amount of truth in this view. It is perhaps less easy to feel comfortable about the certainty of our own intuitions when we find them at variance with the views of cultures for whose moral sense we have considerable respect. I am thinking primarily of ancient Greece. Everyone knows that the Spartans exposed deformed or weak infants, but then no one cares much for Spartan morality anyway. Less often commented on is the fact that both Plato, in the *Republic,* and Aristotle, in his *Politics,* proposes that the state command the killing of deformed infants.[16] In making these recommendations, Plato and Aristotle were merely endorsing the legislative codes said to have been drawn up by the renowned law givers Lycurgus and Solon.

In Roman times, too, we find a moralist like Seneca, whose humanitarian outlook has survived the centuries, advocating infanticide for the sick and deformed.[17] Up to this time, this was thought of as a natural and humane solution, obviously preferable to the alternative of a miserable life for both parents and children. We find nothing resembling the doctrine that the lives of all born of human parents are sacred in the pre-Christian literature.

There can be no doubt that the change in European attitudes to abortion and infanticide is a product of the coming of Christianity. What is especially important to note about this change, for the purposes of the present discussion, is that the change had a special theological motivation in the new religion; that is to say, the change occurred not because of some general broadening of people's moral concern that was part of a more enlightened moral outlook, but because of the Christian doctrine that all born of human parents have immortal souls and are destined for an eternity of bliss or for everlasting torment. This central belief of the new religion placed a yawning gulf between *homo sapiens* and all other species, so far as the significance of their lives was concerned. To kill a human being was an act of fearful significance, since it consigned him or her to an eternal fate. Moreover this idea was coupled with another doctrine that made abortion and infanticide still more terrible. As the sixth century Saint Fulgentius says in his treatise *De Fide:*

It is to be believed beyond doubt that not only men who are come to the use of reason, but infants, whether they die in their mother's womb or after they are born, without baptism in the name of the Father, Son and Holy Ghost, are punished with everlasting punishment in eternal fire, because although they have no actual sin of their own, they carry along with them the condemnation of orignal sin from their first conception and birth.[18]

This was the orthodox view of the Latin Church. The unborn fetus, from the moment it acquired its soul, was destined to rise again on the day of judgment and face its Judge. If its responsibility for the sin of Adam had not been removed by baptism, it was doomed to hell for ever. No wonder that while previously abortion and infanticide had been looked upon as not crimes at all, or if crimes, then far less serious than the murder of an adult, after the coming of Christianity they were often thought of as worse than ordinary murder. Nor was this doctrine merely current among scholarly theologians. It was embodied in various early Christian laws. The Lex Bajuwariorum, one of the medieval Germanic codes, expressly provides for a daily compensation for children killed in the womb, on account of the daily suffering of those children in hell; and other codes provide for distinctively cruel modes of execution for mothers who kill their infants.[19] As W.E.H. Lecky puts it in his classic *History of European Morals:* "That which appealed so powerfully to the compassion of the early and medieval Christians, in the fate of the murdered infants, was not that they died, but that they commonly died unbaptised."[20]

Over the centuries of Christian domination of European thought, the moral ideas based on these doctrines took a firm hold. They became part of the basic moral beliefs of most Europeans. They were not seriously challenged until the eighteenth century, when rationalist thinkers started to question various religious dogmas. Then Bentham, among others, pointed out that the law's treatment of infanticide ignored the differences between this act and ordinary murder. He referred to the killing of an infant by an unmarried mother as

what is improperly called the death of an infant, who has ceased to be, before knowing what existence is,—a result of a nature not to give the slightest inquietude to the most timid imagination; and which can cause no regrets but to the very person who, through a sentiment of shame and pity, has refused to prolong a life begun under auspices of misery.[21]

The challenge to theological doctrines that gave rise to the doctrine of the sanctity of human life has, by and large, succeeded. The challenge to the moral attitudes themselves has made slower progress. Laws against abortion have been substantially weakened or abolished in many countries, but a doctor may still be charged with murder if he kills an infant, no matter how retarded. My brief historical survey suggests that the intuitions which lie behind these laws are not insights of self-evident moral truths, but the historically conditioned product of doctrines about immortality, original sin, and damnation which hardly anyone now accepts; doctrines so obnoxious, in fact, that if anyone did accept them, we should be inclined to discount any other moral views he held. Although advocates of the doctrine of the sanctity of human life now frequently try to give their position some secular justification, there can be no possible justification for making the boundary of sanctity run parallel with the boundary of our own species, unless we invoke some belief about immortal souls.

Before I finish I should mention one major objection, practical rather than theoretical, to my proposal that we reject the idea of the sanctity of human life. People are liable to say that while the doctrine may be based on an arbitrary and unjustifiable distinction between our own species and other species, this distinction still serves a useful purpose. Once we abandon the idea, this objection runs, we have embarked on a slippery slope that may lead to a loss of respect for the lives of ordinary people and eventually to an increase in crime or to the selective killing of racial minorities or political undesirables. So the idea of the sanctity of human life is worth preserving because the distinction it makes, even if inaccurate at some points, is close enough to a defensible distinction to be worth preserving.

There is no evidence that taking the lives of members of our own species under certain special circumstances will have any kind of contagious effect on our attitudes to killing in other circumstances. Historical evidence suggests the contrary. Ancient Greeks, as we have seen, regularly killed or exposed infants, but appear to have been at least as scrupulous about taking the lives of their fellow-citizens as medieval Christians or modern Americans. In Eskimo societies it was the custom for a man to kill his elderly parents, but to murder a normal, healthy adult was virtually unknown.[22] White colonists in Australia would shoot aborigines for sport, as their descendents now shoot kangaroos, with no discernible effect on the seriousness with which the killing of a white man was regarded. If we can separate such basically similar beings as Aborigines and Europeans into distinct moral categories without transferring our attitudes from one group to the other, there is surely not going to be much difficulty in marking off severely and irreparably retarded infants from normal human beings. Moreover, anyone who thinks that there is a risk of bad consequences if we abandon the doctrine of the sanctity of human life must still balance this possibility against the tangible harm to which the doctrine now gives rise: harm both to infants whose misery is needlessly prolonged, and to nonhumans whose interests are ignored.

Notes

1. See Michael Tooley, "Abortion and Infanticide," *Philosophy and Public Affairs* 2, no. 1 (1972); a similar conclusion seems to be implied by Mary Anne Warren, "The Moral and Legal Status of Abortion," *The Monist* 57, no. 1 (1975).
2. See Henry K. Beecher, "Ethical Problems Created by the Hopelessly Unconscious Patient," *New England Journal of Medicine* 278, no. 26 (1968); Anthony Shaw, "Dilemmas of 'Informed Consent' in Children," *New England Journal of Medicine* 289, no. 17 (1973).
3. Op. cit.
4. G. Deneau, T. Yanagita and M. Seevers, "Self-Administration of Psychoactive Substances by the Monkey," *Psychopharmocologia* 16 (1969), pp. 30–48.
5. See Richard Ryder, *Victims of Science* (London: Davis-Poynter, 1975).
6. This list is a compound of the main indicators of "humanhood" or "personhood" suggested by Mary Anne Warren, op. cit., and Joseph Fletcher, "Indicators of Humanhood: A Tentative Profile of Man," *The Hastings Center Report,* Institute of Society, Ethics and the Life Sciences (Hastings-on-Hudson, N.Y.) 2, no. 5 (1972).
7. For an early report, see R. A. Gardner and B. T. Gardner, "Teaching Sign Language to a Chimpanzee," *Science* 165 (1969); and for a more recent informal summary of progress in this area see the report by Peter Jenkins, *The Guardian* (London) 10 July, 1973, p. 16, reprinted in T. Regan & P. Singer (eds.), *Animal Rights and Human Obligations* (Englewood Cliffs, N.J.: Prentice-Hall, 1976).
8. Op. cit.
9. See note 6.
10. R. S. Duff and A.G.M. Campbell, "Moral and Ethical Dilemmas in the Special Care Nursery," *New England Journal of Medicine* 289, no. 17 (1973).
11. See Jonathan Bennett, "Whatever the Consequences," *Analysis* 26 (1966); Tooley, op. cit.; and Chapters 7 and 8 of this book; for a contrary view, see Chapter 2 of this book.
12. Gerald Leach, *The Biocrats* (Middlesex: Penguin, 1972) p. 197.

13. I owe this point to Jonathan Glover. See his *Causing Death and Saving Lives* (Middlesex: Penguin, 1977), Chap. 7.

14. *New York Times,* 5 Dec., 1973.

15. Edward Westermarck, *The Origin and Development of Moral Ideas,* Vol. 1 (London: Macmillan, 1924), pp. 394–413.

16. Aristotle *Politics* 7.1335^b; Plato *Republic* 5.460.

17. Seneca *De Ira* 1. 15 (referred to by Westermarck, op. cit., p. 419).

18. St. Fulgentius *De Fide* 27 (quoted by Westermarck, op. cit., pp. 416–17).

19. W.E.H. Lecky, *History of European Morals,* Vol. 2 (London: Longmans, 1892), p. 23n.

20. Ibid., p. 23. John T. Noonan has argued (in *The Morality of Abortion: Legal and Historical Perspective,* [Cambridge: Harvard Univ. Press, 1970]) that Christian opposition to abortion and infanticide did not depend on narrow theological doctrines, but on the spirit of the scriptual injunction to love our neighbor as ourself. So Noonan says, "The fetus as human was a neighbor; his life had parity with our own" (p. 58). But if we do not take account of theological doctrines, how can it be explained why, for the Christian, *any* human, including a fetus, is my neighbor, while a horse or a dog is not my neighbor, even though they resemble me more closely than the fetus in important characteristics like sentience and self-awareness, and I have more contact with them and am able to relate to them in a much more neighborly manner? Once this question is asked the influence of theological doctrines becomes apparent.

21. Jeremy Bentham, *Theory of Legislation,* p. 264f. (quoted by Westermarck, op. cit., p. 413n).

22. For the practice of killing elderly parents and other forms of euthanasia among the Eskimo, see the sources cited by Westermarck, op. cit. p. 387, n. 1 and p. 392, n. 1–3; for the rarity of homicide outside such special circumstances and the severe condemnation with which it is regarded among the same people, see Westermarck, op. cit. pp. 329; 330; 331, n. 2; 334.

4 Decisions to Terminate Life and the Concept of Person

MICHAEL TOOLEY

This chapter deals with the moral issues relevant to medical decisions to terminate the life of a human organism. The expression "termination of life" will be used to cover both (1) active intervention to bring about a state of an organism that will cause its death, and (2) a failure to intervene in causal processes that will otherwise result in the death of an organism. I will attempt to distinguish the different cases in which a decision to terminate life is morally justified and to isolate the considerations that are morally relevant to such decisions.

I. Decisions to terminate life: some possibly relevant considerations

There are a number of considerations that different people think relevant to medical decisions to terminate life and that are taken into account in actual medical practice. The following questions capture, I hope, the main ones:

1. Can the organism in question be characterized as a person?
2. If the organism is not a person, is it at least a potential person; that is, such as will develop into a person?
3. If the organism is a person, does he desire his own death, and if so, is that desire a rational one?

4. If the organism is a potential person, will this potential person express a rational desire to die once it becomes capable of expressing such a desire?

5. What quality of life will this person enjoy?

6. What quality of life will this potential person enjoy?

7. What is the cost of maintaining the life of this person?

8. What is the cost of allowing this potential person to become a person, and then of maintaining his life?

9. Are we dealing with an unconscious person whom it is technologically impossible to restore to consciousness?

10. Is the termination of life a matter of active intervention or only a matter of refraining from saving the life of the organism?

11. Are we dealing with a case of "direct" killing or only one of "indirect" killing?

12. Does it require "extraordinary," or only "ordinary" means to keep the person alive?

13. Is the individual suffering from a fatal illness?

There are two ways in which each of these considerations might be relevant to a decision to terminate life. First, it might bear upon the question of whether it is morally *permissible* to terminate life. Secondly, if termination of life is morally permissible, it may be relevant to the question of whether there is any *positive reason* for terminating life.

Given this distinction, the position I believe to be correct is this. First, the only considerations that should be taken into account in deciding whether it is morally permissible to terminate the life of an organism are whether it is a person, whether it has a rational desire to die, how expensive it will be to keep the person alive, and whether one is dealing with a person whom it is technologically impossible to restore to consciousness—considerations 1, 3, 7, and 9. Secondly, if it is morally permissible to terminate the life of an organism, then the considerations which may provide positive reasons for doing so are whether the organism is a person with a rational desire to die or a potential person that will come to have a rational desire to die, how expensive it will be to keep the person alive, what quality of life will be enjoyed by the potential person, and how expensive it will be to allow the potential person to become a person and then maintain its life—

considerations 3, 4, 6, 7, and 8. The remaining considerations—2, 5, 10, 11, 12, and 13—are not in themselves relevant to either issue.

Although many people in the medical professions might well agree with this general view, it is clear that it does diverge, in quite significant ways, from the moral viewpoints most commonly accepted in contemporary medical practice and thinking. The most important differences are these. First, a sharp distinction is usually drawn between killing and letting die, so that, for example, "death with dignity" or passive euthanasia is one thing, active euthanasia quite another. Secondly, a distinction between "direct" and "indirect" killing is sometimes appealed to, especially by Catholic moralists. On this view, a lethal dose of morphine, if there is no other way of alleviating a dying person's suffering, is morally permissible; simply killing the person is not. Thirdly, quality of life considerations are sometimes held to be relevant to the question of whether infanticide is morally permissible in certain cases. Finally, a distinction between "ordinary" and "extraordinary" means of keeping a person alive is sometimes invoked as justification for letting a person die in some cases where it would be possible to keep him alive.

Space does not permit me to comment critically upon the contention that some or all of these other considerations and distinctions are also morally relevant ones. Some of the important issues, however, especially those involved in the distinction between active and passive euthanasia, are discussed in Chapters 7 and 8 of this book. I shall confine myself to discussion of the types of cases where it seems to me that termination of life is morally permissible.

II. Death of persons versus death of biological organisms

Perhaps the first distinction that needs to be drawn is between the death of a person and the death of a biological organism. Expressions such as "right to life" and "sanctity of life" tend to blur this distinction, but its importance can be brought out by considering a case in which there would be a violation of someone's right to life, even though no biological organism had been destroyed. Suppose that one could destroy all of an organism's memories, program in completely new memories (or rather, apparent memories), and alter in an arbitrary manner the attitudes, beliefs, preferences, and personality traits of a human organism. If this were done to me, I would contend that Michael Tooley no longer existed and that a new person had been produced whose body was the body that once belonged to Michael Tooley. This strongly suggests that the right to life is not at bottom the right of an organism to continue to live, but the right of a person to continue to exist as the person he or she is.[1]

Once one realizes that it is the death of a person that matters rather than the death of a biological organism, one is in a position to ask whether there cannot be cases (not as in my reprogramming example where a person, but not an organism, is destroyed) where an organism is destroyed, but not a person. Of course one encounters such cases every day, assuming that at least some nonhuman animals, such as flies, are not persons.[2] But the question of interest here is whether this cannot also be the case with humans. There are three main candidates. First, those who hold that abortion is a morally neutral act generally do so on the ground that destruction of a human fetus is destruction of a biological organism that is not yet a person. Secondly, there are cases in which one is dealing with a human that was once a person, but which has suffered extensive brain damage of such a sort that it is no longer a person. Finally, there are cases in which a human infant has a brain which is defective in such a way that it is incapable of ever becoming a person. In these three cases the destruction of a human organism apparently does not involve the destruction of a person.

This is not to say that the three cases are morally on a par. The least problematic case is that of a human organism that never has been, and never can be, a person. It seems plausible to hold that, considered in itself at least, the destruction of such an organism is no more wrong than the destruction of a nonhuman animal which is not a person.

The case of a human organism that was once a person may be more complicated in some cases, since the person may, for example, have expressed a desire for his body to be kept alive even if his brain should be irreparably damaged. It seems unlikely that a person who distinguished between his continued existence as a person and the continued existence of his body as a mere biological organism would have such a desire. But even where such a desire that one's body be kept alive does exist, violation of that desire is not at all comparable to the destruction of a person, and would require nothing like the justification that violation of a person's desire to continue to exist as a person requires.

The most problematic case is that of abortion. For here, in contrast to the other two cases, one is dealing with an organism that is at least a potential person, and some would contend that it is seriously wrong not only to destroy persons, but also potential persons.

This does not, however, affect the basic point here, namely, that there is a critical distinction between the death of a person and the death of a biological organism, and it is the former that is morally significant. As a result, it would seem that there are cases in which the destruction even of an adult human being is not even a prima facie violation of anyone's right to life.

III. Different situations in which termination of human life is justified

There are at least three very different types of cases in which the termination of a human's life is justified and which arise in medical practice. It is critical to separate these cases, since they involve quite different types of justification.

First type of case: Nonpersons

The first sort of case is where one is dealing either with a human that was once a person, but which can no longer be so characterized due to extensive brain damage; or with a human that, due to a defective brain, never has been, and never can be, a person. I would also include under this first type of case abortion and infanticide involving normal human organisms. However such cases are ethically less clear-cut since they raise the additional question of the morality of destroying potential persons, and I shall confine my discussion here to the other cases.[3] I will, however, touch upon the issue of infanticide in a later section.

What objection could there be to the termination of life in such cases? Some would object that it is just a basic moral principle that it is wrong to kill innocent human beings, without exception. However I think that a little reflection will convince one that this is not a plausible candidate for a basic moral principle.[4] Suppose that one encountered organisms belonging to a different species that enjoyed all the psychological states and capabilities characteristic of normal adult members of the species homo sapiens. Then surely it would be just as wrong to kill normal adult members of that species as to kill normal adult human beings. Membership in a particular biological species is not in itself morally significant. There must be an underlying moral principle that explains both why it is wrong to kill normal adult human beings and why it is wrong to kill normal adult members of this other species we are imagining. The underlying principle will state that it is wrong to kill any individual, regardless of what species it belongs to, which possesses certain psychological capacities or enjoys certain psychological states. The principle that it is wrong to kill humans will then be derived from this more basic principle, together with relevant empirical facts about the psychological states and capacities generally enjoyed by humans. And as a result, it will not prohibit the killing of human organisms that do not possess the relevant psychological states and capacities.

But even if it is not intrinsically wrong to kill human organisms that are not, and never can be, persons, it might be contended that such actions ought to be prohibited on the ground that allowing them would have the consequence that people would come to accept the killing of humans who are persons, or at least potential persons. The quick answer to this argument is that there is no reason at all to believe that the empirical claim on which it rests is true. However, I will comment at greater length upon this general line of argument when I discuss a parallel objection that is frequently urged against allowing voluntary euthanasia.

It would seem, then, that the killing of humans that are not, and never can be, persons, is not morally objectionable either in itself or in virtue of its consequences. But even if it is granted that this first sort of case is morally unproblematic, serious problems do arise when one attempts to set out a more specific philosophical characterization of cases of this sort and when one attempts to formulate usable medical criteria. The main barrier to a satisfying characterization of cases of this first sort is the question, What properties must something possess in order to be a person, in the ethically relevant sense? There has been surprisingly little serious discussion of this important and difficult question. I will turn to the issue in the final section of this chapter.

One need not know, however, exactly what a person is in order to be justified in saying that some human organisms are not persons. The least problematic case is that of a human whose brain has been damaged to such an extent that it is in an irreversible coma, for it is surely a necessary condition for being a person that one can enjoy states of consciousness. So if an organism can never be conscious, it cannot be a person. But even this case is less clear-cut than it at first appears, for reasons to be discussed in section IV.

Second type of case: Voluntary euthanasia

Here we are concerned with situations in which a person exists, but his state is such that he has a rational desire that his life be terminated; that is, a desire to die that is in accordance with an estimate of his own long-term self-interest that is based upon the best information available. Termination of life in such cases does not involve the violation of anyone's right to life, even though it does involve the destruction of a person. The reason is roughly, though not exactly, that one has a violation of a right only where one has an action which violates the corresponding desire. This account is only a first approximation, since there are cases in which one would regard the killing of someone as seriously wrong—and, moreover, as seriously wronging the person killed—even though the victim wished to be killed. An example is where a person is suffering from momentary depression. A more accurate account would be in terms of what is in an individual's long-term *interest*, rather than in terms of what is in accord with his present desires. This is why suicide may be problematic in a way that voluntary euthanasia is not. It is often reasonable to believe that suicide is not in one's long-term interest, whereas this is not the case with voluntary euthanasia if it is restricted to cases where a person is undergoing suffering that cannot be eliminated and which is sufficiently intense that he prefers death to life and will continue to do so.

Why, then, do many people view voluntary euthanasia as morally objectionable?[5] Some view it as wrong because they think that one has not only a right to life, but an *obligation* to go on living. The latter belief is usually found in conjunction with certain religious views: there is a creator who does not want us to shorten our lives even to avoid pain which renders death more attractive than life. Let me dismiss this view by saying, first, that I see no reason to believe that there is a creator, let alone one with a desire that others perform actions that are in no one's interests; and secondly, that even if one thought there was a god with such a desire, it is far from clear why one should act in accordance with that desire, unless one is prepared to accept the rather hardy view that a creator is free to choose whatever standards of right and wrong he wishes.

Another common objection to voluntary euthanasia is the contention that it will lead to compulsory euthanasia—the so-called "wedge" or "slippery slope" objection. Thus G. K. Chesterton says:

Some are proposing what is called euthanasia; at present only a proposal for killing those who are a nuisance to themselves; but soon to be applied to those who are a nuisance to other people.[6]

What reason is there for believing that this is so? If someone were to advocate sexual activity, and a critic were to object that while only voluntary sexual activity is being advocated at present, the proposal will soon be extended to cover compulsory sexual activity, i.e., rape, the critic would hardly be taken seriously. If the analogy is a fair one, the objection is certainly preposterous.

To understand how intelligent people could ever have taken this line of argument seriously, I think that one needs to bring out into the open a contrast between two very different ethical positions. One position has been called the "sanctity of life" view.[7] This is an unhappy label, for a variety of reasons. In the first place, the moral viewpoint in question is concerned only with human life, not with life in general. More important, the label makes it psychologically easy to lump together a number of very disparate principles in unthinking fashion.[8]

For our purposes it is critical to distinguish between the following principles, all of which are suggested by discussion of the value or sanctity of human life: (a) it is a good thing for there to be some human beings; (b) the more humans there are, the better; (c) every human has a right to life; (d) it is always wrong to kill an innocent human being. These principles are quite distinct. The first implies that it would be bad to destroy the human race, but says nothing about individual humans. The second principle implies that contraception of any sort is prima facie wrong. The third principle implies that murder is wrong, but has no implications with respect to suicide or voluntary euthanasia. Those last two are excluded by the fourth principle.

It is perhaps worth emphasizing that, even if one thought one or more of these principles was sound, one could not view any of them as plausible candidates for *basic* moral principles, for they all involve reference to a particular biological species—*homo sapiens*—and we surely do not want to maintain that membership in a particular biological species is in itself a morally relevant characteristic. My reason for emphasizing this is that I think that the realization that none of these principles can plausibly be viewed as basic moral principles forces one to reflect seriously upon issues that otherwise could easily be evaded, such as the issue of whether it is wrong to destroy not only persons, but also potential persons.

What is of primary interest here, however, is the difference between principle c and principle d. A person who accepts the sanctity of life view accepts both principles, but views principle d as more basic than principle c: the reason that murder is wrong is that it is always wrong to kill an innocent person.

The second ethical position is very different. It might be labeled the "right to life" position but can be more accurately described as the view that persons have a right to continued existence. On this view the relevant obligation is an obligation not to *murder* people. Principle c is accepted, but principle d rejected.

What I want to suggest, then, is that people such as Chesterton fail to distinguish between the sanctity of life view and the view that persons have a right to continued existence, and as a result conclude that if someone is willing to allow suicide and voluntary euthanasia, it must be the case either that he accepts the sanctity of life view as a prima facie principle but allows exceptions to it when it is socially useful to do so, or else that he views decisions to terminate life not as moral decisions at all but as decisions to be made simply on the basis of "social utility." *If* either of these things were generally the case, there would be some reason to claim that people who accept voluntary euthanasia will come to accept compulsory euthanasia for those who cannot contribute to society. However, it will rarely be the case that an advocate of voluntary euthanasia accepts the sanctity of life view but allows exceptions on grounds of social utility, and even rarer for such a person to hold that there are no moral principles relating to decisions to terminate life. Almost always, the advocate of voluntary euthanasia simply has a different view as to what the appropriate moral principle is. Namely, that people have a right to life, but that, as in the case of other rights, this is a right that an individual can waive, at least under certain conditions. The upshot is that while compulsory euthanasia is contrary to the moral outlook that he accepts, suicide and voluntary euthanasia presumably are not. The fact that he accepts the latter thus provides no reason at all for thinking that he will also come to accept the former. The conclusion, then, appears to be that once the distinction between the sanctity of life position and right of persons to continued existence position is made explicit and kept firmly in mind, the wedge argument is seen to rest upon a confusion.

There is an important issue concerning the scope of voluntary euthanasia that ought to be at least briefly considered. In the normal case, the individual not only has a rational desire to die, but is capable of *expressing* that desire. But doesn't one also want to allow euthanasia in some cases in which an individual lacks the capacity of expressing his desires? What, for example, is one to do in cases in which the individual who is suffering terribly from a terminal illness is (1) an infant, (2) a child that has not yet learned to talk, (3) an adult who is completely paralyzed, or (4) a human who has been reduced by accident or disease to a "vegetable" existence and is no longer capable of communicating with others?

People who advocate euthanasia in cases of the third and fourth sort sometimes appeal to the notion of *prior consent* and maintain that euthanasia without expressed contemporaneous consent is morally permissible if the individual has previously indicated that he does not wish to continue to live in the specific state that he is now in.

I do not feel that this treatment of cases of types three and four is entirely satisfactory. To begin with, I think they should be treated very differently. In the case of a totally paralyzed adult, one is dealing with a person and it does then make sense to speak of voluntary euthanasia. But in the case of an individual who has really been reduced to a "vegetable" existence devoid of any capacity to interact with others, one might wonder whether it is right to say that a person still exists.

Secondly, I think it is clear that one does not want to restrict voluntary euthanasia without expressed contemporaneous consent to those cases in which prior consent has been given. Suppose that someone is suffering from an extremely painful disease that is incurable and such that all who suffer from it prefer death to life provided that they do not have any moral objection to euthanasia. Suppose further that the person in question is known not to disapprove of euthanasia, but that, unfortunately, he has been struck by another disease that has paralyzed him, so that he cannot now request that his life be ended, and that he has neglected to make a prior request that he be killed in such circumstances. I would think the right thing to do might be to terminate that person's life. For although he cannot now express such a desire, there surely could be excellent evidence that if he could do so, he would request that his life be ended.

The appeal to prior consent is also of no help in the case of a child that has not yet learned to use language. Here too I would contend that if it is morally certain that the child is in such a state that anyone in that state prefers death to life, then it is justifiable to end the child's life, even though there has been no expression of consent, either now or previously.

This line of thought should not be confused with a "quality of life" approach. The contention is not that if a child is destined to live a rather unhappy life, it is morally permissible to kill him. My view is that, prima facie, it is never morally permissible to kill a person, no matter how low the quality of his life, as long as the person himself prefers continued existence to death. Euthanasia before consent is possible is justified only if it is known that the person is suffering and will continue to do so at such a level that it can be assumed he prefers death to life and would express such a preference were he able to do so.

Finally, there is the case of an infant suffering from some very painful condition. How this case should be viewed depends upon whether infants are persons. If they are persons, it will be just another case in which an individual would request that his life be terminated if he were able to do so. But if infants are not in fact persons, then one will not be able to treat it as a case of voluntary euthanasia. I will return to the question of infanticide in a later section.

Third type of case: The cost of maintaining life

This final type of case involves a person who wants to go on living, but the cost of keeping him alive is so great that letting him die is the lesser of evils. This sort of case is agonizing in a way that the first two are not, since it involves an action that is seriously contrary to the interest of the individual primarily involved.

The idea that it may sometimes be right to allow someone to die because it will be very expensive to keep him alive distresses many people, and they try in various ways to find some less threatening way of describing the situation. Perhaps the most common is by appealing to a distinction between killing and letting die, and then holding that killing is seriously wrong in a way that merely letting die is not. In contrast, it seems to me that letting a person die who wants to live is, prima facie, seriously wrong, and can only be justified if it is a lesser of evils.

Another attempt to make these situations seem less distressing involves drawing a distinction between "ordinary" and "extraordinary" means of keeping a person alive: one has an obligation to employ ordinary means of keeping a person alive, but not extraordinary ones. My view is that whether a method of keeping a person alive is ordinary or extraordinary is not in itself morally relevant. I would agree that one is often under no obligation to use extraordinary means to sustain life, but when this is true the reason is not the extraordinary nature of the techniques but the fact that they are very expensive.

What I want to do now is to attempt to indicate why this third sort of case, though inevitably distressing in the way that any decision which involves a serious conflict of interests is distressing, is not morally objectionable. The first and least controversial point is that there are limited resources available for saving lives, and if the cost of keeping a given person alive is too great, one will be able to save more lives either by diverting the resources to other patients or to medical research. But I would also insist that one should not assign unlimited weight to lengthening a person's life. This is certainly desirable, but it is also desirable to increase the quality of life, and it seems to me that there are instances in which the right choice is to increase the quality of life for a number of people, rather than to use resources to keep a single person alive. This sort of choice will rarely arise when one is dealing with a particular individual, but it certainly arises when it comes to a decision about the allocation of resources. One has to decide, for example, how much money should be put into the construction of dialysis machines and into training and employing people to operate them and how much into research into arthritis. One also has to decide how much money should be put into the development of life-saving technology and how much into nonmedical social programs.

One way of looking at this situation is to notice that individuals do not generally assign unlimited weight to maximizing the length of their lives. Most of us are willing to ride in a car in order to see a movie, thus increasing our happiness slightly, even though we know that the chance of getting killed in an automobile accident is significantly greater than the likelihood of dying in an accident while sitting at home.

Where everyone has a reasonable personal income, there is a very fair solution to the question how much should be spent keeping an individual alive. One can allow each person to decide how much of his income he wishes to use, not to improve the quality of his life but to invest in insurance to guard against possible occurrences which would necessitate large expenditures in order to keep him alive. This approach allows each individual to establish his own priorities with respect to the relative distribution of his resources between the two goals of improving the quality of his life and maximizing his life expectancy. There is no need for a general societal decision which is imposed upon everyone. Each person can decide for himself the extent to which he wants to sacrifice quality of life for sheer length of life.

There are two rather different subcases which fall under this third category. The one I have been focusing upon so far involves a *conscious* person. But one also has the case of a *comatose* individual where, although it may not be too expensive to keep the person alive, there is no method available for bringing the person back to consciousness. This case is sometimes confused with cases of the first type. They are really very different. In cases of the first type, such as brain death cases, the person in question no longer exists and terminating the life of the human organism is not killing any person. In the case of a comatose individual the person still exists, and if it were technologically possible to revive him, it would be as seriously wrong to destroy the organism, or to let it die, as it would be to destroy a sleeping human, or to let one die.

In the case of a comatose individual one is once again in the realm of cost/benefit analysis. One must weigh the likelihood that some method of reviving the person will be discovered and the value of preserving a person's life—primarily the value to the person himself—against the cost of keeping him alive. The case differs from that of a conscious person in that in sustaining the life of a conscious person one is satisfying his desires, whereas in keeping a comatose individual alive one will have contributed to his happiness only if some way of reviving him is discovered. If the probability of this happening is very small, the cost which will justify not keeping him alive may be much less than that which would justify letting a conscious person die. But the relevant moral principles are the same in the two cases.

This concludes my survey of three types of cases in which I believe the termination of a human life is morally justifiable. I also want to suggest that these are the only sorts of cases which arise in medical contexts in which such action is morally permissible.

IV. Death: Concept, criterion, and indicators

The first type of case described above in which termination of life is morally permissible was that involving an organism that is not a person. There were three important subcases: (1) an organism that was once a person but is no longer one; (2) an organism that never has been and never can be a person; (3) an organism that has the potential to develop into a person but is not yet one. I will touch upon the second and third cases in section V. Here I want to consider some of the issues involved in the first subcase.

I noted in section II that the term "death" is ambiguous when applied to sentient organisms: one may be referring either to the death of the biological organism or to the death of the associated person. There is a further possible ambiguity, since one can speak of the death of a sentient being that is not a person in cases where there is no death of a biological organism. Consider, for example, a lower animal that will never again enjoy states of consciousness, owing to brain damage. In short, one can have: (i) the death of a person; (ii) the death of a sentient being; (iii) the death of a biological organism. The cases upon which attention tends to be focused in discussions of the concept of death are ones in which one has both i and ii but not iii. It is important to realize, however, that there are cases in which the death of a person occurs without either the death of a sentient being or the death of a biological organism.

The primary issue here is sometimes described as pertaining to the *definition* of death, the suggestion being that our very concept of death is in need of revision. I think this is a slightly inaccurate way of describing the situation. The morally relevant concept of death is that of the death of a person, conceived of either as the complete ceasing to be of a continuing subject of mental states or as the severing of all relationship between such a continuing subject and the biological organism with which it has been associated. But this is the way that death has always been conceived. What is in need of revision is not the concept of death, but the traditional *criterion* of the death of a person: death of the biological organism.

There are three tasks to be carried out in establishing an account of death adequate for purposes of medical decision making. First, one must set out a philosophical analysis of the morally relevant concept of the death of a person. Secondly, one must provide physiological and/ or behavioral criteria for the death of a person. Finally, one must specify tests which will be extremely reliable indicators of the satisfaction of the physiological and/or behavioral criteria of death.[9]

The central task involved in giving an adequate philosophical analysis of the concept of the death of a person will be to isolate the morally relevant sense of "person" and to supply appropriate criteria of personal identity. It is important here not to assume that our ordinary concept of a person incorporates precisely those properties that are morally significant. A number of alternative accounts are available, and it is far from clear which is correct. I will return to this question of the ethically relevant concept of a person in section VI.

The philosophical analysis of the concept of a person will be expressed in psychological terms. But in order to be able to determine when a person has died, one must be able to specify states that are in principle publicly observable and that are either identical with, or else correlated with, the relevant mental states. This is the second task—the setting out of behavioral and/or physiological criteria of death. These criteria, however, may be highly theoretical in nature. So it is necessary to specify *operational* tests that can be easily carried out and that will enable one to determine whether the physiological and/or behavioral criteria for the death of a person are in fact satisfied.

The most familiar proposal for a revised criterion of death is *brain death*. This is a very natural suggestion, given that a person is a continuing conscious subject and consciousness is dependent upon the central nervous system. If the brain is dead, there is no longer any possibility of consciousness; hence it would seem correct to say that the person has died.

This suggestion provides a fruitful starting point for discussion.

Perhaps the place to begin is by asking what is meant by "brain death." It certainly is intended to cover cases in which an organism's brain has been completely destroyed. And it does seem clear that in such a case the person has died. Suppose, for example, that an individual's brain is completely destroyed in an accident but the rest of his body is kept alive artificially. Even if one had complete information about the structure and states of his brain immediately before the accident, were able to construct an exact replica of it, and transplant it into his body, one would not have succeeded in reviving the person. One would only have created a replica of the person, making use of what was once his body.[10]

But what is meant by "brain death" in cases where one is dealing with something less than total destruction of the brain? I think that what is normally meant in such cases is that the individual has a permanently nonfunctioning brain, or at least a brain that is permanently nonfunctioning in some respect which results in irreversible coma.[11] But what does it mean to characterize the brain as "permanently nonfunctioning"? One is presumably saying not merely that it will never again begin to function on its own, but that there is no way that one can repair the damage. But isn't this relative to the present state of medical technology? Wouldn't it be possible in most cases to freeze the brain and then wait until technology advanced to the point where the damage, including that due to freezing, could be repaired? But if all that one is asserting is that it is *not now* technologically possible to repair it, it is surely inaccurate to speak of a *permanently* nonfunctioning brain. What one would have, surely, is not a criterion of the death of a person but, at most, a characterization of one sort of situation in which the cost of maintaining an organism until it becomes technologically possible to repair its brain, and thus revive the person, is too great to warrant its being done.

What is needed is a distinction between two different types of brain damage. These will differ not with respect to the possibility of repair, but with respect to what psychological states and capacities the damaged parts of the brain are causally related to or identical with. The critical philosophical issue is that of the criterion of personal identity. Suppose, for concreteness, that memory is essential for personal identity. That is, that the mental states associated with this biological organism today belong to the same person as the mental states associated with this organism yesterday only if there is some way of linking them together by means of memories. It would then follow that if at any point in time the states of the central nervous system which are the basis of memory states (or identical with them) were destroyed, the person who had existed would cease to be. Even if one could repair the damage and program in the same sort of mental states as had previously existed, this would not serve to revive the person: it would only create a replica of the original person.

Suppose, in contrast, there is a certain part of the brain that has nothing to do with memory, but which is the basis of consciousness. If it were destroyed, there would be no reason for concluding that the person had died. If it some day became possible to repair this sort of brain damage, one would not say that one had produced a replica but that one had revived the person who had existed previously. So if one maintained that termination of life would be justifiable in a particular case of this sort, the justification would have to be that it was impossible at present to repair the brain damage and that the expense of keeping the organism alive until it would become possible was so great, or the likelihood of such a breakthrough within the lifetime of the individual so small, that the expenditure was unwarranted. The critical point is that one would then have not a case of the first sort, where a person no longer exists, but a case of the third sort, where letting a person die is the lesser of evils.

My criticism, then, is that the proposed brain-death criterion fails to distinguish these two very different cases. The result is a confusion between, on the one hand, a physiological criterion of the death of a person and, on the other, a physiological state of affairs which makes it morally justifiable to terminate the life of a biological organism *either* because the person is no longer alive *or* because it is not presently possible to revive the person, and the cost of keeping the organism alive in the hope that it will become possible in the future to revive the person is too great to warrant the investment.

In the context of actual medical decision making about whether to terminate life, this distinction may, at least at present, be of little practical relevance. For I think there is little doubt that a cost/benefit approach leads to the conclusion that one ought to terminate the life of an organism in an irreversible coma due to a nonfunctioning brain which cannot presently be repaired, even if the damage does not involve the destruction of those states upon which personal identity is based.

To sum up, if "brain death" is construed as covering only cases in which there is complete destruction of the brain, it constitutes a sufficient condition for the death of a person, but not a necessary one. The suggestion that one construe "brain death" more broadly so that it also covers cases in which an organism is in an irreversible coma due to a permanently nonfunctioning brain is of no assistance, since strictly speaking there is no brain that cannot in principle be repaired given appropriate technological advances. While if "brain death" is construed as covering cases in which the organism is in a coma owing to brain damage that is at present impossible to repair, what one has is not a criterion of death but a description of conditions under which one is probably justified in terminating the life of an organism, assuming that the cost of keeping the organism alive is sufficiently great. To formulate an adequate criterion of death, one will first need to clarify the appropriate criterion of personal identity, and second to determine what states of the brain those psychological states upon which personal identity rests are identical with, or causally dependent upon. The resulting criterion of death will not be brain death; it will be the destruction of those parts of the brain upon which personal identity rests.

V. The problem of infanticide

Of all the areas of medical decisions relating to the termination of life, perhaps the one in which thinking is least satisfactory is that of infanticide. This is not surprising, since the topic is a very emotional one, and the issues raised are far from simple.

One of the ways in which contemporary medical practice has attempted to cope with the problem of infanticide has been by appealing to a distinction between active and passive infanticide. This distinction does help one to deal with some of the more agonizing cases, and it is a distinction that is quite widely accepted. But as was mentioned in the discussion of euthanasia, some philosophers have called into question the view that there is a serious moral difference between killing and letting die, and they maintain either that there is no moral difference or that it is not such that the one sort of act can be seriously wrong in circumstances in which the other is not. (This position is set forth by Rachels in chapter 7.) If this point of view turns out to be right, the distinction between active and passive infanticide will have to be set aside as morally irrelevant.

But if one abandons the appeal to this distinction, what is one to say about infanticide? Is it morally acceptable, or is it, as many believe, in itself seriously wrong? In order to arrive at an adequate answer to this question, one must come to grips with the following difficult issues:

1. What properties must an organism have in order to be a person?
2. Is a human infant a person?
3. If a human infant is not a person, is it only persons that it is seriously wrong to kill, or is it also seriously wrong to destroy *potential persons*?

I do not want to discuss these issues in detail here, but some points should at least be noted in passing. First, if one holds that abortion is not in itself seriously wrong, one cannot consistently reject infanticide on the ground that it involves the destruction of a potential person: a fetus is equally a potential person. Secondly, even if it is not clear exactly what psychological properties something must have in order to be a person, it is apparent that it is going to be very difficult to argue that a human infant is a person without also holding that adult members of some nonhuman species—such as chimpanzees—are persons, thus implying that it is also seriously wrong to destroy them, for the mental life of adult members of many nonhuman species is surely not inferior to the mental life of human infants.

Is a human infant a person? I have suggested elsewhere that it is capacities such as self-consciousness and the ability to envisage a future for oneself and to have desires about that future that serve to distinguish persons from sentient beings that are not persons. I will touch upon the reasons for this view, and important alternatives to it, in the final section of this chapter. The point to notice here, however, is simply that if this view is correct, it may well turn out that human infants are not persons, since it is far from clear that human infants possess self-consciousness or that they are capable of envisaging a future for themselves and of having desires about such a future.

Since I do not believe that human infants are persons, but only potential persons, and since I think that the destruction of potential persons is a morally neutral action, the correct conclusion seems to me to be that infanticide is in itself morally acceptable. But even if one disagreed with this view, either on the ground that human infants are generally persons or on the ground that it is wrong to destroy even potential persons, there would still be at least three situations in which one might well hold that it was morally permissible to terminate the life of a human infant.

First, just as it is possible for an adult human to suffer brain damage so that it is no longer a person, some infants presumably suffer from brain defects of such a nature that they do not possess the capacity of developing into persons. To decide when this is true would require a precise understanding of the properties something must have to be a person. Until this is done one can hardly be very confident about classification in individual cases. But there surely are such cases. And in these cases it would seem that there is no moral objection to terminating the life of such a human, since in doing so one is destroying neither a person nor even a potential person.

Secondly, there may be cases in which the cost of keeping a human infant alive is so great that it is better to use society's resources in some other way. People often accept the view that in such cases there is a significant moral difference between passive infanticide and active infanticide, but this would be a mistake. What is relevant here is not a distinction between killing and letting die. The relevant factor is that the cost of keeping an individual alive may sometimes be very great, with the result that letting him die is, regretfully, the lesser evil. The failure to see this, and the belief that it is the killing/letting die distinction which is morally significant, has unfortunately led many people to conclude that merely allowing defective infants to die, when it would require only a relatively simple and inexpensive operation to save them, is morally unproblematical. It has also led people to the incredible conclusion that given a choice between allowing an infant to endure a slow and painful death—say, by starvation—and painlessly terminating its existence, the former action is morally preferable.

Thirdly, there may be cases in which an infant is suffering to such an extent, and will continue to do so, that it seems virtually certain that it either prefers death to continued existence or will do so as soon as it becomes capable of having such a desire. In such a case termination of the infant's life is akin to voluntary euthanasia and thus surely justified.

But what seems to me illegitimate in such cases is any appeal to *quality of life* considerations. The question in the third case is not whether the individual is destined to enjoy a rich and satisfying life, but whether it will at least be a life that he himself will prefer to death. It is only if the quality of his existence will be so bad that he will prefer death to continued existence that one can appeal to this third sort of justification for terminating an infant's life, *if* one assumes that a human infant is a person.

On the other hand, quality of life considerations may legitimately enter in if one assumes that an infant is not a person and that infanticide does not violate anyone's right to continued existence. For in that case one is merely deciding what potential persons should be allowed to become actual, and the rational approach would seem to be to decide on the basis of the quality of life which the potential person is likely to enjoy if allowed to develop into an actual person.

To sum up, I think there are at least four major shortcomings in much contemporary medical thinking about infanticide:

1. There has been a failure to determine whether it is only persons, or also potential persons, that it is seriously wrong to kill.

2. There has been a failure to ask what properties something must possess in order to be a person.

3. Quality of life considerations have been allowed to enter into the question of infanticide in an illegitimate way by those who hold that even though infanticide is usually seriously wrong, it may be justified in some cases if the quality of life the individual will enjoy is rather low. This position seems indefensible, for if infanticide is in general seriously wrong, the reason surely is that it violates the individual's right to continued existence. Then one is in effect saying that violating someone's right to continued existence can sometimes be justified if the quality of life he is going to enjoy will be rather low. This seems clearly unacceptable.

4. Finally, the distinction between killing and intentionally letting die has been erroneously used to justify letting defective infants die when what is morally significant in this context is the possibly immense cost of keeping an individual alive. The acceptance of this error has, in turn, led people to the very unhappy conclusion that allowing such an infant to die, even if it is a slow and painful death, is morally preferable to a painless termination of its life.

VI. Ethics and the concept of a person

The concept of a person plays a critical role in ethics. This is especially true of medical ethics, where, I have argued, the concept of a person is crucial in any attempt to think clearly about the moral issues involved in decisions to terminate life. Yet its importance for such decisions has often been overlooked, and when its relevance has been noticed, it has usually been taken for granted that there is no difficulty in saying exactly what the morally relevant concept of a person is.

It seems to me that, on the contrary, it is far from obvious precisely what the relevant concept of a person is. Thus one of the main things I want to do in this final section is to set out, and comment upon, some alternative accounts of the concept of a person that are involved in fundamental ethical principles. But I also want to ask how one is to decide which account is the correct one.

Basic moral principles and the concept of a person

One of the primary ways in which the concept of a person is important is that it enters into the formulation of ethical principles dealing with the conditions under which one seriously wrongs something by destroying it. Yet it is easy to overlook this. If asked to set out moral principles stating when one does and does not wrong something by destroying it, many people might respond by offering the following:

It is seriously wrong to kill humans.
It is not seriously wrong to kill nonhuman animals.
It is not seriously wrong to kill plants.
It is not seriously wrong to destroy nonliving things.

These principles might seem to cover the ground, and yet they do not involve the concept of a person. So what reason is there for holding that the concept of person is essential?

The answer to this was mentioned earlier, near the beginning of section III, namely, that the possibility of a nonhuman species whose members are capable of using language and that have experiences, thoughts, and so on, shows that the above principles are not plausible candidates for the role of *basic* moral principles, where a moral principle is basic for an individual if and only if his acceptance of it does not depend upon his acceptance of some *nonnormative, factual* belief. Such underlying moral principles will be free of reference to particular species, being formulated instead in terms of species-neutral concepts such as those of a person and a potential person.

Clarifying the form of the basic moral principles involved has a number of beneficial consequences. In the first place, once we realize that some principles that we firmly adhere to are not basic but derivative, we may be more open to the thought that those principles may in fact be mistaken, since they may rest upon mistaken nonnormative beliefs. Most people in the Western world believe that there is generally nothing especially problematic about the killing of nonhuman animals, provided it is done painlessly. But if this is correct, it is not a basic moral principle. It would be, for most people, derived from the basic moral principle that it is persons that it is seriously wrong to destroy, together with the nonnormative claim that nonhuman animals are not persons. But when things are looked at this way, are we really so confident that nonhuman animals are not persons? I think that when we turn to consider some alternative accounts of the concept of a person, it will become clear that the traditional Western view of nonhuman animals is very much open to doubt.

Another beneficial consequence is that it makes possible more fruitful discussion of topics such as the morality of abortion and infanticide. Discussion of the question of abortion, even among philosophers, is often couched in terms of the misleading question of whether a fetus developing inside a human mother is itself a human being. Whereas what one should be asking, and will, if one thinks in terms of basic moral principles, is first, whether a human fetus is a person, and secondly, whether it is seriously wrong to destroy potential persons.

Alternative accounts of the concept of a person

Perhaps the place to begin is by distinguishing between those accounts of the concept of a person according to which whether an entity is a person is determined simply by its intrinsic (or nonrelational) properties, and those accounts according to which it is a matter, at least in part, of its relations to other things. The latter view is much the less common one, although, for example, some theologically-oriented thinkers appear to have held that part of what makes members of the human race persons is their unique relationship to a deity.

Relational accounts of the concept of a person deserve serious consideration, even though most people find them quite implausible. Here, however, I shall have to set aside such accounts and confine the discussion to views which hold that it is an entity's nonrelational properties that make it a person.

What, then, is the most plausible nonrelational account of the concept of a person? A natural place to begin is with the claim, which most people would accept, that something cannot be a person unless it is sometimes in some mental state or other.[12] The point to notice about this claim is that the concept of a mental state is a concept that people construe in different ways. This means that the widespread agreement to the claim that something is not a person unless it enjoys mental states is to some extent only apparent agreement. The account of the concept of a mental state that a dualist will offer diverges radically from the accounts a logical behaviorist and an identity theorist will offer. This divergence will be reflected in the ethical principles each advances.

The main ethical difference between these accounts lies in their implications for the rights of robots. If there were a machine capable of behavior indistinguishable from human behavior, then both the identity theorist who offers a relational or functional account of the concept of a mental state and the behaviorist would have to admit that the machine in question would enjoy mental states comparable to those enjoyed by humans and so would be a person. But if the distinction between a biological person and a mechanical person is not morally significant in itself, then one will be forced to ascribe to robots whatever rights one ascribes to normal adult humans. It will then be wrong to injure or torture robots, and it will be seriously wrong to destroy them, no matter how easily duplicates can be produced.

The dualist, in contrast, holds that the fact that robots would have minds in the behaviorist and in the identity-theorist sense is not morally relevant. The critical question is whether they would enjoy states of consciousness—thought of as private states, not even in principle publicly observable, to which the individual who has them has logically privileged access. Many dualists hold that one would not be justified in believing that machines whose behavior is comparable to that of normal adult humans enjoy mental states in this morally relevant sense.

The conclusion, in short, is that since the concept of a person enters into some of one's basic ethical principles, and since the concept of a person is the concept of something which has mental states, the analysis one adopts of the concept of a mental state will affect the judgments one makes about how certain sorts of things ought to be treated. As technology advances, the issue of robot rights might become a serious practical problem.

Let us turn now to the critical question, What *more* is required, beyond the mere having of mental states, to make something a person? This question arises for almost everyone, regardless of what theory of the nature of mental states one accepts, for virtually everyone will grant that there are some organisms that have mental states—and in particular, sensations, experiences, states of consciousness (however such states are construed)—but which are not persons in the ethically relevant sense.

Let us briefly examine some possible answers to this question. A natural one is:

1. A person is an entity that has experiences occurring at different times and linked together by memory.

This account is capable of different interpretations, depending upon what one counts as experiences linked together by memory. Isn't it true that even animals very far down the evolutionary ladder remember their experiences? They certainly modify their behavior in response to their experiences. Are we then to say that such animals are persons, and that it is therefore seriously wrong to destroy them?

The natural response here is, I think, to distinguish between remembering construed in a purely behavioristic way and remembering interpreted as involving a disposition to have thoughts about the event remembered. Let us interpret 1 as involving only the behavioristic sense of memory and formulate a second alternative:

2. A person is an entity that has experiences occurring at different times and linked together by memory in a sense involving a disposition to have thoughts about previous experiences.

When one brings in this nonbehavioristic construal of memory, it is much harder to say what counts as a person. The case of human babies and many nonhuman animals will be difficult to settle. In part, the issue is one of the relationship between the ability to have thoughts and the ability to use language. Some philosophers have held that the former presupposes the latter. If this were so, then 2 would lead to the conclusion that human babies and virtually all nonhuman animals are not persons. But it is far from clear that the ability to have thoughts presupposes linguistic capability. There are, for example, psychological facts about animal learning sometimes discussed under the label of "insightful learning." The interpretation of these facts is not uncontroversial, but it is tempting to think that certain sorts of problem solving ability exhibited by animals that do not possess a language are evidence for the occurrence of thought episodes.

A rather different view of the nature of a person is that:

3. A person is an entity that enjoys *intentional* states.

This view seems to me objectionable on at least two grounds. The first is that it would seem to imply that a robot whose behavior was indistinguishable from that of an adult human would be a person. One can imagine a machine that was disposed to behave just like a human, but which had no experiences at all. Putting the objection in this form seems to presuppose a dualistic view of the mind. But this presupposition can be avoided by considering instead a machine whose behavior is like that of humans except that it never ascribes any sensations or other experiences to itself. It seems to me that such an entity would have intentional states, but that, lacking states of consciousness, it would not qualify as a person.

The simplest way of meeting this objection is by revising 3 to:

4. A person is an entity that enjoys both states of consciousness and intentional states.

My objection to this suggestion—and also my second objection to 3— is that it implies that most animals are persons. Animals certainly enjoy sensations and other states of consciousness, and we attribute beliefs and desires, which are intentional states, to most animals. One might try to maintain that while we do speak of animals as having beliefs and desires, this is really a mistake. What we should say is only that they behave *as if* they had beliefs and desires. But why should we say this? Perhaps the main reason offered is the claim that it is language that is the source of intentionality. The intentionality of beliefs and desires is parasitic upon the intentionality of linguistic utterances in such a way that if an organism cannot use language, it cannot enjoy any intentional states at all. I believe that this view of intentionality is untenable, but it would take us too far afield to attempt to refute it here.

A fifth possible view is:

5. If an entity has experiences occurring at different times that are unified by memory (interpreted as involving a disposition to have thoughts about earlier experiences), then that entity might well be called a *self*; that is, a continuing subject of experiences and other mental states. But before it can be considered a person in the morally relevant sense, it must also possess *self-consciousness*. A person is thus a continuing subject of experiences and other mental states that recognizes itself to be such a continuing subject of mental states.

This view has been around for a long time, a number of people having held that the critical difference between humans and (most) nonhuman animals is that while the latter possess consciousness, it is only the former who possess self-consciousness. But one might well ask why it is not enough simply to be a self. Why should it also be important to be aware of this fact?

Except for 3, the accounts mentioned have been gradually more stringent with respect to the entities allowed the status of persons. A final view, which proceeds even further in that direction, is suggested by Benn:

6. "I characterize a natural person as someone aware of himself, not just as process or happening, but as agent, as having the capacity to make decisions that make a difference to the way the world goes, as creatively initiating changes in the world that he intends shall make things 'better'; he is conscious of himself as capable of having projects that constitute certain existing states 'important' or 'unimportant,' and in relation to which he can assess his own performances as successful or unsuccessful. And, as a kind of meta-project, he has the overarching enterprise of making of himself something he can esteem."[13]

That an entity of this sort is a person is surely right. What is not clear, however, is that only entities having all of the characteristics mentioned are persons. Perhaps the most pressing ground for doubt is this. Consider a human who believes that his behavior and mental life are completely determined. Such an individual would view himself not as an agent in the sense intended here, but as a mere "process or happening." But does one want to say that such a human would not be a person and hence not have a right to life?

A derivation of the morally relevant concept of a person

The six accounts of the concept of a person mentioned above are not that different from one another. Still I think that one should feel disturbed that there are these alternatives, and more so that it is not clear how one decides what the correct account is. I want to suggest one way of attempting to cope with this problem. The fundamental idea is that although the moral injunction not to kill persons (against their will) is a basic moral principle in the sense that it is not plausible to regard it as derivable from other moral principles *together with factual claims,* this does not preclude its being derived from *moral principles alone.* If one can find more fundamental moral principles that entail a principle stating what sorts of things it is intrinsically wrong to destroy, one will have determined in effect the relevant concept of a person.

One way of approaching the issue is to broaden one's base and to consider other ethical principles besides the principle that it is wrong to kill persons against their will. Another basic principle to which most people are deeply committed is this:

It is wrong to inflict pain upon conscious organisms, regardless of whether or not they are persons.

It would be nice if one could find some more general principle or principles from which one could derive both this principle, which is not restricted to persons, and the principle that it is wrong to kill persons.

What might such a moral general principle be? One familiar candidate is the following:

The frustration or nonfulfilment of desires and preferences is always an *intrinsically* undesirable state of affairs, the undesirability being proportional to the strength of the desire or preference in question. (It might not, of course, be extrinsically undesirable.)

An individual who accepted this as a basic moral principle could attempt to use it to justify both the claim that it is wrong to inflict pain upon conscious organisms, regardless of whether they are persons, and the claim that it is wrong to murder persons. In the case of the former, the account would turn simply upon the facts that pain is a state that a conscious organism desires to be free of, and that it is a state that generally hinders an organism in its pursuance of other desires.

As for the injunction not to kill persons against their will, the approach might be along the lines that the reason it is wrong to kill persons is that they are *things that can envisage a future for themselves, and that have desires about those future states of themselves,* and thus killing such entities makes it impossible for these desires to be satisfied.

This provides an explanation of why it is wrong to kill some animals, such as normal adult humans, but not wrong to kill others, such as oysters. In the case of the former there is a desire to continue to exist as a conscious subject of experiences and other mental states, and killing is wrong because it prevents this desire from being satisfied. Killing oysters, in contrast, is not wrong, so long as it is done painlessly, since oysters presumably do not possess a concept of themselves as continuing subjects of experiences, and thus cannot envisage a future for themselves, and so are incapable of having a desire to go on living which will be denied satisfaction if they are killed.

Some comments are in order. The first is that desires here cannot be construed in a purely behavioristic way. One might construct a machine that would have a desire to survive in the behavioristic sense; that is, it would be disposed to behave in ways that increase the likelihood of its survival. More important, even plants and lower animals would have a desire to survive if "desire" is interpreted behavioristically. In the present context, then, a desire for something must be construed as, roughly, a disposition to act in ways that will increase one's chance of getting that thing, together with a disposition to have the thought that one is disposed to act in such ways. Desire in this sense, while not itself a state of consciousness, involves reference to states of consciousness.

Secondly, the prohibition against killing is very strong. The derivation suggested provides an explanation of this feature. The principle that was appealed to states that the wrongness of frustrating a desire is proportional to the strength of the desire. The desire to continue to exist as an ongoing subject of experiences and other mental states is usually extremely strong, especially since many of the other desires one has cannot be satisfied unless one continues to exist.

Finally, notice that such a derivation of the principle that one ought not to kill persons also has the advantage of automatically accounting for *exceptions* to that prohibition. Thus, if one believes that suicide is not seriously wrong in itself, even though it certainly involves the destruction of a continuing subject of mental states, one has the immediate explanation that the reason it is not wrong is that the individual in question does not have a desire to go on living that would be violated by his killing himself.

This suggested derivation of the injunction against killing persons provides, in effect, an account of what it is to be a person in the morally relevant sense, and an account that diverges somewhat from all of the views advanced earlier:

7. Something is a person if and only if it is a continuing subject of experiences and other mental states that can envisage a future for itself and that can have desires about its own future states.

It is worth noticing that there is, however, a fairly close relationship between this view and the fifth. To be capable of envisaging a future for oneself as a subject of experiences and other mental states, one must be capable of having the concept of a continuing subject of experiences, and of recognizing oneself as such a continuing subject. In short, one must be capable of self-consciousness. So something cannot be a person as defined by the seventh account unless it at least has the *capacity* for self-consciousness.

I think that the characterization of a person as a continuing subject of experiences and other mental states that can envisage a future for itself and have desires about the future is essentially correct, and that the derivation suggested is plausible. Even if this is so, one is still left with the question of how, if at all, one is to justify the basic moral principle upon which the derivation rests. To pursue this issue would lead us to the very core of metaethics. And in any case my primary concern here has not been to defend one particular answer to the question, "What is a person?" Rather, my aim has been to stress the importance of that question if one is to formulate basic moral principles that will enable one to deal adequately with the ethical issues involved in decisions to terminate life. The tendency to think not in terms of the concept of a person but in terms of an individual's being a member of a particular biological species—*homo sapiens*—has resulted in a great deal of confused ethical thinking. The situation has been further aggravated by the appeal to distinctions that are not morally relevant in themselves, particularly the distinctions between killing and letting die and between direct and indirect killing. It is only when these distinctions are swept aside and the concept of a person is adequately clarified and allowed to assume a central role in our ethical thinking that we can hope to have an acceptable account of the conditions under which the termination of life is morally justified.

Notes

1. One might grant that the paradigm case of the right to life is the right of persons to continue to exist, but hold that potential persons also have a right to life, which in that case is the right of something to become a person. I have argued against this view in my papers on abortion and infanticide. See, especially, sections 3 and 5 of "A Defense of Abortion and Infanticide," *The Problem of Abortion,* ed. Joel Feinberg (Belmont: Wadsworth, 1973).

2. It is commonly assumed, in Western society, that *no* nonhuman animals are persons. I am strongly inclined to think that this view is mistaken. There is some helpful discussion of the question of the moral status of animals in Leonard Nelson's "Duties to Animals" and in Roslind Godlovitch's "Animals and Morals," both available in *Animals, Men, and Morals,* eds. Stanley and Roslind Godlovitch (London: Taplinger, 1972).

3. For arguments in support of the view that the destruction of potential persons is not morally wrong, see section 5 of "A Defense of Abortion and Infanticide."

4. A moral principle is basic for a person if and only if his acceptance of it is not dependent upon any of his nonnormative, factual beliefs. That is, no change in his nonnormative beliefs would cause him to abandon the principle in question.

5. For a vigorous statement of a variety of objections to voluntary euthanasia, see Yale Kamisar's article, "Euthanasia Legislation: Some Non-Religious Objections." There is some forceful criticism of Kamisar's views in Glanville Williams's "Euthanasia Legislation: A Rejoinder to the Non-Religious Objections." Both articles are contained in *Euthanasia and the Right to Die,* ed. A.B. Downing (New York: Humanities Press, 1970).

6. G.K. Chesterton, "Euthanasia and Murder," *American Law Review* 8 (1937) p. 486.

7. See chapter 3.

8. An example of this is provided by Daniel Callahan in his paper, "The Sanctity of Life," *Updating Life and Death,* ed. Donald R. Cutler (Boston: Beacon, 1968). Under the so-called principle of the sanctity of life—a principle that he himself admits is "indeterminate and vague" (p. 199)—Callahan introduces a number of more substantive principles whose only relationship is that they all deal with what humans have a right to do or with what it is wrong to do to humans or with the desirability of there being humans!

9. See chapter 6 for further discussion and references.

10. A dualist could conceivably deny this—but to do so he would have to hold that minds are causally associated, not with brains, but with bodies. One could then maintain, first, that destruction of the brain does not entail the death of the person, and secondly, that construction of a new brain does not involve the creation of a new person. But this position is radically implausible, since there are excellent reasons for holding that whenever there are cerebral states, there also exist mental states and thus that in constructing a new brain one is also creating a new person.

11. For a statement of the view that irreversible coma due to a permanently nonfunctioning brain is the correct criterion of death, see "A Definition of Irreversible Coma: Report of the "Ad Hoc" Committee of the Harvard Medical School to Examine the Definition of Brain Death," Henry K. Beecher, available in Cutler, op. cit., pp. 55–63. For other references, see chapter 6.

12. The main grounds that might be offered for rejecting even this innocuous-looking claim can be brought out as follows. Consider the science fiction example of a member of the species *homo sapiens* that has been assembled, sophisticated Frankenstein fashion, in the laboratory. If the organism were to be destroyed before it had been brought to consciousness, one would have destroyed something that never enjoyed any mental state. Yet some might feel that it would be seriously wrong to destroy such an entity and take this as grounds for regarding the entity as a person.

What I should attempt to do here is to convince the person that the reason he feels it is wrong is that he thinks it is wrong to destroy not only persons, but also potential persons. And surely this is a plausible explanation, for if the organism did not possess the capacity of enjoying a mental life, one should hardly be tempted to view its destruction as seriously wrong.

13. Stanley I. Benn, "Persons and Environmental Ethics," p. 8. This is a revised version of the Presidential Address to the Australasian Association of Philosophy Conference in Canberra, August 1974. For a slightly briefer formulation of this view, see pp. 99–100 of Benn's "Abortion, Infanticide, and Respect for Persons," Feinberg, op. cit.

5 Moral Rights and Permissible Killing

DAN W. BROCK

In what types of cases that arise in the practice of medicine is it morally permissible to kill human beings? Michael Tooley, in the preceding chapter, has proposed an answer that is at least along the general lines of the view I would support. Much of my own discussion will consist of further elaboration of this kind of position, elaboration which will involve revisions of both theroretical and practical significance in the categories Tooley labels voluntary euthanasia and the cost of maintaining life. My discussion will largely involve working out some implications of a particular type of normative moral theory for the question of terminating human life in medical settings. However, the very substantial and often heated disagreement that arises over these issues amounts to more than simply disagreement over the implications of the kind of view I shall develop. Rather, it arises in large part because participants in the disputes hold general moral views of fundamentally different sorts. In the emotionally charged context in which these discussions often take place, and where the specifics of particular cases often occupy much of the attention, the deeper sources of the moral disagreement encountered is often obscured. I shall begin then with a brief attempt to illuminate some of those sources.

I

How one divides and distinguishes substantive moral theories is largely a matter of convenience, in the sense that it depends on the purpose of the inquiry at hand and the usefulness to that inquiry of carving up the geography of normative ethics in that particular way. No general distinctions between types of normative theories which delineate broad categories of such views are *the* correct distinctions or categories; any quite general distinctions will at the very least blur differences that are important in other contexts. Moreover, though I shall talk of three different types of moral theories with regard to their implications concerning the killing of human beings, it is not the case that we can neatly divide up real persons into holders of one or another of these types of moral view. Rather, for many if not most persons, two or even all three of the different types of moral positions have some appeal and place in their moral reasoning; this helps account for the uncertainty and internal conflict many of us experience in considering concrete cases in this area.

The first sort of moral view is what Ronald Dworkin has called goal-based and what is more commonly termed consequentialist, utilitarian, or teleological.[1] Most generally, it views morality as concerned with the production of desirable or valuable states of affairs or experiences— commonly human happiness, welfare, or desire satisfaction; their production is the goal of morality. Human actions are morally evaluated in terms of their tendency to promote these goals, and right action is that action which, among the alternatives open to an agent, maximizes these valuable consequences for any and all persons affected. The consequences for any one person count for no more than for any other simply because of who that person is; it is a matter of the amount of, for example, human happiness or desire satisfaction produced, and not of who produces it or who receives it. The morally significant features of persons in the goal-based moral view are simply their roles as subjects, recipients, or vessels of the experiences that the theory holds to be valuable; so long as the causal consequences for morally valuable experiences remain the same, persons from this moral point of view are fully interchangeable in any situation. In this goal-based view, killing a human being is morally justified if and only if doing so maximizes the production of the goals of the theory, however they are specified, and is morally wrong if it does not; killing is morally evaluated according to its promotion of the goals the theory specifies as valuable.

The two other sorts of moral theory are what philosophers commonly call deontological. Each makes an appeal at the most basic level to a different sort of moral notion, whose logical form carries implications for the sort of actions that are morally justified according to the theory as well as for the general focus the view employs. These are what Dworkin has labeled duty-based and rights-based moral views. Both provide a focus, though of different sorts, directly on human deliberation, choice, and action which is not derived solely from the consequences of that action for the production of valuable experiences. A duty-based moral view posits a moral ideal for a person in the form of a set of moral commitments, constraints, or prohibitions of behavior that can be violated only at the cost of one's moral integrity, at the cost of becoming morally evil or corrupt. This kind of moral position focuses directly on individual decision and action, and evaluates that decision and action not solely on the consequences it brings about. It might be thought of as positing certain limits on how one can act toward others beyond which a person cannot pass without becoming evil. Such prohibitions will usually concern what one deliberately does to other persons, what are sometimes loosely called one's projects, as opposed, for example, to what one simply fails to prevent. The prohibitions may be, though they need not be, absolute prohibitions which no conflicting moral consideration can justify violating.[2] The Catholic position that the direct killing of an innocent human being is always wrong is an example from moral theology, and the common view that deliberate torture of human beings is always wrong, is unthinkable for a moral person, serves as a secular example. The moral categories of a duty-based view are all constraints on our action to which we must conform at the peril of our moral integrity. These constraints commonly derive from the general idea of relations between persons, and the moral requirement that what we do to others be justified by features of that specific other, and our relation to him.[3] Duty-based views attempt to account for the intuition that a person has a special responsibility for what *he* deliberately and directly does to others, different from his responsibility for the actions of others. In this sense, duty-based views take the distinction between persons more seriously than do goal-based views, and focus on persons as agents whose own deliberate actions put them into morally significant relations with specific other persons. In most duty-based views, not killing human beings is a basic moral duty in the theory.

Finally, compare a view that appeals generally, and in particular with regard to the issue of killing, to moral rights that persons are asserted to possess. Rights function differently than duties in that they delineate areas in which the person possessing the right is at liberty to act as he sees fit and to act in his own interest as he understands it, as opposed to delineating specific constraints to which he must conform. Rights specify, as well, areas of behavior in which it is wrong, at least without special justification, for others to interfere with the rightholder's exercise of his right, or to fail to provide that to which the rightholder has a right if and when he calls for it. We may choose to exercise our rights or not as we see fit. Rights-based views emphasize a view of persons as capable of forming purposes, of making plans, of weighing alternatives according to how well they fulfill those plans and purposes, and of acting on the basis of this deliberation. Rights protect our exercise of these capacities, capacities whose exercise is often associated with the notion of autonomy, independent of how doing so promotes goals specified as valuable. We might say that while both duty- and rights-based views focus on individual action in a way that goal-based views do not, duties focus on constraints on action while rights focus on unconstrained choice. For a rights view, killing a human being will be wrong because it violates his right not to be killed; it wrongs the one killed, by violating *his* right, in a more direct manner than occurs on either a goal or duty view.

We might then summarize that in a goal-based view morality is concerned with the production of valuable experiences; in a duty-based view with the conformance of human action to prohibitions necessary to the maintenance of moral integrity; and in a rights-based view with the exercise and preservation of moral rights and the free choice they protect.

All of this is, of course, extremely sketchy and a great deal more could profitably be said in delineating and sharpening the nature of the three sorts of views and the many variants each may assume. I hope it is sufficient, though, to suggest the radically different implications for the issue of killing that the three positions have. All three views, we may assume, hold killing persons to be seriously wrong, but they differ on why it is wrong and in turn on when it is wrong. Consider the following cases:

Case A. Jones has a terminal, incurable disease. It completely prevents him from leading a normal life, causes him considerable though not unbearable pain and suffering, and he is expected to die from it within roughly a year; he has no relations or friends who care about him. Jones explicitly requests that everything be done to keep him alive as long as possible, even though his treatment is fantastically expensive and exhaustive of medical resources. Because of unique features of Jones' medical situation, if he is killed now it is likely that new medical knowledge will be obtained that will enable alleviation of the suffering of other similar patients.

Case B. Smith has terminal, incurable cancer. It completely prevents him from leading a normal life, causes him considerable though not unbearable pain and suffering, and he is expected to die from it in roughly a year. His treatment is expensive, but such that his family can afford it without undue stress. Smith is fully in command of his rational faculties, has given long and serious thought to his situation, and has decided he wants to die because life in his present condition is not worth living. He is unable, in his present situation, to bring about his own death, and requests another (his doctor, wife, etc.) to do so. He will only die if steps directly intended to kill him are taken.

If we take a goal-based view and act to maximize the balance of good consequences for all affected, then it seems reasonable to conclude that in Case A Jones ought to be killed. There seems no reason to suppose that cases of this sort, where the happiness of all affected will be increased by someone's being killed, do not occur with some frequency. Duty- and rights-based views will both hold killing Jones to be wrong in A, the former because doing so would violate the doctor's duty not to kill and so violate his moral integrity, the latter because Jones has a moral right not to be killed that he has neither waived, forfeited, or failed to exercise. Case B makes clear the difference in the rights- and duty-based views. For the rights view, Smith has waived his right not to be killed by explicitly requesting his doctor to kill him, and so it is morally permissible for his doctor to do so; no right of Smith's is violated and no wrong done him. For the duty view, the moral constraint is on how the physician (or wife) can permissibly behave to avoid moral corruption and avoid doing evil; that constraint need not be affected by the wishes of others. Smith would be viewed as asking the physician to act evilly, a request the physician is morally required to refuse, and which in no way need affect his duties in the case.

Much more could be said about these cases, filling in details and answering objections, to support the interpretations I have given them in the three different sorts of moral views, but I shall not attempt that here. I have only wanted to suggest how the *form* of the overall moral theory or view that one holds can lead people in substantially different directions on questions of killing within medical settings. As already noted, few of us fall neatly and completely into one of these three moral camps, but rather what is more often the case is that each of us feels at least some of the plausibility of each of these three ways of looking at the morality of killing; we experience what might be called *intra*personal disagreement on these issues, as well as *inter*personal disagreement. Most people's actual moral views are a complex of these three different sorts, the parts of which are in continual and often shifting tension. This intrapersonal complexity can come at the price of internal conflict and lack of coherence in one's overall moral views, which in turn can generate motivation for bringing all one's particular moral positions into conformity with one or another of the sorts of moral views I have delineated, as one way of regaining coherence in one's moral views.

It is, of course, quite natural to want to move from the delineation of different kinds of moral theories and their implications in a particular area such as killing, to the task of determining which is the correct, true, or most justified theory. In what sense if any this can be done is, of course, perhaps the central issue of ethical theory, but an issue which would take us far afield if considered here. This much, however, is worth adding. If one holds, as I do, a view on the justification of normative ethical positions similar in major respects to John Rawls's view of justification and reflective equilibrium, with its implications for a coherence account of normative ethical theories, then the task at hand is to work out the implications of different moral theories on various moral issues in order to match them up with what Rawls calls our considered moral judgments on those issues.[4] I am more inclined than I believe Rawls is to expect that the reflective equilibrium of different persons will not converge on a single view, but rather will tend to divide at least along the lines of the three different forms of moral views I sketched above. If so, it is all the more important to be clear about precisely where and how they do diverge. In the remainder of this chapter I shall take up that task by exploring some implications of a rights-based view, a view that holds killing to be morally wrong because it violates a person's moral right not to be killed.

II

If we begin with a moral right of a person not to be killed, then the issue of morally permissible killings becomes a question of when that right is not sufficient for the moral wrongness of killing a human being. One class of case will be the human being's failure to have the properties of personhood necessary and sufficient for possessing the right not to be killed; he is not the sort of being who has the right at all. This is Tooley's first class of case of morally permissible killing, and I shall not discuss it here. A second class of case is the person's having forfeited his right not to be killed. Killing in self-defense is the most prominent example, and in some views capital punishment falls into this class as well. However, I can think of few if any significant cases in the medical context that plausibly fit the forfeiting category, and so shall set it aside as well.[5] The third class of case is that in which the right-holder has waived his right not to be killed, the category Tooley labels voluntary euthanasia. This class is prominent in the medical context, and I shall begin with Tooley's account of voluntary euthanasia in order to bring out what I believe is a more acceptable account of rights, the right to life, and so the category of voluntary euthanasia. The fourth class of case is when a person's right to life, or right not to be killed, is justifiably overridden by some competing moral consideration, the category Tooley labels the cost of maintaining life. I shall argue that these cases cannot be adequately handled in the way he suggests. They require appeal to a theory of justice or fairness. Moreover, thinking of these cases in terms of rights justifiably overridden, as opposed to how conflicting interests are resolved or accommodated, may shed a rather different light on them. I should add before proceeding that, throughout the remainder of this chapter, I shall be considering cases in which terminating a person's life is *morally* justified, apart from either what the law at present allows, or ideally ought to allow. I believe that morality here should form the basis for legal policy, though it is, of course, not the case that what is morally permissible or prohibited should *ipso facto* be legally permissible or prohibited.

How should we understand the category of morally permissible termination of human life which Tooley labels voluntary euthanasia? He characterizes it as "cases in which a person exists, but his state is such that he has a rational desire that his life be terminated; that is, a desire to die that is in accordance with an estimate of his own long-term self-interest that is based upon the best information available." The claim that the presence of a desire to die means that killing a person does not violate his right not to be killed is based on a general account of the nature of rights and of the conditions in which they are and are not violated. Tooley assumes, in my view correctly, that the right to life is like other rights, in its form or logic, though its content differs. But he has ignored two aspects of the nature of rights, and as a result has produced a defective account of voluntary euthanasia.

First, to avoid violating A's right to x when I deprive A of x, it is not enough that A simply not desire x. A must have consented or granted permission to me to deprive him of x; he must have waived his right to x. For example, suppose I have no desire to vote in the next election, and Jones removes my name from the list of eligible voters. Jones has wrongly deprived me of my right to vote even though I did not intend to exercise my right; I have a moral (and legal) complaint against Jones for violating my right, even though I had no desire to vote. He has deprived me of that to which I have a right without my authorization or consent—without my having waived my right. If this is correct, and if the right to life is understood as structurally similar to other rights, then to avoid violating my right to life it is necessary not just that I desire to die but that I have consented to be killed, or waived my right not to be killed.

By concentrating on the rightholder's present desire for the object of his right rather than whether or not the right has been waived, Tooley misses an important aspect of rights that adds to their usefulness and value in facilitating our control and prediction of our future. His analysis of the conditions under which rights are violated suggests that if someone gives you permission to kill him in certain circumstances, you do not have a right to do so if, when he is actually in those circumstances, you find that he wants to go on living; it is not prior permission or consent to be killed, but the present desire to die, which would be morally necessary. I believe this is mistaken. The granting of permission or waiving of a right may, like the granting of authority to another to act for us or in our name, be either revocable or irrevocable; e.g., the law allows one to give up certain rights to property by establishing an irrevocable trust (where one's subsequent desire at future times for the trustee to exercise certain rights is not necessary to his having those rights) or a revocable trust (where such a continuing desire is necessary in the sense that without it, one may revoke the trustee's right to act with regard to the property). The waiving of one's right not to be killed in specified circumstances should likewise be able to be revocable or irrevocable. A person might wish it to be irrevocable if, for example, he believed that human life should only be lived when one was in possession of certain capacities and faculties, and should not be prolonged beyond that point, but believed that he might be, for various reasons, what could be called weak-willed in such circum-stances, and would then have and act on a desire to continue living. In such a case, a person might have good reason to waive irrevocably his right not to be killed under specified circumstances. When those cir-cumstances arose it would not be necessary for the desire to be present for it to be morally permissible for another to kill him. There is nothing morally objectionable, in itself, in our present self binding our future self in a way which will be contrary to the desire of the future self. This is a function in part of the fact that we each view ourself as one single self that continues over time, so that it is *my* future that my present action seeks to control.[6] Odysseus lashed himself to the mast for just such purposes, an alcoholic may keep no liquor in his house so that it is not available when he wants it in the future, and in fact persons often perform actions which are structurally of this sort. That particular rights may be waived irrevocably allows us to control our future in ways that would otherwise not be possible.

Many persons, of course, do not possess such an ideal, and realize that their desires may change with time and as conditions change. Thus, they have good reason to make their consent for another to kill them under specified circumstances revocable should they in fact not desire to die when in those circumstances, and especially since dying is the most irreversible of occurrences: one cannot, as with other events which may turn out to be unwanted, "make the best of it" and try to recoup one's loss, as with a bad bet or investment. With a revocable waiving of one's right not to be killed, then, the presence of the desire to die at the later time is relevant only in establishing that the person does not wish to revoke his waiving. As a practical matter, it seems that both irrevocable and revocable waivings of one's right not to be killed under specified circumstances are intended by different persons, for example in so-called Living Wills, and so it is important to be clear, as is usually not done, about which is intended. Some requests for euthanasia specify it only for conditions where one will then not be in a position to confirm or deny one's present desire to waive that right, and here the issue of revocability is not of practical importance.

The more important aspect of rights that Tooley ignores is that their possessor may waive them, or give consent for acts that would otherwise violate them, for reasons that need not accord with the best available estimate of his long-term interests. This issue is far too complex for a full treatment here, but let me at least roughly suggest how I believe the matter is correctly conceived. A person's interests are not simply equivalent to the objects of his present desires at any point in time; rather, he may be mistaken about his interests and so desire things not in his best interests. This is because while what a person desires is ascertained (in a rather complex way) by what he says he wants and what he pursues, what his interests are is ascertained (again, probably in a rather complex way) by what promotes his welfare or good, with the latter having an objective status independent to some degree of what he simply happens to desire. Consequently, other persons may at times be better judges of what best promotes our interests than we ourselves are. On the other hand, it is important that though the concept of interests has this objective status, what that objective content is, and how it is determined, is often controversial, so that what best serves a person's interests is often a contested question. Tooley's account suggests that a person's desire to waive his rights is rational only when that desire is in his overall best interest, and only when it is does it justify other persons acting in ways that would, in the absence of the desire, violate his rights. While he does not take up the issue, this account suggests as well that our exercise of our rights ought only to be protected from interference by others when that exercise is in our best interests. But if rights were understood in these ways, their character would be substantially different from what I believe it is, and something significant and valuable about rights would be lost. Rights

protect our freedom to act in the areas the right covers even in ways
that may not be in our overall best interests, and so may not be rational
in Tooley's sense. This feature reflects first a view of persons as able to
form purposes, weigh alternative actions according to how they fulfill
those purposes, and to act on the result of that deliberative process;
and second, it reflects a value placed on our autonomy or self-determination in making such choices and directing our lives, a value that is
not simply derived from our choices best promoting our welfare,
happiness, or interests. That our view of rights in fact has this feature
can perhaps best be shown with an example. Whatever the more basic
moral right from which they are derived, Americans are considered to
have a right to marry whom they wish and to choose the occupation
they wish. Others may try to convince one that a particular choice of
mate or job is a great mistake, that it is not in one's best interests;
however, even if on the best evidence available they are clearly correct,
one's right is still to make and act on one's own choice, to marry the
wrong person and take the wrong job. It would be wrong for others to
forcibly prevent one from doing so. These examples concern preventing a person from exercising his rights. Consider a case of waiving
rights where it is not in the best interests of the rightholder to do so.
My property rights make it the case that others would act wrongly in
taking property that is rightfully mine, but if I choose to give large
sums to a foolish cause even when it is clearly not in my best interests
to do so, representatives of that cause do not violate my rights in
taking it.

Now while rights protect our freedom to act in ways that need not be
in our best interests, it is not the case that they are sufficiently strong to
make interference in the exercise or waiving of a right taken in the
interests of the rightholder never justified. The issue is, When does a
rights-based view permit paternalistic intervention which violates a
person's rights? There is not space to develop a full account of paternalism here, but I will at least indicate the way in which my treatment
of it would differ from Tooley's treatment of voluntary euthanasia.[7]

In the areas of behavior which they cover, rights give protection to
our uncoerced choice and action. As indicated above, an institution of
rights presupposes that persons have capacities to form purposes,
weigh alternatives, and act, and reflects in turn the value most of us
place on being free to exercise these capacities without interference

from others, a process we value for its own sake as part of an ideal of human excellence and not simply as instrumental to human happiness or some other goal. In this view, we will want others to act paternalistically towards us only when our *capacities* to form purposes, weigh alternatives, and act are seriously defective, only when we are clearly subject to a serious defect of reason or will. The forms such defects can take are various and I shall not say more about them here, except to emphasize that the mere judgment by another that one's express desires will not best serve one's interests, even where on the evidence that judgment may be considered by most to be correct, is not sufficient to demonstrate incompetence and to justify paternalistic intervention contrary to those desires. It is the freedom to decide for ourselves as we see fit what direction our life will take, even when others may with good reason disagree, that our moral rights are designed to protect.

Since paternalistic action must be taken for the good of the person involved, I am doubtful whether it is ever the case that killing a person could be justified on paternalistic grounds in the face of a strong and continuing desire on that person's part to live. The difficult issue is whether we should on paternalistic grounds discount his desire to die. Pressing this question further would require a full account of paternalism. But enough has been said to suggest why for a rights-based view a request to be killed need not be in the person's overall long-term interest to be a valid request, though there will be some cases where, because the person is not competent to exercise and waive his rights, paternalistic grounds may justify invalidating his request to die. The practical implication of this point is that in specifying when they wish euthanasia to be performed on them, persons should not be restricted by any particular conception of rational desires or of their long-term interests.

We can conclude that in standard cases of voluntary euthanasia, the desire to die must actually be expressed—that is, consent given to be killed and thus waiving one's right not to be killed—but the desire or request need not always be a present desire and need not always be rational in the sense of best serving the person's long-term interest.

I want now to turn to cases where a person is unable to express his desire either to die or to go on living, unable to waive or insist on his right not to be killed. If we include as well cases where paternalistic intervention is justified because the person is no longer competent to exercise his rights, as in many cases of advanced senility, then this class of case is probably of considerable practical importance. Is it reasonable to construe any such cases as instances of voluntary euthanasia, and if so which?

Tooley proposes one extension of the category of voluntary euthanasia. He concentrates on two cases of persons suffering from some extremely painful, incurable disease, a disease in which everyone who has it prefers death to life, and of whom it is known that they do not disapprove of euthanasia: a child who has not yet learned a language, and an adult who is paralyzed and cannot make his desires known to others. Both examples are designed to allow us to be virtually certain that the person in fact has, and will continue to have a desire to die, but just cannot express that desire to us. On my account of the right not to be killed, and of the conditions under which killing does not violate that right, these are not cases of voluntary euthanasia because voluntary euthanasia requires consent to be killed, a waiving of the right not to be killed.

Compulsory euthanasia, on the other hand, means a person is killed who is capable of waiving his right not to be killed should he so desire and explicitly declines or refuses to do so, or has not yet done so. These examples of Tooley's actually constitute a third sort of case—the potential victim who is unable to give or withhold consent to be killed, unable to waive or decline to waive his right not to be killed. The plausibility of assimilating these examples to standard cases of voluntary euthanasia is that they suggest that we have sufficient evidence to be virtually certain that, were the person capable of waiving his right not to be killed, he would do so. I have no substantial quarrel with assimilating these cases to the category of voluntary euthanasia so long as it is clear that doing so is legitimate not just because of evidence of a desire to die, but because that evidence strongly supports the counterfactual that the person would waive his right not to be killed were it possible for him to do so.[8]

The more frequently encountered case, however, is a person who is capable neither of competently waiving or declining to waive his right not to be killed, where we have no decisive evidence regarding what he would do if he did not lack this capability. This case cannot be assimilated to the category of voluntary euthanasia, although it is more typical of what physicians and families actually encounter. It might well be wondered whether they ever encounter cases of the sort Tooley imagines, where virtual certainty exists about the person's desire though he is incapable of expressing the desire. Such certainty in his examples is based on the fact that everyone in similar circumstances who can express such a desire, in fact does so; but do we ever have evidence of this sort? It is well known that in many persons a desire to live may persist in the face of the most severe, incurable and incapacitating suffering; especially, but certainly not only, or even usually, with persons who believe euthanasia is wrong. Could we ever be certain that the case before us, where the person is incapable of consenting or declining to consent to be killed, was not of this sort? Surely, given the unpredictability of the strength of the will to live in any particular person, physicians must usually, if not always, be uncertain about whether a patient in cases of this sort would wish to and consent to be killed.

It is important to distinguish two sorts of cases in which a person is unable to make his wishes known—in the first he is undergoing extreme and continual suffering, whereas in the second he is relatively free from suffering. In the second case, and in the absence of a prior waiving of the right to life for situations of this sort, it is difficult to see what evidence could strongly support the belief that the right would be waived were it possible to do so. Since infringing upon such a fundamental moral right is an extremely serious moral wrong, I believe that in cases of the second sort one should assume that the right not to be killed would not be waived. Where the patient is undergoing extreme suffering as well, the case for a general policy of erring on the side of not violating the right to life, by assuming that the right would not be waived, is less persuasive. A moral theory asserting the existence of fundamental moral rights will quite likely include as well a right of persons to have extreme suffering relieved by others, at least where it is possible for others to do so with little cost or risk of harm to themselves.[9]

But if we can only relieve someone's suffering by killing him or by significantly shortening his life, as in fact is often true, then we have in such cases two rights which conflict, and we can avoid violating one only at the cost of violating the other. Arguing that one should always act so as to err on the side of not violating a fundamental moral right when there is significant danger of doing so is of no help here. In such cases, I believe we should obtain all the available information about the person relevant to what right *he* would choose to waive in such circumstances (including, of course, his views, if they are known, on euthanasia); we must then decide, often under considerable uncertainty, which right it is reasonable to believe he would waive under the circumstances. In such cases, we will have to act on a balance of the evidence, and rarely with the luxury of virtual certainty about whether the person would waive his right not to be killed.

Note that the less information we have about what the specific person in question would choose in the circumstances, the more our reasoning will have to resemble that of what a normal, rational person would choose in the same circumstances. And, in such cases, quality of life considerations will enter into our decisions to a greater extent than Tooley suggests, since the considerations that would be the basis of the argument that a rational person would desire to die (e.g. that he is suffering from an extremely painful, incurable disease which completely incapacitates him) are quality of life considerations. They show that the quality of life of that person, if his life is not now terminated, will be exceedingly and tragically low. The difficulty with quality of life considerations is not in their entering into any euthanasia decisions at all, but in insuring that they only enter into the question of what a normal, rational person would do in cases where the actual person is unable to waive or decline to waive his right not to be killed, and we do not know what he would do if he could do so. Tooley seems to me quite right—showing that someone's quality of life is or will be very low can never of itself justify terminating his life.

III

The second type of case of morally permissible termination of human life that I want to discuss is that in which the right to life is overridden by some competing moral consideration. Tooley describes these as cases where a person wants to continue to exist, but the cost of keeping him alive is so great that letting him die is the lesser of two evils. He does not say much about the weighing or balancing process that should be used, but does insist that it is wrong to assign unlimited weight to lengthening human life as against improving the quality of human life, and at one point characterizes the process generally as cost/benefit analysis. He is correct that it is sometimes justified to terminate a person's life against his wishes (self-defense is another important though nonmedical instance already cited), but he does not make clear what moral issues are involved and so the kind of reasoning that justifies doing so. It is important to bring out some of these issues.

Some of the issues concern the allocation of scarce resources. In this case appeal to cost/benefit analysis is of limited help; perhaps it is better to say that such an appeal presupposes the appropriateness of consequentialist or utilitarian reasoning in an area where it is most controversial and in my view least adequate.[10] What is needed instead is a theory of distributive justice. To see this, first consider the simpler case where only saving lives, i.e. choosing which lives to save, but not improving the quality of lives, is involved. Cost/benefit reasoning would seem to tell us to always save the most lives possible. However, if saving lives is not always to be given priority over improving the quality of lives, then such reasoning will require us to weigh different lives as well according to the expected value they will produce. The life of a great benefactor of mankind, such as a brilliant medical researcher, will count for far more than the life of a good-for-nothing ne'er-do-well. We should save the "more valuable" members of society before and in preference to the "less valuable," and should save a "more valuable" life even in preference to saving several "less valuable" lives if the difference in value is large enough. This result in itself seems to me sufficient to discredit utilitarian, cost/benefit reasoning on the issue of killing.[11] However, I do not wish to rest the case against such reasoning on this interpretation, and so shall assume that cost/benefit reasoning requires only weighing lives against lives, with no life to count for more than any other life; it then seems to produce more acceptable results. Where we have sufficient resources to save only some but not all, we should attempt to save the most lives possible. Consider the following:

Case C. We have a limited amount of life-saving medicine needed by two groups of persons. Jones, the only member of group A, needs all the medicine to survive, whereas Brown and Black, the two members of group B, each need only ½ the entire amount to survive.

If we are to save the most lives possible, then we should give the medicine to Brown and Black, thereby saving two lives instead of only one if the medicine is given to Jones.[12] We can say to Jones, "If you consider the situation impartially and imagine that you do not know to which group you belong, then you would agree that we should save Black and Brown in B, for if you don't know to which group you belong, that solution would maximize your own chances of being saved." Or we could say to Jones, "Saving Black and Brown is not unfair to you because if you consider the situation from a fair initial position where you don't know what dosage you will turn out to require and so to which group you will belong, you would accept that we should save Black and Brown." This latter way of putting the argument to Jones is important—it suggests that we want to be able to justify to Jones the fairness to him of our action, and as well that we might not always be able to do so.

Consider another case.

Case D.   The situation is identical to that in Case C, except that now Jones is a member of a minority that has been systematically and unjustly exploited by the majority to which Brown and Black belong. It is only as a direct and known result of this exploitation in which Brown and Black have taken part that Jones requires a higher dosage of the medicine for it to be effective.

Were it not for the prior exploitation all three would require equal amounts of the medicine, though there would still be only enough for two, in which case fairness would seem to require a random selection of two among the three to be saved. Thus, if circumstances were not unjust, Jones, as well as Black and Brown, would have an expected probability of being saved of 2/3. As a result of Black's and Brown's exploitation, if we save the most lives possible, Jones has no chance of being saved. Could we still say to Jones that saving the most lives possible is fair or just to him? It seems to me clear that we could not. Rather, Jones could say that to treat him fairly, all three should have an equal probability of being saved, as they would have had in the absence of his unjust treatment at the hands of Black and Brown, which in this case could be achieved by a random selection between saving Jones or saving both Brown and Black. Or, Jones might alternatively argue that he should have the same two-thirds probability of being saved that he would have had in the absence of the unjust exploitation to which he was subject. In real world conditions, of course, things are rarely as clearcut as the example makes them, and so whether simply saving the most lives possible is fair or just to those not saved will in turn often be controversial and unclear. But I would at least suggest that there is a moral requirement of fairness, which is independent of cost/benefit reasoning, and which makes it incumbent on us to explore and consider arguments from fairness in such life-saving situations. I do not believe considerations of fairness should always override considerations of utility maximization, but only that they should sometimes do so; it is difficult to say anything general about how precise trade-offs should be made here. I would add that such life-saving situations occur not only at the level of a physician in possession of scarce life-saving therapy, but as well at policy-making levels in the political process where decisions are made to allocate funds for research or medical delivery systems for different life-threatening diseases.

Next, consider a case where we must weigh saving lives against other benefits, specifically, improving the quality of other persons' lives.

Case E. Suppose rich Jones promises Smith that if Smith will kill Doe, he (Jones) will give a large sum of money to arthritis research. Smith correctly believes that this is the only opportunity in the near future to raise funds for arthritis research and relieve arthritis suffering, and that he can kill Doe with no one else learning of it.

Would Smith be morally justified in killing innocent Doe as the lesser of two evils in order to lessen the suffering and improve the quality of life of arthritis sufferers? Since the distinction between killing and letting die is not, in my view, *in itself* morally significant, it seems that if we simply attempt to maximize benefits and minimize harms we must say that (if Jones's donation is large enough) Smith would be morally justified in killing Doe. Yet cases like this are far more morally troubling than such utilitarian, cost/benefit analysis makes them, and not just for those who mistakenly appeal to the killing/letting die distinction. All can agree that Smith's killing Doe would be *prima facie* wrong because, on the cost/benefit view, it involves the cost of Doe's death, or because, on the rights-based view, it violates Doe's right to life. But is this the only moral consideration to be weighed against the cost of failing to further arthritis research if Doe is not killed? What has been left out again is that it would be unfair or unjust to single out innocent Doe for death to benefit arthritis sufferers. "Why should my life be sacrificed, why me and not others?" Doe might say. Doe is being used merely as a means to improve the lives of others, quite apart from whether *he* deserves to be so disadvantaged for the benefit of arthritis sufferers. A net gain in benefits or reduction of harms or evils from killing Doe, which cost/benefit, utilitarian reasoning might establish, could not show that Smith's action is fair or just *to Doe*. Once again, what is needed here is a comprehensive theory of distributive justice.

Now, just what constitutes an adequate theory of distributive justice is a notoriously complex and controversial issue; it is a major area of contention among moral and political philosophers, as well as the public at large. Tooley's proposal of a fair method for making allocations between lengthening of life and quality of life considerations is therefore, in its simplicity, extremely attractive. He suggests that when everyone has a reasonable personal income, the fair solution is to "allow each person to decide how much of his income he wishes to use, not to improve the quality of his life, but to invest in insurance to guard against the possible occurrences which would necessitate large expenditures in order to keep him alive." This solution is also designed to avoid the well-known problems of the interpersonal comparison of utility and of finding morally defensible methods of social choice or decision.[13]

It will be sufficient to point out two difficulties with this solution to see that it has neither the advantage nor simplicity it promises. First, note that if this is to be a fair solution to the distribution problem, we must stipulate not just that at the outset everyone has a reasonable income, but that everyone has a fair income; only if we begin from a fair status-quo point will the application of fair procedures produce a fair or just outcome. This may seem a quibble, but it is not, for it makes clear that Tooley's proposal does not avoid the need for a theory of the fair or just distribution of income and wealth. And it means as well that so long as substantial injustices persist in the distribution of income and wealth, personal financing of life-saving medical treatment, whether through purchase of insurance or otherwise, will result in substantial injustices in the allocation of such treatments.

Second, setting aside the issue of justice or fairness, we cannot avoid the problems of the interpersonal comparison of utility and of social choice, and so do not have a sound basis for making cost/benefit calculations in the manner Tooley proposes. Successful medical research has some of the attributes of what economists call "public goods"; it makes possible new therapeutic knowledge and procedures which will be generally accessible to members of society. But it is not entirely possible to restrict the benefits of medical research to those who pay for the research when participation in its financing is voluntary, as it would be with Tooley's insurance scheme. Medical research in this respect is similar to such goods as public parks and a system of national defense. There will be a tendency for rational self-interested persons to understate their preferences for public goods, e.g. Tooley's case of arthritis research, because they can benefit from the decisions of others to support the supplying of the goods. This so-called "free-rider" problem in the provision of public goods requires a collectively made and enforced decision to insure that public goods will be provided in amounts reflecting the real preferences of the group. This suggests that a social decision is necessary in order to provide an optimal allocation of funds between life-saving and quality of life programs on cost/benefit grounds. This is a special problem in the present case where we must weigh what appear to be largely incommensurable goods—the saving of some lives versus the improvement in the quality of other lives. Cost/benefit analysis is only of limited usefulness in such decisions.

There is one other common approach to decisions concerning patient treatment that seems to provide a way around some of these conflict-of-interests issues. A common model of the doctor-patient relationship is one in which the doctor is viewed as the agent of the patient and who is to act in the interest and for the welfare of the patient alone. Sometimes this model is restricted to the physician's relationship to the dying patient, where it is asserted that his concern should be solely with the dying patient's welfare: the physician should adopt what has been called a patient-centered ethic.[14]

Decisions about a patient's treatment, including institution or withdrawal of treatment which will hasten or prolong the patient's death, are to be made solely according to how his welfare or interests are affected. This model for treatment decisions has the effect of drastically limiting the conflict of interests category of morally permissible killing. Recall our earlier Case A in which Jones has a terminal disease. He wishes to be kept alive as long as possible, but because of unique features of his medical situation, if he is killed now it is likely that new medical knowledge will be obtained that will enable alleviation of the suffering of other similar patients. The patient-centered model of the doctor-patient relationship would preclude any effects on the interests of persons other than the patient (whether provision of benefits or prevention of harms) from being weighed in the physician's decision about Jones's treatment.

Perhaps more common instances where the interests of others are significantly affected are those in which continued use of life-sustaining therapies will have disastrous consequences for the psychological and financial well-being of the patient's family. Here again, the patient-centered model of the doctor-patient relationship precludes any consideration of effects on a patient's family in decisions concerning treatment. In terms of a right to life, the patient-centered model gives a particularly strong interpretation to the right to life and indicates when it can be justifiably overridden—it does not allow the conflicting interests of others ever (except perhaps in cases of choosing whom to save and whom to kill or let die) to override the patient's right to life. I am doubtful of how closely physicians in fact adhere to such a model of the doctor-patient relationship in their practice, but, more important, it is by no means clear why they should adhere to it. If there is a class of case involving conflicts of interest in which the termination of human life is morally justified because the effects on the quality of life of others weighs against lengthening the life of the patient, then this doctor-patient model is badly confused and promotes faulty reasoning about an important group of cases.

Where does this leave us with regard to conflict of interests cases? I have suggested that moral considerations of justice and fairness are involved in cases where we must choose which lives to save. And they appear again in cases where saving or lengthening lives must be weighed against improving the quality of lives. Neither Tooley's insurance scheme, nor a patient-centered model of the doctor-patient relationship seems to be a defensible way of meeting these issues. In the moral view I have been elaborating in this paper, the two central issues in the question of when the right to life is overridden by competing considerations remain to be answered. The first concerns the strength or importance of the right to life compared to other moral rights and considerations and to quality of life considerations. The second concerns the fair or just distribution *between* persons of benefits and burdens when saving a life comes into conflict with other considerations. On this second question, I have been content here to argue that utilitarian, cost/benefit reasoning is inadequate, and that the point at which termination of life is morally permissible cannot be settled without some appeal to a theory of distributive justice. Developing such a theory, or even simply applying an already developed theory such as that of John Rawls in his *A Theory of Justice,* is far too complex and lengthy a task to be attempted here. At the very broadest level, the issues include: the allocation of resources between health care and other nonhealth care interests; the allocation of resources to different sorts of health care needs, for example life-saving versus nonlife threatening; and the extent and basis of any particular individual's legitimate claims on those resources. Unless undue weight is placed on the killing/letting die distinction, we cannot hope to decide when it is morally permissible to kill within the practice of medicine without coming to grips with these broader issues of distributive justice.

With regard to the first issue—the relative importance of the right not to be killed as opposed to other moral rights and considerations—I believe an adequate position will have to account for the special importance normally accorded to the right to life without at the same time according it absolute priority. This special importance reflects, most importantly, two things. First, it reflects the way in which life itself is a necessary condition for carrying out and pursuing all our other life plans and purposes; it is not merely one purpose or project among others, which if taken away could have some other project, with its attendant satisfaction, substituted for it. Second, it reflects the way in which each person's life is uniquely important to him/her and the fact that gains to others in their well-being cannot compensate me, and my life, for its loss; loss of life itself is not able to be compensated for *inter*personally, by benefits gained by others, in the way that satisfactions can be compensated for *intra*personally. The two factors help explain the special importance of the right to life in somewhat different ways. The first factor helps account for the special importance given loss of life in comparison with other harms and benefits, the second for the limits on the possibility of compensating one person for the loss of his life by gains in benefits provided, or harms prevented, to others. Perhaps further development of these and related considerations will yield some insight into the relative strength of the right to life. In the whole category of morally permissible termination of life when the cost of maintaining it is too high, most of the necessary analysis remains to be done; I hope here only to have brought out what some of the issues are, and by so doing to suggest some directions which further inquiry must take.

Notes

1. Ronald Dworkin, *Taking Rights Seriously,* ch. 6 (Cambridge, Mass.: Harvard University Press, 1977). My characterization of the three types of moral views owes much to Dworkin's discussion.

2. If the moral prohibitions are absolutist prohibitions, then to remain coherent they must be restricted to something like what we deliberately do to others, since one might find oneself in a situation where, whatever one did, the prohibited effect (e.g. someone's death) would come about as a result. Cf. Thomas Nagel, "War and Massacre," *Philosophy and Public Affairs* 1 (1972), pp. 123–44. Neither Nagel, nor anyone else to my knowledge, has made clear precisely how the distinction between what one does, and what merely happens as a result of what one does, should be drawn.

3. This requirement is developed by Nagel, "War and Massacre."

4. See John Rawls, *A Theory of Justice,* (Cambridge, Mass.: Harvard University Press, 1971), especially ch. 1 and sec. 87; also Rawls, "The Independence of Moral Theory," *Proceedings of the American Philosophical Association* 48 (1974–75), pp. 5–22.

5. There is an important issue that, while not strictly a case of forfeiting rights, is quite closely related—the relevance, if any, to claims for medical care of the patient's own responsibility for his disease or condition. I have in mind cases where the patient could have avoided the condition if he had chosen to; for example, emphysema acquired as a direct result of heavy smoking.

6. For a contrary view on personal identity over time, its implications for moral theory in general, and binding our future selves in particular, see Derek Parfit, "Later Selves and Moral Principles," *Philosophy and Personal Relations,* ed. Alan Montefiore (Montreal: McGill-Queen's University Press, 1973).

7. I have discussed paternalism, with specific reference to the involuntary commitment of the mentally ill, more fully in "Involuntary Civil Commitment: The Moral Issues," *Mental Illness: Law and Public Policy* eds. Baruch Brody and H. Tristram Englehardt, Jr., (Dordrecht, Holland: Reidel, forthcoming).

8. My colleague Dr. Sidney Cobb has suggested to me that cases of the sort Tooley imagines rarely occur, at least with adults, because loss of cerebral function to the point at which communication becomes impossible is usually associated with relief of pain and suffering.

9. See, for example, David Richards, *A Theory of Reasons for Action* (Oxford: Clarendon Press, 1971) pp. 185–89, and Rawls, *Theory of Justice,* pp. 338f.

10. Precisely how cost/benefit analysis should be understood is not clear. It can be conceived merely as an analytic tool or procedure in which the costs and benefits of alternative courses of action are estimated. I shall associate it as well with a normative principle of a consequentialist or utilitarian sort according to which a course of action ought to be performed if, and only if, it produces at least as good overall consequences (benefits less costs) as alternative possible actions.

11. A good discussion of the implications of utilitarianism for killing in general is contained in Richard Henson, "Utilitarianism and the Wrongness of Killing," *The Philosophical Review* 80 (1971), pp. 320–37.

12. That we need not always save the most lives possible is argued, on somewhat different lines than I have taken, by Elizabeth Anscombe, "Who Is Wronged?" *Oxford Review* (1967), and saving the most lives possible is defended by Gertrude Ezorsky, "How Many Lives Shall We Save?" *Metaphilosophy* 3 (1972) pp. 156–62.

13. An excellent discussion of these problems can be found in A.K. Sen, *Collective Choice and Social Welfare* (San Francisco: Holden-Day, 1970).

14. This view is advocated in, among other places, Leon Kass, "Death as an Event: A Commentary on Robert Morison," *Science* 173 (20 August 1971) pp. 698–702.

6 The Definition of Death and the Right to Die

JOHN LADD

Discussions of euthanasia often involve questions concerning the definition or redefinition of death and involve questions concerning rights such as the right to life or the right to die. From the philosophical point of view, most available discussions of death that employ these two categories seem very simple-minded. They almost always fail to take into account the distinctive logical properties of definitions in general or of rights in general, properties that philosophers have discussed rather extensively. In this chapter, I shall argue that due attention to these logical properties of definitions and of rights will help us to see more clearly what can and what cannot be done with definitions and rights in this context. In particular, it will make us wary of taking them as ready-made categories to be used without further ado in ethical discussions concerning death. I am not suggesting that we ought to abandon them altogether, only that we must take a more sophisticated attitude toward them than is generally found in the literature on euthanasia.[1]

Part I: The definition of death

There is a rapidly growing literature concerned with the definition of death, i.e. with establishing criteria for determining whether a person is alive or dead as well as for determining the moment of death.[2] Before the advent of modern medical technology, the stoppage of respiration and the circulation of the blood were universally accepted as sufficient signs of death.[3] However, the new technology has made it possible to reverse these stoppages and to "bring a person back to life," e.g. after cardiac arrest. We now have to cope with the fact that some vital functions can be sustained even though others have ceased. There are all sorts of intermediate stages between life in the full sense and death in the full sense, and we are faced with the problem of where to draw the line. Strictly speaking, however, the problem is not one simply of drawing a line; rather it is a problem of deciding which particular functions or set of functions are essential to human life and what signs shall be taken as indicating the presence or absence of these functions.

There are, of course, practical exigencies that make the question of determining the occurrence of death of more than purely academic interest. The dramatic development of techniques of organ transplantation has made this question peculiarly urgent, because if one waits too long after death before removing an organ, the organ will begin to deteriorate. There are also a number of legal issues that hang on the definition of death, e.g. issues relating to such things as inheritance or culpability for murder.

Nevertheless, even though there has been a great deal of writing on the definition of death and the problem of defining death is an urgent practical problem, little attention has been given by those concerned with the subject to the notion of definition itself, despite the fact that there is a considerable philosophical literature on the subject of definition going back to Plato and Aristotle and continuing down to the present. This neglect of the philosophical literature on definition is especially unfortunate because in recent years philosophers have devoted special attention to the distinctive properties of the kinds of definition that are used in ethics, law and science.[4]

If we wish to proceed philosophically in the matter of defining death, we need to ask a number of preliminary questions. What kind of definition is being sought? What will the definition be used for? What standards of propriety should be used for deciding whether or not a proposed definition is the correct one or whether it is the best definition? And, finally, is there any reason to assume that there is only one definition of death? May there not be a number of correct definitions valid respectively for the different contexts in which they are used?

A few preliminary observations in regard to these questions about definitions will be helpful. First, it is obvious that since a definition of death will be used for important practical purposes, the kind of definition that is required cannot be an arbitrary stipulative definition, as are some mathematical and scientific definitions. Therefore, any definition of death that is proposed needs to be defended by arguments that will show it not to be arbitrary. Moreover, as a practical definition with practical import a definition of death will, of necessity, be value-laden; in Stevenson's terms, it will be a "persuasive definition," since anyone proposing a definition of death will *ipso facto* be advocating certain courses of action or nonaction. Hence, some sort of ethical justification of the definition is required. Finally, inasmuch as any definition of death is likely to be controversial, if discussion is to be rational, argumentation is required. Thus, for a number of reasons, a definition of death requires a full-fledged rational vindication; appeals to intuition, to medical practice or to authority are not enough.

Second, following Wittgenstein and other recent authors, we must assume that not only is it possible, but it is highly likely that the concept of death is not definable at all in the strict sense. Many of our concepts, as Wittgenstein pointed out, are not univocal but are "family-resemblance" concepts, open-textured; and for that reason are incapable of definition in terms of necessary and sufficient conditions.[5] Achinstein has argued that even scientific concepts like copper or acid are not definable in this sense; that is, it is not possible to specify all those properties that are logically necessary and sufficient to justify classifying a thing in a certain way.[6] Such concepts are often called "cluster-concepts"; that is, they refer to a cluster of properties such that the possession of a number of them is sufficient to justify classifying a thing as a certain kind of thing, but no single one of these properties is of itself necessary or sufficient for this purpose. The properties in a cluster are generally called *criteria.*

Considerations such as those just mentioned suggest that we might well ask whether we are dealing with a single, univocal concept of death or with a family-resemblance concept. It is conceivable that there might be a biological, a medical, a legal, a moral, a theological and a metaphysical concept of death, none of which are the same except in a family-resemblance sense. (I shall return to this point later.)

Finally, a few observations should be made about "medical" definitions of death. One of the chief difficulties in finding a medical definition of death that will be specific enough to pinpoint the moment of death comes from the physiological fact that dying is a process, and different parts of the body, different functional systems and organs, cease functioning at different times.[7] The fact is not simply that dying is a continuous process but that it is also a multiple process, so that theoretically at least there are a number of different processes the termination of any one of which could be used as a definition of death.[8] For obvious reasons, the kinds of processes that are the most plausible ones to use in a definition of death are brain processes of some kind, since stoppage of circulation or of respiration, if not reversed, will lead quickly to death of the brain.[9] There have been a number of definitions of death based on the concept of brain death originally formulated by the Ad Hoc Committee of the Harvard Medical School to Explore the Definition of Brain Death.[10] The criteria set forth in this document consist of: (1) unreceptivity and unresponsivity, (2) no movements or breathing, (3) no reflexes, and (4) flat electroencephalogram. All tests are to be repeated after twenty-four hours. (These criteria are slightly modified in more recent versions.)

In regard to medical definitions of death, two points are worth noting. First, the only requirement for a definition of death that is generally agreed upon to be absolutely necessary is that the condition designated by the definition be *irreversible*. Indeed, medical discussions of the definition of death focus almost exclusively on irreversibility as the test of the correctness of a definition and virtually the only consideration advanced for or against a particular definition in the medical literature relates to the reversibility or irreversibility of the processes in question.

It goes without saying that irreversibility is not sufficient, for we must be able to specify which particular function has been lost irreversibly. The emphasis in the medical literature on irreversibility is easy to understand, because the determination that a certain function has been destroyed irreversibly is a scientific matter, a question on which medical scientists are the experts, whereas other questions about the definition of death, e.g. which particular function must be destroyed irreversibly, may also be questions for philosophers, theologians, or lawyers. I shall presently try to explain why irreversibility is such an important element in the concept of death.

Second, in considering definitions of death it is important to distinguish between clinical *signs* (or indicators) of death and *criteria* (or determinants) of death.[11] Following current philosophical usage, I shall use the term "criteria" to stand for those properties that pertain to the meaning of "death." "Signs" will be used to stand for clinical evidence that the criteria have been fulfilled. Thus on certain accounts, electrocerebral silence, apnea (absence of spontaneous respiration), and deep coma (unresponsivity) would be signs of brain death. Brain death, in turn, would be a criterion of death, for to be brain dead would be part of the meaning of "being dead," if that is the definition in question. Signs are directly observable and as such are called "clinical signs of death." The conditions inferred from them are the criteria of death. (They may reflect what Achinstein calls the "underlying structure.")[12] The distinction between signs and criteria is a logical one representing the distinction between contingent connections that are established empirically and connections that are logical and necessary.[13] Thus, for example, the connection between a clinical sign such as a flat EEG and what it signifies, e.g. brain death, is an empirical connection founded on observation. Whether or not the total destruction of the brain is a necessary condition of death, or a criterion of death, is not an empirical question at all: it is a question of meaning or of conceptual analysis.

The distinction that I have just drawn between signs and criteria suggests an interesting philosophical question, namely, whether the clinically observed factors in a given definition of death, e.g. unresponsivity, are simply signs of an irreversible physiological condition that constitutes death, e.g. brain death, or whether these factors are themselves criteria of death, i.e. constitutive of death in the sense that they are part of what we mean by being dead. In other words, if unresponsiveness plus a number of other observable conditions are manifestations of brain death, do we want to say that the person in question is dead because his brain is dead, or do we want to say that he is dead because he makes no responses? Which represents death, the cause or the effect? The problem suggests that sooner or later we may be forced to choose between a behavioristic and a physiological definition of death. Or must we settle for a cluster concept?

Behind this general problem of signs versus criteria, or of clinical observations versus inferred conditions, lies the more general issue concerning what it is that we are trying to determine when we ask whether someone is dead. Death has traditionally been defined as the departure of the soul from the body. Contemporary philosophers prefer to say that death is the ceasing to exist of a person. Are we to assume that when the brain (or part of the brain) ceases to function that the soul has departed or that the person ceases to exist? Is irreversible coma sufficient to say that this event has occurred? How could such questions be settled?

It is difficult for us not to picture dying as the soul leaving the body, just as a person leaves his house. This creates a mythological concept of death. We feel that if a person can no longer make certain responses or if his brain is dead, then the soul must have left. But we will not get anywhere with the problem of defining death, until we divest ourselves of this picture. The first thing we have to do is to demythologize the concept of death, for if we fail to do so we will look for realities in places where they do not exist and we will not see them where they do exist. We will, for example, picture the soul quietly resting in the body of a comatose person, waiting to be released when the brain stem ceases to function! The picture forces on us a mythology that there is still something in the body as long as any part of the brain continues to function.

It appears that we are working with two quite different conceptions of death, a mythological conception and a medical conception; the first views death as an event, like leaving the house, and the second views it as a process, like a house burning down. But the picture theory of concepts is not only misleading, it generates false dichotomies. The only way out of the apparent impasse between these two conceptions is to take a cue from Wittgenstein and think of concepts, like the concept of death, as tools, tools that we use for various purposes in our social discourse and transactions with one another.[14] Different concepts, according to Wittgenstein, operate in different ways; their functions are as diverse as the functions of the handles in the cabin of a locomotive. The concept of death might be likened to a handle that turns things off. But like a handle in a locomotive, the concept of death can only be understood by showing its relation to other concepts that we use in practical life. In order to show this we must return to the notion of definition.

The purpose of definition

The criterion of a good definition is that it serves its purpose well, for definitions, like concepts in general, are tools. Hence, our first task in seeking a definition is to ask what the definition will be used for. Definitions in general may be regarded as rules for connecting the term (or concept) to be defined, generally called the *definiendum,* with the terms (or concepts) that define it, generally called the *definiens.* Very roughly speaking, a definition of death is supposed to connect death in its ordinary meaning (the definiendum) with certain physiological facts, functions or processes. Just how this is to be done depends on the prior logical properties of the definiendum; in particular, what the concept of death is to be used for. (It might be used, for example, for an ethical, legal, or theological purpose.)

It is presumed that here we are concerned with ethical issues, so that we can answer this question about the use of the concept of death from the ethical point of view. If our ethics is Kantian, as mine is, that would mean that we are interested in death as it relates to treating persons as ends and not merely as means. If our purposes are legal, on the other hand, the concept might be used to settle certain kinds of conflicts of interest, say, with regard to an inheritance.

In general, then, the kind of definition that we are looking for in a definition of death is a practical definition; that is, one that takes into account how the concept functions while at the same time providing criteria for applying the concept to particular kinds of processes or events. The difference in purposes explains why the definition of the death of, say, a tree differs from the definition of the death of a person.

The two sides of a definition may become clearer by relating them to what Kovesi calls the *formal* and the *material* elements of a concept.[15] The formal elements, according to Kovesi, are connected with what the concept is used for; that is, they pertain to the point of calling something a so-and-so; the material elements, on the other hand, consist of what are often called the "criteria" for the application of the concept. As Kovesi points out, most concepts of a practical nature are open-textured, since the material elements or criteria will change as conditions change. The formal element, in contrast, is fairly constant, for it is what enables us to bring a thing under a rule: "without the formal element, we cannot follow a rule in using a term."[16] For example, it is the formal element in a concept like the concept of murder that allows us to bring a certain act under a rule, e.g. against murder; whereas the material element in the concept of murder determines what is to count as murder. As Kovesi points out, the material elements cannot be enumerated in a final list, as is required in a definition in the strict sense. For the same reasons, it might be argued that concepts like the concept of death cannot, strictly speaking, be defined in the sense of providing a definitive list of the necessary and sufficient conditions for applying them. The open texture of concepts such as these is what makes them cluster concepts.

Uses of the concept of death

Let us see what light Kovesi's distinction between the formal and the material elements of a concept can shed on the controversy surrounding the definition of death. We may begin with the formal aspect of the concept of death and ask: What is the point of saying that someone is dead or, to be more specific, of saying that a person died at a certain time?

There are, of course, a number of different answers to this question. In general terms, it is obvious that when a person dies certain readjustments—psychological, social and legal—are required on the part of other individuals and on the part of society. Let us ignore wider metaphysical, theological, phenomenological and psychological functions of the concept of death and focus on some obvious practical reasons why we need to know that a person has died and the time of his death.

First, we need to know that a person has died, and the time of his death, for a variety of specific legal purposes; such as the determination of inheritance or taxes, or the remarriage of the spouse.[17]

Second, we need to know that a person is dead in order to know when and when not to apply criminal statutes, e.g. statutes concerning murder or homicide: if a man is already dead, you cannot kill him.[18]

Third, if we know that a person has died, we are free to terminate treatment: turn off the respirator, cease feeding, cease administering drugs.[19]

Finally, if a person is dead we can do various things with the body: perform an autopsy on it, remove organs from it for transplantation, bury it.

Every one of the points mentioned involves a rule of one sort or another such that the ascription of death to a person brings the rule into operation. In order to determine whether or not any of these rules is operative, a moment of death must be specified. For certain purposes the time designation may be given in very general terms, but in any case, death must be categorized as a dateable event. Death must also be taken to happen to a person as an integral unit; that is, it is the person as a whole that dies the death and not just some part of him. In that regard his personhood is simple and indivisible, not separable into parts or distinguishable into degrees. Finally, death must be irreversible, for the actions they permit have effects that cannot be undone. In sum, for all the purposes mentioned in our list, death must be thought of as *momentary, holistic* and *irreversible.*[20] These, then, are the formal requirements of the concept of death by virtue of which it can be used as a practical, moral, and legal concept.

Let us now turn to the material aspects of the concept of death, i.e. the criteria to be used for determining what counts as being alive or dead for purposes of the kinds of rules that I have mentioned. It is obvious that physiological processes can never exactly match the formal requirements of these practical rules. Formerly, it was possible to use the breakdown of general bodily systems as a criterion of death, e.g. the cessation of respiration or of heartbeat. But now these roughly matching criteria will not do, since we have artificial means for continuing the processes in question. Thus, even if at one time there were criteria that were approximately momentary, holistic and irreversible, now, in certain cases at least, the required kind of criteria are no longer available. We should not be surprised at this, however, since the material elements in almost any concept change as conditions change.

Of course, it might be argued that the Harvard criteria effectively satisfy these requirements. The trouble with the Harvard criteria is that they are too stringent; in some cases, they make possible the indefinite prolongation of life-support, and in other cases some of the procedures required seem to be unnecessary. Perhaps more important for us is the real likelihood that future advances in neurology will make it possible to resuscitate parts of the brain artificially. So that even if criteria like the Harvard criteria work today, they may be out-of-date tomorrow, if they are not already.

But even granted that the Harvard criteria or other criteria of brain death provide sufficient conditions of death, they certainly do not establish the necessary conditions of death. Yet, for purposes of definition we need all the necessary conditions as well as a sufficient condition of death; there are lots of sufficient conditions of being dead that are of little help practically. For example, having been born in A.D. 1000, or having been decapitated or cremated are sufficient conditions of being dead, but they are obviously not necessary. A necessary condition of death is, of course, logically equivalent to the absence of a sufficient condition of life—and who is to say what that is?

Sometimes, indeed, it is even difficult to specify an unexceptional, sufficient medical condition or set of conditions of death. If we consider the criteria customarily applied by physicians, including such things as absence of respiration or heart beat, or flat EEG for a certain time, it is evident that under normal conditions they are sufficient conditions of death, but under abnormal conditions they are not; for example, the test of flat EEG does not apply under hypothermia or when drugs have been used.

Considerations such as these, as well as the constant development of new tests, go to show that, as has already been suggested, the material element in the concept of death is open-textured and subject to change. In this sense, death cannot be defined at all in the sense of providing a complete set of necessary conditions that are jointly sufficient for the occurrence of death. But as we shall see presently, the quest for a definition of death runs into even greater difficulties, difficulties of a logical nature that arise as a result of trying to define death under conditions created by modern medical technology.

For the time being, let us leave aside the large proportion of death determinations that create no new problems and focus on the new kind of case that medical technology has created for us. The critical fact is that the new technology has given us the power to control dying; that is, to control the timing and manner of death. We may not be able to reverse the deterioration of most life-sustaining functions, but we can continue at will some of the processes that we used to refer to as signs of "life," i.e. processes the termination of which formerly served as criteria of death. Since some of these functional changes can now be reversed, e.g. cardiac arrest, they can no longer be used as criteria of death—in a simple-minded way, at least.

The result of these new developments is not simply that we are confused because things have become more complicated, but that by acquiring the power to control such things as the time of death we have created a paradox. For *this new power undermines the practical functions that the concept of death is designed to perform;* the formal element in the concept of death presupposes that the moment of death is not subject to manipulation, i.e. that death is irreversible, while the material elements that determine what is to count as death have now become subject to manipulation through the advance of medical technology, i.e. they are reversible. Paradoxically, if we can postpone death by keeping a person on a respirator, then we cannot use the occurrence of death to justify turning off the respirator. A person would be dead only if we turn off the respirator, but we can turn off the respirator only if that person is dead.

It is unnecessary to examine other paradoxes resulting from our new power to manage death. All of them are due to the fact that we are now able to select at will the time at which the rules mentioned in the list above will come into operation. With sufficient cunning this kind of manipulation can be used for all sorts of purposes. It is clear that Generalissimo Franco's death was managed by the politicians for their own special purposes. So far in the United States the manipulation of death has been governed chiefly by the interests of institutional medicine, lawyers and the suppliers of health care equipment and materials; but one can imagine situations where the timing of death might be manipulated for even more insidious purposes.

To summarize this part of the chapter: a presupposition of death in its formal aspect is its being beyond human control, i.e. its irreversibility. This presupposition no longer holds true in a number of cases. That means that the point of calling a person dead or alive at a certain time has been undermined—under some circumstances, at least. We can, of course, stipulate a definition of death for particular purposes, but a general all-purpose defintion of the old-fashioned sort is probably no longer possible.

In the final analysis, the question we have to face is whether to change the criteria (the material element) or to change the rules that employ the concept of death as a category. In any case, it is clear that we need new categories and new rules; either different categories of death, or new rules concerning what can or cannot be done. In fact, of course, we have already moved in the direction of changing both the criteria and the rules; for example, what is happening in practice with regard to the latter is that issues concerning the determination that death has occurred are now simply bypassed when decisions need to be made concerning the continuation or termination of treatment.[21] Perhaps that is all to the good. As far as the law is concerned, a revamping of legal concepts and rules relating to death will probably soon be necessary for the same sorts of reason.[22] For, although traditionally law has devised many ways for coping with situations in which a person's death has been deliberately hastened (e.g. by murder), it has not yet had to cope with situations in which death is deliberately delayed to suit the interests of other parties, e.g. to secure an inheritance, to avoid being convicted of murder, or to provide organs for transplantation.

Part II: The issue of rights

It should be clear from the foregoing discussion that, in many cases at least, the real ethical question is no longer the question of how to define death. It has now become the question: Who is to control the manner and timing of death in its *formal* sense; that is, who is to decide when to terminate treatment and when to begin the other actions and procedures that were previously regarded as depending on the occurrence of death? Questions of control of this sort are generally construed as questions about rights.[23] Who, then, has the right to decide? And equally important, who does *not* have the right to decide?[24] The right to decide certain matters is generally contingent upon other rights that one possesses. We must therefore examine the whole question of rights in the area of medical decision making.

The prevalent use of the concept of rights in discussions of ethical issues relating to the prolongation of life, euthanasia, and the prevention of cacothanasia provides a nice illustration of de Tocqueville's contention that Americans tend to turn every question into a legal question and to discuss political and social issues in the language of the law.[25] Ethical issues concerning life and death are thought to hinge on rights such as the right to life, the right to die, the right to be treated, the right to refuse treatment, the right to decide when to turn off the respirator. Our next task, therefore, will be to examine the assumption that moral issues concerning decisions about life and death should be handled as questions about rights.

In the present context, we might assume that such rights come into play as the result of the futility, perhaps the paradoxicality, of basing the rightness or wrongness of any of the actions involved here on the definition of death. In cases like the Quinlan case, for example, the real issue is not whether the person in question is dead or not, but whether or not to turn off the respirator; this question in turn hinges on the question of who has the right to decide that treatment should be terminated.[26]

Let us now examine this concept of rights more carefully. Our concern is with what are called "moral rights," "natural rights," or "human rights," rather than with strictly legal rights.[27] Moral rights may be regarded as rights that ought to be recognized, promoted and protected by positive law and institutional regulations, even though, in fact, they may not be.[28] A just state or institution is one that incorporates moral rights into its system of laws, regulations and procedures to the highest degree possible. If this assumption about moral rights is correct, then we may expect moral rights to have somewhat the same formal logical structure as legal rights. Otherwise, the term "rights" has no meaning and there is no point to using it. In order to understand what is at issue in the appeal to rights like those mentioned, e.g. the right to life, we must begin by examining the formal, logical structure of rights in general.[29]

I shall assume along lines suggested by Hohfeld's analysis that a moral right, like a legal right, represents a moral (or legal) relationship between persons: the person who possesses the right and the person, or set of persons, against whom the right holds, that is, who are obligated by the right.[30] I shall call the former the *right-holder* and the latter the *right-ower*.[31]

A number of questions must be asked about any alleged right.

First, *who are the parties in the relationship?* (Who is the right-holder and who is the right-ower?) Following tradition, it is useful to distinguish between rights held against a particular person or group and rights held against everyone, that is, rights that are said to "avail against the whole world." These are usually called rights *in personam,* rights that impose duties on specific persons, and rights *in rem,* rights that impose a duty on everyone. I should like to add a third possible set of right-owers, an indeterminate group of persons, they might be called "people" or "society"; or, if you wish, "we" (or "us"). Rights of this kind correspond to what McCloskey calls "welfare rights."[32] I shall call them *ideal rights.* The notion of ideal rights will be explained and defended later in the chapter.

Second, *what kind of performance or forbearance is required of the right-ower?* Here we may provisionally distinguish between positive rights, rights that require positive acts of some sort or other, and negative rights, rights that require nonperformances, e.g. noninterference.[33] The question of whether a right is positive or negative becomes relevant to the issue of euthanasia when we ask what sort of performance or nonperformance is required by the alleged right to life or the alleged right to die: Do they require positive acts of one sort or other, or do they require only forbearances, e.g. the abstention from killing or the abstention from treatment. Just how the line is to be drawn, however, is far from clear in many concrete instances.[34]

Third, *a number of questions arise about the formal properties of an alleged right.* How and when can it be exercised? Can it be waived or not? Can it be alienated or abrogated? Can one person exercise the right of another person on his behalf, as a proxy? Is the right in question a prima facie right or is it an absolute right in the sense that it can never by overridden? In connection with the formal properties of a right, we must also be told what other secondary rights follow from it, such as the right to compel others to comply or the right to reparation for violations of a right.

Finally, *anyone who asserts that there is a right must be prepared to tell us where the right comes from; that is, its source or basis.* Rights may arise out of contracts (or promises), out of positions and roles, out of conditions and circumstances, and out of various acts of oneself or of others. Theologians maintain that some rights, e.g. the right to life, were given to man by God; natural rights are supposed to stem from the nature of man as a rational, social animal. Liberal philosophers often suppose that rights are based on interests of one sort or another. Still others maintain that rights are based on needs. Unless the proponent of a right is able satisfactorily to answer this question about the source or basis of the right, his claim that there is such a right, either in general or in a specific instance, must be rejected. The burden of proof rests on the proponent of the right to show that there is such a right by showing where it comes from.

It is clear that, with regard to any of the rights mentioned earlier, such as the right to life or the right to die, all four of these questions must be answered before we can understand what the right-claim itself involves and before we can evaluate it.

As far as legal rights are concerned, there is generally no difficulty in answering these questions. Take, for example, the right to refuse treatment. (1) The patient is the right-holder and the physician is the right-ower. (2) Forbearance from treatment is the performance required. (3) It need not be exercised; and, of course, it is usually not exercised. (4) The right originates in the common law rules relating to assault and battery.[35] Whether or not there is a moral right, as distinct from a legal right, to refuse treatment is still, in my opinion, an open question.

It is not as easy to get answers to the same questions about the right to life or the right to die. Proponents of these rights are generally rather vague about who the right-owers are as well as what kind of performances are required of them. They are also vague about how the rights are to be exercised, whether they can be waived or not, etc.[36] And finally, they are usually vague about where the supposed right comes from.[37] Apart from purely legal answers concerning such alleged rights, the absence of specific answers to questions about them in the moral context suggests that the appeal to them may often be more rhetorical than substantial.

But even supposing that these four questions can be answered satisfactorily, there is still some question about the suitability of using the rights model for the kinds of predicament that were mentioned in the Introduction: What kinds of answers does the appeal to rights like the right to life or the right to die provide for questions raised by these predicaments? Some of the difficulties in using the rights model to answer these questions will emerge if we take a closer look at the formal character of right-claims.

Functions of the concept of rights

Rights have been called a "moral commodity," and indeed they are very important things to have. To have a right is to have a very strong claim, and demands based on rights are very strong demands. However, rights do not make up the whole of morality; there are many other good moral reasons for doing or refraining from doing something besides the fact that someone has a right requiring us to do it or to refrain from doing it. Compassion, devotion, love, sympathy, care and responsibility are all morally good and provide morally worthy motives for conduct; but it hardly seems correct to say that anyone has a right to them—at least, without further ado. For that reason, these two different kinds of ethical requirement are sometimes subsumed under the headings of justice and charity, respectively.[38]

For our purposes, we may regard rights as creating duties (or obligations); but they are duties of a very special kind of stringency, what Kant calls "perfect duties"; that is, acts that it would be wrong not to do. Accordingly, we do not ordinarily praise a person for doing something that is required by a right; rather, if he fails to do it, we censure and condemn him. The nonfulfillment of a right is occasion for moral indignation, whereas the fulfillment of the right is not something that we have to be grateful for. The formal negativity of the rights-duty relationship places rights in a very special moral category.

The second thing to be noted about rights in general is that they are peremptory. Rights are the sort of thing that one may demand rather than simply request or plead for.[39] If one has a right, one is by that very fact authorized to take certain measures to secure what it is a right to; in addition to demanding it, one may take other measures, including sometimes resorting to coercion or self-help. Having a right in law gives one a ground for enforcing one's will on others through the legal machinery.

A third formal feature of rights is a kind of asymmetricality between the right-holder and the right-ower. The right-holder has the option of exercising or not exercising the right; the right-ower, on the other hand, has no option if the right-holder wants to exercise the right. The right-ower has no choice; he has to do what is demanded by the right-holder, even if he thinks that it is imprudent or undesirable for the right-holder or for himself.[40] (Throughout this discussion I am ignoring exceptions that might be due to unusual circumstances or other overriding conditions.)

Finally, there is a kind of opacity involved when rights are used to determine what one ought to do. The only relevant consideration that ought to move the right-ower is the fact that the right-holder wishes to exercise his acknowledged right.[41]

Let us apply this last consideration to the supposed right to die.[42] If a right-holder has such a right, then, as right-owers, we have no choice as far as fulfilling his wish to die is concerned and, more importantly, we are not permitted to bring in other moral considerations, e.g. the intrinsic merits of his dying or staying alive, in deciding what to do. Even if his wish to die is entirely capricious and irrational, we are bound to aid and abet him in accomplishing it, simply because he has a right to die and chooses to exercise that right.[43]

There is another formal aspect of the rights model that, in my opinion, makes it a peculiarly inappropriate model for resolving issues of life and death. The appeal to rights automatically places a person in an adversary position vis-à-vis the right-ower. The closer and more intimate one's relationship to another person is, the less appropriate is the appeal to rights. Thus, rights are more typically invoked in our dealings with strangers than they are in our relationships with those we love and care for. Perhaps this fact explains why the appeal to rights in situations involving, say, racial discimination is more suitable than it is in familial situations. Rights are appealed to when other relationships break down.[44]

It should be observed that the rights model that we have been dealing with here is a *proprietary model*. That is why we find throughout the discussion of rights like the right to life and the right to die a constant reference, explicit or implicit, to notions like "property," "title," and "possession." Rights are said to be "moral commodities," it is assumed that we "possess" or "own" our body, our life is said to be the property of God. Many of the difficulties that I have pointed out in connection with the rights model are due to the proprietary nature of the rights, for property is typically the kind of thing that a person is permitted to exclude others from and is permitted to "use" and "enjoy" without having to account to others. Furthermore, a proprietary model of rights excludes any reference to virtue. In the extreme instance, it vindicates a Shylock-Scrooge attitude towards morality. One of the morally questionable consequences of a slavish adherence to the proprietary model is that it forces us to construe ethical decision making as the prerogative of one of the parties involved in the dying situation, as against the other parties. Thus, either the doctor or the patient has the exclusive right to decide about what is to be done. This kind of exclusive decision-making right is incompatible with the kind of joint decision making of all the concerned parties that is required by a full theory of moral responsibility.[45]

That is not to say that proprietary rights are never relevant considerations in determining the rightness or wrongness of a particular course of action. To maintain that would, of course, be absurd.[46] It is often quite to the point to be able to appeal to that kind of right (and, of course, to legal rights) in situations where there is an absence of trust and communal feeling. Still, to invoke rights in a discussion of what ought to be done about a dying person makes dying a public and impersonal issue.

Perhaps death is in fact becoming just that, an impersonal matter from which love, compassion and care are excluded. Growing institutional control over dying has made the rights-model more useful than it would be if people were allowed to die in their homes.[47] For, as formal organizations, institutions such as hospitals are not persons; hence they are incapable of love and compassion. Indeed, I am prepared to argue that they are also incapable of morality, for moral responsibility is something that can only be predicated of persons.[48] No wonder, therefore, that the institutionalization of contemporary medicine has turned death into cacothanasia.

The institutionalization of medical care and care for the terminally ill forces us to decide whether decisions about life and death ought to be impersonal or personal. By an "impersonal" decision I mean a decision made on the basis of rules alone, including rules about rights; a personal decision, on the other hand, is made on the basis of many other sorts of consideration. Ideally, it is a shared decision involving all the persons concerned consulting with each other, reached after careful reflection on the particular circumstances of the case and taking into account all the various considerations for and against possible courses of action.

Sometimes, as I have already suggested, the proprietary model of rights is the only means available for coping with impersonal decision making on the part of hospitals and doctors. However, it may not be appropriate when considerations of a more personal and humane nature are involved. The rights-model is obviously quite unsuitable for the moral relationship between the patient and his family and friends (and among friends we may include the humane physician and health care team). Neither the right to life nor the right to die seems adapted to a situation of concern and trust.

The trouble with both the definitional and the rights approach to issues connected with euthanasia is that they are rule-bound. Both approaches are concerned with establishing a rule that will provide a clear-cut decision-making procedure. They have enormous appeal because they promise to give us a mechanical model for reaching decisions in every case relating to the control of death and they assure us that these decisions will be certain, uniform and "objective." The search for this kind of decision procedure reflects what John Dewey used to call "the quest for certainty." It may be psychologically reassuring or politically advantageous to have such a procedure, but the issues before us are obviously not capable of being resolved in a slot-machine fashion. We buy certainty at a cost, the cost of sacrificing moral excellence, virtues, and ideals. Blind devotion to rules will not, ultimately, help us to live well or to plan well for the end of life. For example, the blind use of rules to determine the manner and timing of a person's death, e.g. by impersonal institutions or impersonal physicians, makes morally responsible and autonomous decisions on the part of the dying patient impossible; it places them out of bounds. A person who wishes to end his life so that others will not have to suffer unnecessarily and will not to have to bear extraordinary burdens resulting from the futile prolongation of his condition is simply not permitted to do so by the generally accepted rules. Even if the so-called right to die is adopted as a rule, it is unclear that it would apply to situations of this kind, for it is difficult, if not impossible, to frame impersonal rules to cover situations where self-sacrifice or heroism is involved.

Furthermore, as I have argued throughout this chapter, new conditions have made some of the rules we have been using obsolete. They often have precisely the effect opposite from their original intent. For example, the right to life and other related rights were originally intended to protect an individual against the trespass of others, i.e. to protect his personal integrity, his body and his life, against intrusion by others, especially by public authorities. Nowadays, the same right is used *against* the individual to impose the will of others on him. Both the right to life and the right to die, if conceived as proprietary rights, are rights that are used to impose the will of one person on another. The difficulty with them is that they are too specific, too stringent, and too abstract (in the sense of ignoring the context of the case in hand) to fulfill the moral purposes that concern us. It is unclear that they really protect the moral integrity of the individual and the integrity of his moral relationship with others. For that purpose we need an entirely different kind of right, one that is not legalistic (like rights based on the proprietary model) and one that will reinforce a morality of trust, compassion and responsibility. This new kind of right might be called "the right to be virtuous"! for one can think of it as following from the need to be virtuous and as having its basis in virtue. I shall call rights of this kind *ideal rights.*

Ideal rights

Ideal rights, according to the conception of them that I propose here, are unlike proprietary rights in several respects. To begin with, they represent *principles* rather than *rules,* to borrow a useful distinction from Ronald Dworkin.[49] Rules are black and white, so to speak; either a case comes under the rule or it does not. Principles are more general and flexible. They serve as guidelines rather than as categorical determinants of conduct.

Ideal rights have a much wider scope than the proprietary rights that we have been considering. They are general, rather than determinate, not only with regard to right-owers, but also with regard to what is required by the right. As McCloskey puts it, such rights are rights *to* something rather than rights against somebody.[50] Examples are the right to health, the right to a job, the right to an education; in sum, ideal rights are the kind of rights asserted in, say, the UN Declaration of Human Rights.[51] They refer to things that society owes all of us, that government ought to provide, that our institutions ought to respect, and that all of us ought to work for.

Why are such things called "rights" rather than "needs," "social ideals," or "social goals"? It is obvious that ideal rights are connected with the all of these other things, but the point of calling them "rights" is to emphasize their peremptory character. As rights they legitimate making demands and sometimes they may even justify the use of coercive measures for the purpose of securing them. In other words, ideal rights are not dependent for their realization on the kindness or good will of others, say, of political leaders, administrative officials, hospitals, or professional medical practitioners like physicians. They are something "owed" to us. In this respect, they represent demands of justice rather than of charity.

On the other hand, unlike proprietary rights they do not create particular obligations binding on particular persons or on everyone. Rather, they represent collective obligations on the part of society; accordingly, they do not impose an obligation on me as an individual but only on me as a member of society.[52] If, for example, there is a right to health care, it is not a right that creates an obligation for any particular physician; rather, it imposes an obligation on society as a whole to make adequate health care available to all of its members. By the same token, neither the right to life nor the right to die (in dignity) are rights that create particular obligations for particular people, e.g. for a particular physician. Instead, they are rights of individuals which society should seek to secure for everybody.

Another characteristic of ideal rights is that they are positive rights; that is, they require positive action of some kind or other rather than simple abstention from certain kinds of action (i.e. noninterferences). Indeed, they may require complexes of actions of one sort or another; they require us, for example, to establish rules and practices, to allocate resources, and to make policy decisions with a view to furthering them. Thus, one way of implementing the ideal right to die (with dignity) might be to adopt legislation establishing a legal right to die as has been done in California and some other states. The ideal right to life, on the other hand, requires us to promote and to protect the lives of the living by providing such things as food, shelter, health care and a safe environment, rather then merely to prolong the life of the dying. A society that fails to advance these ideal rights has abdicated its responsibility for the welfare of its citizens. Insofar as it fails in this regard, it is an unjust society. I trust, no one feels that our own society has done enough either for the living or for the dying as far as securing and protecting their ideal rights are concerned.

Just as specific rights, proprietary and legal, relating to life and death ought to have their basis in ideal rights, so ideal rights in turn depend on the nature of social life, not merely for the way in which they are exercised and satisfied, but also for their basis in the moral nature of human interrelationships. Ideal rights are rights to all the means that are necessary for living a good life. By a "good life" I do not simply mean a happy or successful life, but also a morally good life; that is, a decent, honest and caring life, a life of interpersonal responsibility—a virtuous life. Ideal rights relate to things that a society ought to provide for its members so that they will be able to live a good life; that is, a moral life constituted by moral relationships such as relationships of responsibility and caring.

Now as ideal rights, both the "right to life" and the "right to die" have a similar foundation for both concern things that are usually necessary elements in a good (moral) life. Life itself is obviously a necessary condition of being moral; this point is brought out clearly by Kant in his lecture on suicide where he states that, although "life is not to be highly regarded for its own sake," it is wrong to commit suicide because "it annuls the condition of all other duties."[53]

The right to die, if it is construed as the right to determine the manner and timing of one's own death, would also seem to follow as a necessary part of a good life, for dying should be something that relates a person intimately to others as a moral agent and that is closely bound up with his personal moral values and ideals. In taking away this control from a person, one has deprived him of an essential element of moral responsibility and moral personality.[54] Society should recognize the ideal right to die a good death, a death that is not simply a painless and dignified death, but one that could have moral quality. But once again it should be noted that both of these rights are ideal rights and not rights in the narrow sense. If we construe them in the latter sense, we end up with paradoxes and absurdities.

Ideal rights, as conceived here, are based on a person's moral needs, the need for the kind of things that may be necessary to carry out his moral ends, his moral aspirations and his moral responsibilities. If you want a slogan: Moral ends justify ideal rights. In this sense, rights are means rather than ends. It follows that, other things being equal, the claim to an ideal right by an individual is invalidated if the end is a bad one or the means are unnecessary. In this sense, the exercise of an ideal right does not depend exclusively on the option of the right-holder. The right to die, if construed as an ideal right, is not opaque, as are proprietary rights; accordingly, it does not require that society permit or help a person to choose the timing and manner of his death if his decision is quite capricious and arbitrary, e.g. if he does it to spite his family or his doctor. Nor, on the other hand, does the right to life of and by itself authorize an individual to interfere with another person's dying.

Nevertheless, construed as an ideal right, the right to die places *society* under an obligation to permit and to facilitate a person's control over his own death and dying in accordance with his moral ideals and aspirations, or his idea of his moral responsibilities and of what is right—in sum, his conscience. Exactly how this ideal right is to be implemented in practice, e.g. in the law and in the rules and practices of the health care system, is a complicated matter; but in principle it is not impossible. The subsumption of the "right to die" under the right to privacy or right of personality, as was done by the New Jersey Supreme Court in the Quinlan case, is a move in the right direction.[55] Perhaps the right to privacy can furnish a new legal category for the kind of cases resulting from our recently acquired power to control the timing and manner of death.

Summary

At the beginning of the chapter, I tried to show that new medical technology has rendered obsolete some of the traditional ways of coping with death ethically. Specifically, the power to control dying and death by dissociating the various organic components of dying and prolonging the function of these bodily systems separately has made it impossible always to apply the traditional moral rules relating to death. The difficulties encountered in applying the traditional rules suggested that we try to cope with moral problems connected with death through the concept of rights. An examination of the concept of rights revealed that the rights model is unsuitable for our purposes if it is conceived as a proprietary model. The principal objection to both the definitional and the rights approach is that they depend on more or less inflexible rules, rules that are often inappropriate in the light of changing conditions, but, more importantly, that are morally objectionable because they undermine the place of virtue in interpersonal relationships involving death and dying, namely, virtues like compassion, understanding and responsibility. As an alternative I proposed a new type of rights model, which I called "Ideal Rights." Ideal rights are positive demand rights of an open-ended and flexible sort with a wide scope. They place society and its institutions under an obligation to provide its citizens with the means to a good life, which, of course, includes a good death—the original meaning of "euthanasia."

Notes

1. Some of the points made here, particularly those relating to rights, are amplified in my "Legalism and Medical Ethics," in John Davis et al., eds., *Biomedical Ethics,* (New York: Humana Press, 1978).
2. For a survey, see Robert M. Veatch, *Death, Dying and The Biological Revolution* (New Haven: Yale University Press, 1976), chap. 1 and 2. See also, Leonard Isaacs, "Death, where is thy distinguishing?" *Hastings Center Report,* vol. 8, no. 1 (February 1978), pp. 5–8. The most detailed analysis from the medical point of view is to be found in Julius Korein, *Definitions of Death* (New York Academy of Science, 1978).
3. "Death. The cessation of life; ceasing to exist; defined by physicians as a total stoppage of the circulation of the blood, and a cessation of the animal and vital functions consequent thereto, such as respiration, pulsation, etc." *Black's Law Dictionary,* 4th ed. (St. Paul, Minn.: West Publishing Co., 1951), p. 488.
4. For a brief survey, see Irving M. Copi, *Introduction to Logic,* 5th ed. (New York: MacMillan, 1978), chap. 4, "Definition." For a discussion of definitions in science, see Peter Achinstein, *Concepts of Science* (Baltimore: Johns Hopkins Press, 1968).
5. Ludwig Wittgenstein, *Philosophical Investigations,* trans. G.E.M. Anscombe (New York: MacMillan, 1953), no. 67.
6. See Achinstein, *Concepts of Science,* chap 1.
7. See Robert S. Morison, "Death: Process or Event?" Reprinted in Peter Steinfels and Robert M. Veatch, eds., *Death Inside Out* (New York: Harper and Row, 1975).
8. There are now "several dozen different sets of criteria," says Dr. Julius Korein. Quoted in the court proceedings in the Quinlan case. *In the Matter of Karen Quinlan.* (Arlington, Vir.: University Publications of America, 1975), vol. 1, p. 355.
9. See Korein, *Definitions of Death* Preface.
10. *Journal of the American Medical Association* 205:337–40 (5 August 1968).

For a recent version, see "An appraisal of the criteria of cerebral death," *Journal of the American Medical Association* 237:982–86 (7 March 1977).

11. It should be noted that there is considerable variation in terminology in the literature on the definition of death. In includes "indicators," "signs," "symptoms," "determinants," and "criteria." For our purposes, it is best to adhere to the terms used by philosophers.

12. See Achinstein, *Concepts of Science*, pp. 51 ff.

13. In traditional philosophical terminology, signs reflect synthetic connections and criteria reflect analytic connections.

14. "Think of the tools in a tool-box . . ." *Philosophical Investigations*, nos. 11, 12.

15. See Julius Kovesi, *Moral Notions* (New York: Humanities Press, 1967). As will become clear shortly, what I have called the mythological and the medical conceptions of death correspond very crudely to these two elements.

16. Kovesi, *Moral Notions*, p. 37.

17. For an elaboration of this point, see Roger B. Dworkin, "Death in Context," *Indiana Law Journal* 48 (summer 1973), pp. 623–46. In their reply, Professors Capron and Kass seem to assume without argument that an essentialist definition, i.e. a single, universally valid definition, is possible and desirable. Kovesi's *Moral Notions* shows why they are mistaken.

18. There have been a number of legal cases in which the issue has turned on the question of whether and when a person is dead. See, for example: Commonwealth *v.* Siegfried Galston. Massachusetts Supreme Judicial Court S-879 (1977). In this case, Galston attempted to use the fact that his victim had been taken off a respirator by doctors as a defense against the charge of murder. Using the Harvard definition of death, the Massachusetts Supreme Court decided that the victim was already dead when he was taken off the respirator and so was killed not by the doctors but by Galston, as charged.

19. Thus the Ad Hoc Harvard Committee recommended that: "the patient be declared dead before any effort is made to take him off the respirator. This declaration should not be delayed until he has been taken off the respirator and all artificially stimulated signs have ceased. . . . Otherwise the physicians would be turning off the respirator on a person who is, under the present strict, technical application of law, still alive." op. cit., p. 339.

20. See Roderick M. Chisholm, "Coming into being and passing away," in S. F. Spicker and H. T. Engelhardt, Jr., ed., *Philosophical Medical Ethics: Its Nature, and Significance* (Dordrecht, Holland: Reidel, 1977), pp. 169–82. Chisholm argues that the concepts of coming into being and passing away are not merely physiological concepts and that a person's coming to be and passing away cannot be a gradual process.

21. See, for example, the rules adopted by Massachusetts General Hospital and Beth Israel Hospital in Boston relating to the resuscitation of incurable patients. *New England Journal of Medicine* 295:7 (1976).

22. Sooner or later there will be cases like the Galston case where, however, the body fails to satisfy completely the Harvard criteria. The legal issue, then, would shift from questions about the definition of death to questions about who or what caused the victim's death. It is interesting to observe that the question of causation is discussed by Justice Braucher in his decision in the Galston case, perhaps for this reason.

23. For a general discussion of rights, see Richard E. Flathman, *The Practice of Rights* (Cambridge: Cambridge University Press, 1976). Some of the points made here are explained in greater detail in my "Legalism and Medical Ethics."

24. In a country where we are so jealous of our rights, e.g. against the government, it seems quite an anomaly that there should be so much discussion about who has the right and so little discussion of who does not have the right to decide these matters.

25. See Alexis de Tocqueville, *Democracy in America,* trans. George Lawrence (Garden City, N.Y.: Doubleday, 1966), p. 270.

26. This, as I understand it, was the position taken by Justice Hughes in the Supreme Court decision in the Quinlan case. See *Karen Quinlan,* vol. 2. (See also note 2.) Much to everyone's surprise, Karen Quinlan continued to breathe after being taken off the respirator. This fact provides further evidence for my contention that the question of rights is more basic than the question of the definition of death in these contexts.

27. See Joel Feinberg, *Social Philosophy* (Englewood Cliffs, N.J.: Prentice-Hall, 1973), pp. 55–97.

28. Moral rights, therefore, may be thought of as *potential* legal rights. This view of moral rights is essentially the same as Kant's notion of right (justice) as he presents it in his *Metaphysical Elements of Justice,* trans. John Ladd (Indianapolis: Bobbs-Merrill), 1965, p. 33.

29. See the classical analysis by Wesley Newcomb Hohfeld in his *Fundamental Legal Conceptions* (New Haven: Yale University Press, 1919). For a general account of the logical structure of rights, see Richard E. Flathman, *The Practice of Rights.* A useful collection of articles on rights may be found in A. I. Melden, ed., *Human Rights* (Belmont, Calif.: Wadsworth, 1970).

30. Strictly speaking, a full-fledged account of the practice of rights requires third and fourth parties in the rights-relationship, namely, those who are required to enforce and otherwise recognize the demands created by a right. For details, see Flathman, *The Practice of Rights.*

31. Although Hohfeld is concerned with an analysis of legal rights only, as I have suggested, moral rights are so much like legal rights that it is safe to use Hohfeld's conceptual categories in analyzing them. However, in the following discussion I shall use only one part of Hohfeld's analysis, namely, what he calls "demand-rights." The other kinds of rights mentioned by Hohfeld are immaterial to the issues that concern us here.

32. See H. J. McCloskey, "Rights," *Philosophical Quarterly* 15 (1965), pp. 115–27.

33. This distinction is mentioned in other essays in this volume. In particular, Foot leans heavily on this distinction for her analysis of the difference between active and passive euthanasia.

34. The distinction between "killing" and "letting die" is discussed in several essays in this volume. It is defended in the essay by Foot and attacked in the essay by Rachels. In Chapter 8, I argue that the distinction needs to be clarified.

35. For further details, see Jon R. Waltz and Fred E. Inbau, *Medical Jurisprudence* (New York: MacMillan, 1971), pp. 152–56. See also, George J. Annas, *The Rights of Hospital Patients* (New York: Avon Books, 1975), pp. 79–91.

36. Can one waive the right in the ordinary sense to life? If it is a right, why not?

37. For a useful discussion of the "right to life" in connection with the questions listed here, see H. J. McCloskey, "The Right to Life," *Mind* 84, no. 332 (July 1975).

38. See Chapter 2. For reasons that cannot be detailed here, I have some reservations about this way of dividing up ethics. See my "Legalism and Medical Ethics."

39. Thus Ross writes: "there hangs about the notion of a 'right' the notion of its being not only something which one person should in decency respect but also something which the other person can in decency claim, etc." W. D. Ross, *The Right and the Good* (Oxford: Clarendon Press, 1930), p. 53.

40. Thus Brandt writes: "'X has an absolute right to enjoy, have, or be secured in y' means the same as 'It is someone's objective over-all obligation to secure X in, or in the possession of, or in the enjoyment of y, if X *wishes* it.'" Richard B. Brandt, *Ethical Theory* (Englewood Cliffs, N.J.: Prentice-Hall, 1959), p. 438. Italics have been added.

41. Thus Wasserstrom writes: "To exercise one's right is to act in a way that gives appreciable assurance of immunity from criticism . . . exercising and standing on one's rights by itself needs no defense." Richard Wasserstrom, "Rights, Human Rights, and Racial Discrimination." Rpt. in A. I. Melden, ed., *Human Rights,* p. 99. I have developed the notion of "opacity" in my "Legal and Moral Obligation," in J. Roland Pennock and John Chapman, eds., *Political and Moral Obligation* (New York: Atherton Press, 1970). I am indebted to Peter Williams for pointing out that the notion of opacity also has application to rights. See his "Rights and the Alleged Right of Innocents to be Killed," *Ethics* 87 (1977), pp. 383–94.

42. It should be observed that the "right to die" may variously be conceived as a legal right, as an ideal right, or as a moral right of the proprietary kind under discussion here.

43. As with other rights, we must always add the qualification "other things being equal," for the situation might be such that a person's right to die might be overridden by rights of others.

44. There are other considerations militating against the use of the rights-model in the medical context. I have set them forth in my "Legalism and Medical Ethics."
45. For a fuller account of this kind of moral responsibility, see my "Ethics of participation," in J. Roland Pennock and John Chapman, eds. NOMOS XVI: *Participation in Politics* (New York: Lieber-Atherton, 1975); and my "Legalism and Medical Ethics."
46. See, for example, Wasserstrom's eloquent statement of the importance of rights as a defense against racism. Wasserstrom, "Rights, Human Rights, and Racial Discrimination."
47. This point is discussed in more detail by Duff and Campbell in Chapter 9.
48. See my "Morality and the Ideal of Rationality in Formal Organizations," *Monist* 54, no. 4 (October 1970). I have set forth my conception of moral responsibility in my "The Ethics of Participation." (See note 45.)
49. See Ronald M. Dworkin, *Taking Rights Seriously* (Cambridge, Mass.: Harvard University Press, 1977). Perhaps what I have in mind by "ideal rights" corresponds to what Dworkin calls "background rights."
50. McCloskey, "Rights." (See note 32.) It should be observed that these rights (Ideal Rights) are not what is sometimes called "general" rights; that is rights against anybody and everybody (rights in rem).
51. They are not, however, what Feinberg calls "manifesto rights," for they constitute not only claims but valid claims, their validity being based on their relationship to moral principles of one sort or another, e.g. the principle of respect for others as moral beings.
52. Collective obligations should not be confused with obligations of a collectivity. Collective obligations are shared obligations; whereas the obligations of a collectivity are obligations of a corporate organization, e.g. of a hospital or of a government.
53. Immanuel Kant, *Lectures on Ethics,* trans. Louis Infield (New York: Harper and Row, 1963), pp. 149, 150. A careful reading of Kant's statements about suicide reveals that he does not disapprove of suicide under all circumstances; if it is heroic or noble it is not wrong.
54. This is the rationale for giving people "more control over living and over the indignities of dying," as Duff and Campbell express it in Chapter 9. I have argued for this conception of responsibility in my "The Ethics of Participation." (See note 45.) It should be observed that in many cases the responsibility is a joint responsibility.
55. For the text of this decision, see *In the Matter of Karen Quinlan* (Arlington, Vir.: University Publications of America, 1976), vol. II.

7   Euthanasia, Killing, and Letting Die

JAMES RACHELS

Dr. F. J. Ingelfinger, former editor of the *The New England Journal of Medicine,* observes that

This is the heyday of the ethicist in medicine. He delineates the rights of patients, of experimental subjects, of fetuses, of mothers, of animals, and even of doctors. (And what a far cry it is from the days when medical "ethics" consisted of condemning economic improprieties such as fee splitting and advertising!) With impeccable logic—once certain basic assumptions are granted—and with graceful prose, the ethicist develops his arguments. . . . Yet his precepts are essentially the products of armchair exercise and remain abstract and idealistic until they have been tested in the laboratory of experience.[1]

One problem with such armchair exercises, he complains, is that in spite of the impeccable logic and the graceful prose, the result is often an absolutist ethic which is unsatisfactory when applied to particular cases, and which is therefore of little use to the practicing physician. Unlike some absolutist philosophers, "the practitioner appears to prefer the principles of individualism. As there are few atheists in fox holes, there tend to be few absolutists at the bedside."[2]

A shortened version of this paper (about one-third the length), with the title "Active and Passive Euthanasia," appeared in *The New England Journal of Medicine* 292, no. 2 (9 January 1975), pp. 78–80.

I must concede at the outset that this chapter is another exercise in "armchair ethics" in the sense that I am not a physician but a philosopher. Yet I am no absolutist; and my purpose is to examine a doctrine that *is* held in an absolute form by many doctors. The doctrine is that there is an important moral difference between active and passive euthanasia, such that even though the latter is sometimes permissible, the former is always forbidden. This is an absolute which doctors hold "at the bedside" as well as in the seminar room, and the "principles of individualism" make little headway against it. But I will argue that this is an irrational dogma, and that there is no sound moral basis for it.

I will not argue, simply, that active euthanasia is all right. Rather, I will be concerned with the *relation* between active euthanasia and passive euthanasia: I will argue that there is no moral difference between them. By this I mean that there is no reason to prefer one over the other as a matter of principle—the fact that one case of euthanasia is active, while another is passive, is not *itself* a reason to think one morally better than the other. If you already think that passive euthanasia is all right, and you are convinced by my arguments, then you may conclude that active euthanasia must be all right, too. On the other hand, if you believe that active euthanasia is immoral, you may want to conclude that passive euthanasia must be immoral, too. Although I prefer the former alternative, I will not argue for it here. I will only argue that the two forms of euthanasia are morally equivalent— either both are acceptable or both are unacceptable.

I am aware that this will at first seem incredible to many readers, but I hope that this impression will be dispelled as the discussion proceeds. The discussion will be guided by two methodological considerations, both of which are touched on in the editorial quoted above. The first has to do with my "basic assumptions." My arguments are intended to appeal to all reasonable people, and not merely to those who already share my philosophical preconceptions. Therefore, I will try not to rely on any assumptions that cannot be accepted by any reasonable person. None of my arguments will depend on morally eccentric premises. Second, Dr. Ingelfinger is surely correct when he says that we must be as concerned with the realities of medical practice as with the more abstract issues of moral theory. As he notes, the philosopher's precepts "remain abstract and idealistic until they are tested in the laboratory of experience." Part of my argument will be precisely that, when "tested in the laboratory of experience," the doctrine in question has terrible results. I believe that if this doctrine were to be recognized as irrational, and rejected by the medical profession, the benefit to both doctors and patients would be enormous. In this sense, my paper is not intended as an "armchair exercise" at all.

The American Medical Association policy statement

"Active euthanasia," as the term is used, means taking some positive action designed to kill the patient; for example, giving him a lethal injection of potassium chloride. "Passive euthanasia," on the other hand, means simply refraining from doing anything to keep the patient alive. In passive euthanasia we withhold medication or other life-sustaining therapy, or we refuse to perform surgery, etc., and let the patient die "naturally" of whatever ills already afflict him.

Many doctors and theologians prefer to use the term "euthanasia" only in connection with active euthanasia, and they use other words to refer to what I am calling "passive euthanasia"—for example, instead of "passive euthanasia" they may speak of "the right to death with dignity." One reason for this choice of terms is the emotional impact of the words: it *sounds* so much better to defend "death with dignity" than to advocate "euthanasia" of any sort. And of course if one believes that there is a great moral difference between active and passive euthanasia—as most doctors and religious writers do—then one may prefer a terminology which puts as much psychological distance as possible between them. However, I do not want to become involved in a pointless dispute about terminology, because nothing of substance depends on which label is used. I will stay with the terms "active euthanasia" and "passive euthanasia" because they are the most convenient; but if the reader prefers a different terminology he may substitute his own throughout, and my arguments will be unaffected.

The belief that there is an important moral difference between active and passive euthanasia obviously has important consequences for medical practice. It makes a difference to what doctors are willing to do. Consider, for example, the following familiar situation. A patient who is dying from incurable cancer of the throat is in terrible pain that we can no longer satisfactorily alleviate. He is certain to die within a few days, but he decides that he does not want to go on living for those days since the pain is unbearable. So he asks the doctor to end his life now; and his family joins in the request. One way that the doctor might comply with this request is simply by killing the patient with a lethal injection. Most doctors would not do that, not only because of the possible legal consequences, but because they think such a course would be immoral. And this is understandable: the idea of killing someone goes against very deep moral feelings; and besides, as we are often reminded, it is the special business of doctors to save and protect life, not to destroy it. Yet, even so, the physician may sympathize with the dying patient's request and feel that it is entirely reasonable for him to prefer death now rather than after a few more days of agony. The doctrine that we are considering tells the doctor what to do: it says that although he may not administer the lethal injection—that would be "active euthanasia," which is forbidden—he *may* withhold treatment and let the patient die sooner than he otherwise would.

It is no wonder that this simple idea is so widely accepted, for it seems to give the doctor a way out of his dilemma without having to kill the patient, and without having to prolong the patient's agony. The idea is not a new one. What *is* new is that the idea is now being incorporated into official statements of medical ethics. What was once unofficially done is now becoming official policy. The idea is expressed, for example, in a 1973 policy statement of the American Medical Association, which says (in its entirety):

> The intentional termination of the life of one human being by another—mercy killing—is contrary to that for which the medical profession stands and is contrary to the policy of the American Medical Association.
> The cessation of the employment of extraordinary means to prolong the life of the body when there is irrefutable evidence that biological death is imminent is the decision of the patient and/or his immediate family. The advice and judgment of the physician should be freely available to the patient and/or his immediate family.[3]

This is a cautiously worded statement, and it is not clear *exactly* what is being affirmed. I take it, however, that at least these three propositions are intended:

1. Killing patients is absolutely forbidden; however, it is sometimes permissible to allow patients to die.

2. It is permissible to allow a patient to die if
    a. there is irrefutable evidence that he will die soon anyway;
    b. "extraordinary" measures would be required to keep him alive; and
    c. the patient and/or his immediate family requests it.
3. Doctors should make their own advice and judgments available to the patient and/or his immediate family when the latter are deciding whether to request that the patient be allowed to die.

The first proposition expresses the doctrine which is the main subject of this paper. As for the third, it seems obvious enough, provided that 1 and 2 are accepted, so I shall say nothing further about it.

I do want to say a few things about 2. Physicians often allow patients to die; however, they do *not* always keep to the guidelines set out in 2. For example, a doctor may leave instructions that if a hopeless, comatose patient suffers cardiac arrest, nothing be done to start his heart beating again. "No-coding" is the name given to this practice, and the consent of the patient and/or his immediate family is not commonly sought. This is thought to be a medical decision (in reality, of course, it is a moral one) which is the doctor's affair. To take a different sort of example, when a Down's infant (a mongoloid) is born with an intestinal blockage, the doctor and parents may agree that there will be no operation to remove the blockage, so that the baby will die.[4] (If the same infant were born without the obstruction, it certainly would not be killed. This is a clear application of the idea that "letting die" is all right even though killing is forbidden.) But in such cases it is clear that the baby is *not* going to die soon anyway. If the surgery were performed, the baby would proceed to a "normal" infancy—normal, that is, for a mongoloid. Moreover, the treatment required to save the baby—abdominal surgery—can hardly be called "extraordinary" by today's medical standards.

Therefore, all three conditions which the AMA statement places on the decision to let die are commonly violated. It is beyond the scope of this paper to determine whether doctors are right to violate those conditions. But I firmly believe that the second requirement—2b—is not acceptable. Only a little reflection is needed to show that the distinction between ordinary and extraordinary means is not important. Even a very conservative, religiously-oriented writer such as Paul Ramsey stresses this. Ramsey gives these examples:

Suppose that a diabetic patient long accustomed to self-administration of insulin falls victim to terminal cancer, or suppose that a terminal cancer patient suddenly develops diabetes. Is he in the first case obliged to continue, and in the second case obliged to begin, insulin treatment and die painfully of cancer, or in either or both cases may the patient choose rather to pass into diabetic coma and an earlier death? . . . Or an old man slowly deteriorating who from simply being inactive and recumbent gets pneumonia: are we to use antibiotics in a likely successful attack upon this disease which from time immemorial has been called "the old man's friend"?[5]

I agree with Ramsey, and with many other writers, that in such cases treatment may be withheld even though it is not "extraordinary" by any reasonable standard. Contrary to what is implied by the AMA statement, the distinction between heroic and nonheroic means of treatment can *not* be used to determine when treatment is or is not mandatory.

Killing and letting die

I return now to the distinction between active and passive euthanasia. Of course, not every doctor believes that this distinction is morally important. Over twenty years ago Dr. D.C.S. Cameron of the American Cancer Society said that "Actually the difference between euthanasia [i.e., killing] and letting the patient die by omitting life-sustaining treatment is a moral quibble."[6] I argue that Cameron was right.

The initial thought can be expressed quite simply. In any case in which euthanasia seems desirable, it is because we think that the patient would literally be better off dead—or at least, no worse off dead—than continuing the kind of life available to him. (Without this assumption, even *passive* euthanasia would be unthinkable.) But, as far as the main question of ending the patient's life is concerned, it does not matter whether the euthanasia is active or passive: *in either case,* he ends up dead sooner than he otherwise would. And if the results are the same, why should it matter so much which method is used?

Moreover, we need to remember that, in cases such as that of the terminal cancer-patient, the justification for allowing him to die, rather than prolonging his life for a few more hopeless days, is that he is in horrible pain. But if we simply withhold treatment, it may take him *longer* to die, and so he will suffer *more* than he would if we were to administer the lethal injection. This fact provides strong reason for thinking that, once we have made the initial decision not to prolong his agony, active euthanasia is actually preferable to passive euthanasia rather than the reverse. It also shows a kind of incoherence in the conventional view: to say that passive euthanasia is preferable is to endorse the option which leads to more suffering rather than less, and is contrary to the humanitarian impulse which prompts the decision not to prolong his life in the first place.

But many people are convinced that there is an important moral difference between active and passive euthanasia because they think that, in passive euthanasia, the doctor does not really *do* anything. No action whatever is taken; the doctor simply does nothing, and the patient dies of whatever ills already afflict him. In active euthanasia, however, we *do something* to bring about the patient's death. We kill him. Thus, the difference between active and passive euthanasia is thought to be the difference between doing something to bring about someone's death, and not doing anything to bring about anyone's death. And of course if we conceive the matter in *this* way, passive euthanasia seems preferable. Ramsey, who denounces the view I am defending as "extremist" and who regards the active/passive distinction as one of the "flexibly wise categories of traditional medical ethics," takes just this view of the matter. He says that the choice between active and passive euthanasia "is not a choice between directly and indirectly willing and doing something. *It is rather the important choice between doing something and doing nothing,* or (better said) ceasing to do something that was begun in order to do something that is better because now more fitting."[7]

This is a very misleading way of thinking, for it ignores the fact that in passive euthanasia the doctor *does* do one thing which is very important: namely, he lets the patient die. We may overlook this obvious fact—or at least, we may put it out of our minds—if we concentrate only on a very restricted way of describing what happens: "The doctor does not administer medication or any other therapy; he does not instruct the nurses to administer any such medication; he does not perform any surgery"; and so on. And of course this description of what happens is correct, as far as it goes—these are all things that the doctor does not do. But the point is that the doctor *does* let the patient die when he could save him, and this must be included in the discription, too.

There is another reason why we might fall into this error. We might confuse *not saving* someone with *letting him die*. Suppose a patient is dying, and Dr. X could prolong his life. But he decides not do so and the patient dies. Now it is true of everyone on earth that he did not save the patient. Dr. X did not save him, and neither did you, and neither did I. So we might be tempted to think that all of us are in the same moral position, reasoning that since neither you nor I are responsible for the patient's death, neither is Dr. X. None of us did anything. This, however, is a mistake, for even though it is true that none of us saved the patient, it is *not* true that we all let him die. In order to let someone die, one must be *in a position* to save him. You and I were not in a position to save the patient, so we did not let him die. Dr. X, on the other hand, was in a position to save him, and did let him die. Thus the doctor is in a special moral position which not just eveyone is in.

Here we must remember some elementary points, which are so obvious that they would not be worth mentioning except for the fact that overlooking them is a source of so much confusion in this area. The act of letting someone die may be intentional and deliberate, just as the act of killing someone may be intentional and deliberate. Moreover, the doctor is *responsible* for his decision to let the patient die, just as he would be responsible for giving the patient a lethal injection. The decision to let a patient die is subject to moral appraisal in the same way that a decision to kill is subject to moral appraisal: it may be assessed as wise or unwise, compassionate or sadistic, right or wrong. If a doctor deliberately let a patient die who was suffering from a routinely curable illness, then he would be to blame for what he did, just as he would be to blame if he had needlessly killed the patient. It would be no defense at all for him to insist that, *really,* he didn't "do anything" but just stand there. We would all know that he did do something very serious indeed, for he let the patient die.

These considerations show how misleading it is to characterize the difference between active and passive euthanasia as a difference between doing something (killing), for which the doctor may be morally culpable; and doing nothing (just standing there while the patient dies), for which the doctor is not culpable. The real difference between them is, rather, the difference between *killing* and letting die, both of which are actions for which a doctor, or anyone else, will be morally responsible.

Now we can formulate our problem more precisely. If there is an important moral difference between active and passive euthanasia, it must be because *killing someone is morally worse than letting someone die.* But is it? Is killing, in itself, worse than letting die? In order to investigate this issue, we may consider two cases which are exactly alike except that one involves killing where the other involves letting someone die. Then we can ask whether this difference makes any difference to our moral assessments. It is important that the cases be *exactly* alike except for this one difference, since otherwise we cannot be confident that it is *this* difference which accounts for any variation in our assessments.

1. Smith stands to gain a large inheritance if anything should happen to his six-year-old cousin. One evening while the child is taking his bath, Smith sneaks into the bathroom and drowns the child, and then arranges things so that it will look like an accident.
2. Jones also stands to gain if anything should happen to his six-year-old cousin. Like Smith, Jones sneaks in planning to drown the child in his bath. However, just as he enters the bathroom Jones sees the child slip, hit his head, and fall face down in the water. Jones is delighted; he stands by, ready to push the child's head back under if it is necessary, but it is not necessary. With only a little thrashing about, the child drowns all by himself, "accidentally," as Jones watches and does nothing.

Now Smith killed the child, while Jones "merely" let the child die. That is the only difference between them. Did either man behave better, from a moral point of view? Is there a moral difference between them? *If the difference between killing and letting die were itself a morally important matter, then we should say that Jones's behavior was less reprehensible than Smith's.* But do we actually want to say that? I think not, for several reasons. In the first place, both men acted from the same motive, personal gain, and both had exactly the same end in view when they acted. We may infer from Smith's conduct that he is a bad man, although we may withdraw or modify that judgment if we learn certain further facts about him; for example, that he is mentally deranged. But would we not also infer the very same thing about Jones from his conduct? And would not the same further considerations also be relevant to any modification of that judgment? Moreover, suppose

Jones pleaded in his defense, "After all, I didn't kill the child. I only stood there and let him die." Again, if letting die were in itself less bad than killing, this defense should have some weight. But—morally, at least—it does not. Such a "defense" can only be regarded as a grotesque perversion of moral reasoning.

Thus, it seems that when we are careful not to smuggle in any further differences which prejudice the issue, the mere difference between killing and letting die does not itself make any difference to the morality of actions concerning life and death.[8]

Now it may be pointed out, quite properly, that the cases of euthanasia with which doctors are concerned are not like this at all. They do not involve personal gain or the destruction of normal, healthy children. Doctors are concerned only with cases in which the patient's life is of no further use to him, or in which the patient's life has become or soon will become a positive burden. However, the point is the same in those cases: the difference between killing and letting die does not, *in itself,* make a difference, from the point of view of morality. If a doctor lets a patient die, for humane reasons, he is in the same moral position as if he had given the patient a lethal injection for humane reasons. If his decision was wrong—if, for example, the patient's illness was in fact curable—then the decision would be equally regrettable no matter which method was used to carry it out. And if the doctor's decision was the right one, then the method he used is not itself important.

The AMA statement isolates the crucial issue very well: "the intentional termination of the life of one human being by another." But then the statement goes on to deny that the cessation of treatment *is* the intentional termination of a life. This is where the mistake comes in, for what is the cessation of treatment, in those circumstances, if it is not "the intentional termination of the life of one human being by another"? Of course it is exactly that; if it were not, there would be no point to it.

Counter-Arguments

Our argument has now brought us to this point: we cannot draw any moral distinction between active and passive euthanasia on the grounds that one involves killing while the other only involves letting someone die, because that is a difference that does not make a difference, from a moral point of view. Some people will find this hard to accept. One reason, I think, is that they fail to distinguish the question of whether killing is, in itself, worse than letting die, from the very different question of whether most actual cases of killing are more reprehensible than most actual cases of letting die. Most actual cases of killing are clearly terrible—think of the murders reported in the newspapers—and we hear of such cases almost every day. On the other hand, we hardly ever hear of a case of letting die, except for the actions of doctors who are motivated by humanitarian reasons. So we learn to think of killing in a much worse light than letting die; and we conclude, invalidly, that there must be something about killing which makes it *in itself* worse than letting die. But this does not follow for it is not the bare difference between killing and letting die that makes the difference in these cases. Rather, it is the other factors—the murderer's motive of personal gain, for example, contrasted with the doctor's humanitarian motivation, or the fact that the murderer kills a healthy person while the doctor lets die a terminal patient racked with disease—that account for our different reactions to the different cases.

There are, however, some substantial arguments that may be advanced to oppose my conclusion. Here are two of them:

The first counter-argument focuses specifically on the concept of *being the cause of someone's death.* If we kill someone, then we are the cause of his death. But if we merely let someone die, we are not the cause; rather, he dies of whatever condition he already has. The doctor who gives the cancer patient a lethal injection will have caused his patient's death, and will have this on his conscience; whereas if he merely ceases treatment, the cancer and not the doctor is the cause of death. This is supposed to make a moral difference. This argument has been advanced many times. Ramsey, for example, urges us to remember that "In omission no human agent causes the patient's death, directly or indirectly."[9] And, writing in the *Villanova Law Review* for 1968, Dr. J. Russell Elkinton said that what makes the active/passive distinction important is that in passive euthanasia, "the patient does not die from the act [e.g. the act of turning off the respirator] but from the underlying disease or injury."[10]

This argument will not do, for two reasons. First, just as there is a distinction to be drawn between being and not being the cause of someone's death, there is also a distinction to be drawn between letting someone die and not letting anyone die. It is certainly desirable, in general, not to be the cause of anyone's death; but it is also desirable, in general, not to let anyone die when we can save them. (Doctors act on this precept every day.) Therefore, we cannot draw any special conclusion about the relative desirability of passive euthanasia just on these grounds. Second, the reason why we think it is bad to be the cause of someone's death is that we think that death is a great evil—and so it is. However, if we have decided that euthanasia, even passive euthanasia, is desirable in a given case, then we have decided that in *this* instance death is no greater an evil than the patient's continued existence. And if this is true, then the usual reason for not wanting to be the cause of someone's death simply does not apply. To put the point just a bit differently: There is nothing wrong with being the cause of someone's death if his death is, all things considered, a good thing. And if his death is *not* a good thing, then *no* form of euthanasia, active or passive, is justified. So once again we see that the two kinds of euthanasia stand or fall together.

The second counter-argument appeals to a favorite idea of philosophers, namely that our duty not to harm people is generally more stringent than our duty to help them. The law affirms this when it forbids us to kill people, or steal their goods, but does not require us in general to save people's lives or give them charity. And this is said to be not merely a point about the law, but about morality as well. We do not have a strict moral duty to help some poor man in Ethiopa—although it might be kind and generous of us if we did—but we *do* have a strict moral duty to refrain from doing anything to harm him. Killing someone is a violation of our duty not to harm, whereas letting someone die is merely a failure to give help. Therefore, the former is a more serious breach of morality than the latter; and so, contrary to what was said above, there is a morally significant difference between killing and letting die.

This argument has a certain superficial plausibility, but it cannot be used to show that there is a morally important difference between active and passive euthanasia. For one thing, it only seems that our duty to help people is less stringent than our duty not to harm them when we concentrate on certain sorts of cases: cases in which the people we could help are very far away, and are strangers to us; or cases in which it would be very difficult for us to help them, or in which helping would require a substantial sacrifice on our part. Many people feel that, in *these* types of cases, it may be kind and generous of us to give help, but we are not morally required to do so. Thus it is felt that when we give money for famine relief we are being especially big-hearted, and we deserve special praise—even if it would be immodest of us to seek such praise—because we are doing more than, strictly speaking, we are required to do.[11]

However, if we think of cases in which it would be very easy for us to help someone who is close at hand and in which no great personal sacrifice is required, things look very different. Think again of the child drowning in the bathtub: *of course* a man standing next to the tub would have a strict moral duty to help the child. Here the alleged asymmetry between the duty to help and the duty not to do harm vanishes. Since most of the cases of euthanasia with which we are concerned are of this latter type—the patient is close at hand, it is well within the professional skills of the physician to keep him alive—the alleged asymmetry has little relevance.

It should also be remembered, in considering this argument, that the duty of doctors toward their patients *is* precisely to help them; that is what doctors are supposed to do. Therefore, even if there were a general asymmetry between the duty to help and the duty not to harm—which I deny—it would not apply in the special case of the relation between doctors and their patients. Finally, it is not clear that killing such a patient *is* harming him, even though in other cases it certainly is a great harm to someone to kill him, for as I said before, we are going under the assumption that the patient would be no worse off dead than he is now; if this is so, then killing him is not harming him. For the same reason we should not classify letting such a patient die as failing to help him. Therefore, even if we grant that our duty to help people is less stringent than our duty not to harm them, nothing follows about our duties with respect to killing and letting die in the special case of euthanasia.

Practical Consequences

This is enough, I think, to show that the doctrine underlying the AMA statement is false. There is no general moral difference between active and passive euthanasia; if one is permissible, so is the other. Now if this were merely an intellectual mistake, having no significant consequences for medical practice, the whole matter would not be very important. But the opposite is true: the doctrine has terrible consequences for, as I have already mentioned—and as doctors know very well—the process of being "allowed to die" can be relatively slow and painful, while being given a lethal injection is relatively quick and painless. Dr. Anthony Shaw describes what happens when the decision has been made not to perform the surgery necessary to "save" a mongoloid infant:

> When surgery is denied [the doctor] must try to keep the infant from suffering while natural forces sap the baby's life away. As a surgeon whose natural inclination is to use the scalpel to fight off death, standing by and watching a salvageable baby die is the most emotionally exhausting experience I know. It is easy at a conference, in a theoretical discussion, to decide that such infants should be allowed to die. It is altogether different to stand by in the nursery and watch as dehydration and infection wither a tiny being over hours and days. This is a terrible ordeal for me and the hospital staff—much more so than for the parents who never set foot in the nursery.[12]

Why must the hospital staff "stand by in the nursery and watch as dehydration and infection wither a tiny being over hours and days"? Why must they merely "try" to reduce the infant's suffering? The doctrine which says that the baby may be allowed to dehydrate and wither, but not be given an injection which would end its life without suffering, is not only irrational but cruel.

The same goes for the case of the man with cancer of the throat. Here there are three options: with continued treatment, he will have a few more days of pain, and then die; if treatment is stopped, but nothing else is done, it will be a few more hours; and with a lethal injection, he will die at once. Those who oppose euthanasia in all its forms say that we must take the first option, and keep the patient alive for as long as possible. This view is so patently inhumane that few defend it; nevertheless, it does have a certain kind of integrity. It is at least consistent. The third option is the one I think best. But the *middle* position—that, although the patient need not suffer for days before dying, he must nevertheless suffer for a few more hours—is a "moderate" view which incorporates the worst, and not the best, features of both extremes.

Let me mention one other practice that we would be well rid of if we stopped thinking that the distinction between active and passive euthanasia is important. About one in six hundred babies born in the United States is mongoloid. Most of these babies are otherwise healthy—that is, with only the usual pediatric care, they will proceed to a "normal" infancy. Some, however, are born with other congenital defects such as intestinal obstructions which require surgery if the baby is to live. As I have already mentioned, sometimes the surgery is withheld and the baby dies. But when there is no defect requiring surgery, the baby lives on.[13] Now surgery to remove an intestinal obstruction is not difficult; the reason why it is not performed in such cases is, clearly, that the child is mongoloid and the parents and doctor judge that because of *this* it is better for the child to die.

But notice that this situation is absurd, no matter what view one takes of the lives and potentials of such babies. If you think that the life of such an infant is worth preserving, then what does it matter if it needs a simple operation? Or, if you think it better that such a baby not live on, then what difference does it make if its intestinal tract is *not* blocked? In either case, the matter of life or death is being decided on irrelevant grounds. It is the mongolism, and not the intestine, that is the issue. The matter should be decided, if at all, on *that* basis, and not be allowed to depend on the essentially irrelevant question of whether the intestinal tract is blocked.

What makes this situation possible, of course, is the idea that when there is an intestinal obstruction we can "let the baby die," but when there is no such defect there is nothing we can do, for we must not "kill" it. The fact that this idea leads to such results as deciding life or death on irrelevant grounds is another good reason why it should be rejected.

Doctors may think that all of this is only of academic interest, the sort of thing which philosophers may worry about but which has no practical bearing on their own work. After all, doctors must be concerned about the legal consequences of what they do, and active euthanasia is clearly forbidden by the law. They are right to be concerned about this. There have not been many prosecutions of doctors in the United States for active euthanasia, but there have been some. Prosecutions for passive euthanasia, on the other hand, are virtually nonexistent, even though there are laws under which charges could be brought, and even though this practice is much more wide-spread.

Passive euthanasia, unlike active euthanasia, is by and large tolerated by the law. The law may sometimes compel a doctor to take action which he might not otherwise take to keep a patient alive,[14] but of course this is very different from bringing criminal charges against him after the patient is dead.

Even so, doctors should be concerned with the fact that the law and public opinion are forcing upon them an indefensible moral position, which has a considerable effect on their practices. Of course, most doctors are not now in the position of being coerced in this matter, for they do not regard themselves as merely going along with what the law requires. Rather, in statements such as the AMA statement that I quoted, they are endorsing the doctrine as a central point of medical ethics. In that statement, active euthanasia is condemned not merely as illegal but as "contrary to that for which the medical profession stands," while passive euthanasia is approved. However, if my arguments have been sound, there really is no intrinsic moral difference between them (although there may be morally important differences in their consequences, varying from case to case); so while doctors may have to discriminate between them to satisfy the law, they should not do any *more* than that. In particular, they should not give the distinction any added authority and weight by writing it into official statements of medical ethics.

Notes

1. F. J. Ingelfinger, "Bedside Ethics for the Hopeless Case," *The New England Journal of Medicine* 289 (25 October 1973), p. 914.
2. Ibid.
3. This statement was approved by the House of Delegates of the AMA on December 4, 1973. It is worth noting that some state medical societies have advised *patients* to take a similar attitude toward the termination of their lives. In 1973 the Connecticut State Medical Society approved a "background statement" to be signed by terminal patients which includes this sentence: "I value life and the dignity of life, so that I am not asking that my life be directly taken, but that my life not be unreasonably prolonged or the dignity of life be destroyed." Other state medical societies have followed suit.
4. A discussion of this type of case can be found in Anthony Shaw, "'Doctor, Do We Have a Choice?'" *The New York Times Magazine,* 30 January 1972, pp. 44–54. Also see Shaw's "Dilemmas of 'Informed Consent' in

Children," *The New England Journal of Medicine* 289 (25 October 1973), pp. 885–90.

5. Paul Ramsey, *The Patient as Person* (New Haven, Conn.: Yale University Press, 1970), pp. 115–16.

6. D.C.S. Cameron, *The Truth About Cancer* (Englewood Cliffs, N.J.: Prentice-Hall, 1956), p. 116.

7. Ramsey, *The Patient as Person,* p. 151.

8. Judith Jarvis Thomson has argued that this line of reasoning is unsound. Consider, she says, this argument which is parallel to the one involving Smith and Jones:

> Alfrieda knows that if she cuts off Alfred's head he will die, and wanting him to die, cuts it off; Bertha knows that if she punches Bert in the nose he will die—Bert is in peculiar physical condition—and, wanting him to die, punches him in the nose. But what Bertha does is surely every bit as bad as what Alfrieda does. So cutting off a man's head isn't worse than punching a man in the nose. ["Killing, Letting Die, and the Trolley Problem," *The Monist* 59 (1976), p. 204.]

She concludes that, since this absurd argument doesn't prove anything, the Smith/Jones argument doesn't prove anything either.

However, I think that the Alfrieda/Bertha argument is not absurd, as strange as it is. A little analysis shows that it is a sound argument and that its conclusion is true. We need to notice first that the reason why it is wrong to chop someone's head off is, obviously, that this causes death. The act is objectionable because of its consequences. Thus, a different act with the same consequences may be equally objectionable. In Thomson's example, punching Bert in the nose has the same consequences as chopping off Alfred's head; and, indeed, the two actions are equally bad.

Now the Alfrieda/Bertha argument presupposes a distinction between the act of chopping off someone's head, and the results of this act, the victim's death. (It is stipulated that, except for the fact that Alfrieda chops off someone's head, while Bertha punches someone in the nose, the two acts are "in all other respects alike." The "*other* respects" include the act's consequence, the victim's death.) This is not a distinction we would normally think to make, since we cannot in fact cut off someone's head without killing him. Yet in thought the distinction can be drawn. The question raised in the argument, then, is whether, *considered apart from their consequences,* head-chopping is worse than nose-punching. And the answer to *this* strange question is No, just as the argument says it should be.

The conclusion of the argument should be construed like this: The bare fact that one act is an act of head-chopping, while another act is an act of nose-punching, is not a reason for judging the former to be worse than the latter. At the same time—and this is perfectly compatible with the argument—the fact that one act causes death, while another does not, *is* a reason for judging the former to be worse. The parallel construal of my conclusion is: The bare fact that one act is an act of killing, while another act is an act of letting die, is not a reason for judging the former to be worse than the latter. At the same time—and this is perfectly compatible with my argument—the fact that an act (of killing, for example) prevents suffering, while another act (of letting die, for example) does not, *is* a reason for preferring one over the other. So once we see exactly how the Alfrieda/Bertha argument *is* parallel to the Smith/Jones argument, we find that Thomson's argument is, surprisingly, quite all right.

9. Ramsey, *The Patient as Person*, p. 151.
10. J. Russell Elkinton, "The Dying Patient, the Doctor, and the Law," *Villanova Law Review* 13 (Summer 1968), p. 743.
11. For the purposes of this essay we do not need to consider whether this way of thinking about "charity" is justified. There are, however, strong arguments that it is morally indefensible: see Peter Singer, "Famine, Affluence, and Morality," *Philosophy and Public Affairs* 1 (Spring 1972), pp. 229–43. Also see James Rachels, "Killing and Letting People Die of Starvation," forthcoming in *Philosophy*, for a discussion of the killing/letting die distinction in the context of world hunger, as well as further arguments that the distinction is morally unimportant.
12. Shaw, "'Doctor, Do We Have a Choice?'" p. 54.
13. See the articles by Shaw cited in note 4.
14. For example, in February 1974 a Superior Court judge in Maine ordered a doctor to proceed with an operation to repair a hole in the esophagus of a baby with multiple deformities. Otherwise the operation would not have been performed. The baby died anyway a few days later. "Deformed Baby Dies Amid Controversy," *The Miami Herald*, 25 February 1974, p. 4-B.

8   Positive and Negative Euthanasia[1]

JOHN LADD

It is a well-known fact that many practicing physicians lean heavily on the distinction between negative and positive euthanasia; that is, between "letting a hopelessly incurable patient die" and "killing him." Polls of physicians indicate that a large proportion of them approve in principle and are willing to practice negative euthanasia, whereas only a small proportion approve or are willing to practice positive euthanasia. Many laymen also hold the distinction to be a helpful and valid one.

The question I shall discuss in this chapter is whether or not there is any significant ethical difference between these two types of euthanasia.[2] For example, is there any significant ethical difference between turning off a machine supporting a patient's life and not turning it on in the first place, or between doing something positive to hasten a patient's death and simply letting him die? I shall argue that it is far from clear how the distinction is drawn and how it can be defended ethically.

Absolutism and consequentialism

There are two extreme positions regarding the distinction between negative and positive euthanasia, "letting die" and "killing." Following

Casey, I shall call them *absolutist* and *consequentialist*.[3] The absolutist, as the name suggests, holds that a clear-cut and absolute distinction can be drawn between killing and letting die. The consequentialist, on the other hand, argues that since the consequences of both kinds of acts are the same, there is no significant ethical distinction between them. In the course of the discussion, I shall try to show that neither of these two positions is tenable and that we ought to adopt a third position that might tentatively be called *contextualist*.

The absolutist position, which is advocated by many Roman Catholic theologians, holds that there is a significant difference between doing something evil intentionally and letting it happen as a "by-product," so to speak. It is never right to will evil, even for the sake of a good end. Killing an innocent person is always wrong, but allowing him to die may not be—under certain circumstances. To "consent" to a person's death when one lets him die is morally different from "willing" his death, i.e. killing him. Like God, who only wills what is good but permits evil, man also must will only what is good but may permit evil.[4] The distinction between "consenting" and "willing" depends, in turn, on various obscure scholastic distinctions between different kinds of "voluntary object," "intention," etc.[5] It is not possible in this paper to enter into a detailed critique of the scholastic theory of action. If that were the only ground for accepting the distinction, its basis would be very weak indeed.[6]

The second position with regard to the distinction between killing and letting die is what I have called *consequentialist*. It maintains that only the consequences of an act are relevant for determining the nature of the act and its ethical significance. If letting an incurable patient die has the same consequence as killing him, then the actions are the same. There may, of course, be other relevant differences, e.g. in suffering, in cost, or in saving the life of another person, but for the consequentialist, the end result is the only thing that counts.[7]

This is a position that appeals to persons who are predisposed towards utilitarianism, for, in a slightly different sense of the term, utilitarianism may itself be regarded as a form of consequentialism. According to utilitarianism, only the consequences are ethically relevant to the rightness or wrongness of an act. It is unnecessary for our purposes, however, to enter into a critique of utilitarianism as an ethical theory, since it is possible to hold a consequentialist theory of action without being an utilitarian in ethics. In general, I propose to examine the distinction between killing and letting die on its own merits and without reference to any theoretical support that its defenders or critics may derive from systematic metaphysics or ethics.

The appeal to intuition

Apart from specialized metaphysical doctrines, the usual defense of the distinction between killing and letting die seems to rest on claims of self-evidence, i.e. intuition (in the philosophical sense). Undoubtedly, people often feel intuitively that there is a significant difference between making something happen and just letting it happen; for example, there seems to be an important moral difference between pushing someone into a river to drown and simply failing to jump in and rescue someone if he accidentally falls in. However, the question is whether feelings of this kind are sufficient to establish the philosophical claim that there is a significant ethical difference between the two.

To begin with, appeals of this kind to intuition are tricky, because examples like the one just mentioned are hardly ever unambiguous. Without being told any more about the case, one naturally assumes that there is a difference, say, in motivation, between the two cases mentioned because there usually is. One takes for granted that anyone who deliberately pushes his victim into the water has some kind of malicious motive for doing so, whereas the bystander who refrains from acting may be motivated by fear or indifference. The acts are different because the motives are different. If this explanation in terms of motives is correct, then the relevance of this kind of example for the medical case is questionable, since as regards motives for euthanasia, we ought to assume that there is good will on all sides. Indeed, discussions of the distinction between positive and negative euthanasia, or of euthanasia in general for that matter, are pointless unless it is assumed that personal motivation (for killing or letting die) is not one of the issues.

On the other hand, if we direct our faculties of intuition to medical examples in order to establish an ethical difference between killing and letting a patient die, ambiguities arise due to the haziness of the surrounding conditions of the imagined example. Thus, we might well imagine that under some circumstances it would be better to let a patient with incurable cancer die rather than to kill him because of uncertainties about the prognosis, the amount of pain he would suffer, the possibility of remission, and so on. It is difficult if not impossible to be certain that we are not covertly or unconsciously assuming that there are other relevant differences between a case of killing and a case of letting die besides the one at issue when we try to argue from intuitions.

In sum, intuitions like those mentioned here and in the literature are inevitably subjective and unreliable, simply because it is impossible to isolate an act in imagination and to consider it apart form its context; some kind of background is always part of the perception of it. We are not always cognizant of the background and so are liable to jump to conclusions about differences by failing to take it into account. For these reasons, your perception and my perception of what is allegedly the same kind of case may not be the same at all.

In addition to the difficulties just mentioned with regard to arguments from intuition, it should also be observed that inferences from one kind of case to other kinds of case may be unwarranted, especially the inference from nonmedical cases to medical cases; for the cases may not be analogous. Medical cases are apt to raise quite different sorts of issues from the other types of case; at least, whether they do or not is an open question. One must not forget that the validity of an argument from analogy, which is the kind of argument involved here, depends not only on the previously established similarities between the cases being compared, but also on the denial of any relevant dissimilarities. The greater the number of dissimilarities, which the logicians call the "negative analogy," the less valid the argument tends to be.

The appeal to intuition is not limited to advocates of the distinction between killing and letting die. Consequentialists also employ this method, with opposite results, of course. Thus, we are asked to imagine a situation in which one person pushes a child into the water to drown and to compare it with another situation in which a bystander, who is easily able to rescue the child, just lets the child drown; and we are asked to imagine that their motivations are similar. Is there any significant ethical difference? The consequentialist's intuition says: no.

They also say that there is no significant ethical difference between a doctor's turning off the oxygen when a patient is in an oxygen tent and simply letting the bottle run out of oxygen.

It is obvious that the case, either for or against the distinction between killing and letting die, rests on slippery ground if it depends on intuitions alone. But in addition to the subjectivity of the appeal to intuitions, there are moral objections to the resort to intuition in ethical discussions. The recourse to intuition represents not only a breakdown in argument, a refusal to carry it forward, but also an objectionable attitude towards those with whom one disagrees. It has the effect of saying: "It is so because I say that it is so. You are stupid not to see it."

In order to determine whether or not there is a significant ethical difference between killing or letting die, it is not enough to "feel" that there is or is not a difference, or to claim to "see" the difference or not to see it. We must go further, and explain what the difference is and why it is ethically significant, or, on the other hand, why there is no difference. In order to to this, we must examine in greater detail the ethics of nonintervention, the notions of acts, nonacts and omissions, and a number of other categories that provide the context of the issue of positive and negative euthanasia.

The ethics of letting something happen

Let us turn now to the specifics of the debate concerning the distinction between "killing" and "letting die." The concept of letting die is itself problematic. In order to understand it better, we may start by examining the more general concept of "letting something happen."

First, it should be observed that letting something happen is sometimes culpable, sometimes commendable, and sometimes neutral. Thus, in certain situations, the failure to act may constitute a form of negligence, even criminal negligence, as in the failure to take proper precautions with dangerous objects. And in the case of death, someone who withholds something necessary, such as food or medicine, may be held criminally liable for a person's death.[8] So to say that the doctor "let his patient die" is not a way of absolving him of culpability.

The question naturally arises: when and under what circumstances is letting something (evil) happen culpable, and when and under what circumstances is it commendable or neutral? We might begin by noting a few reasons why people *do* let things happen culpably. It is often easier not to intervene, out of laziness, cowardice or simply the desire to avoid becoming involved or committing oneself. Here one thinks of the Kitty Genovese tragedy, where numbers of people let her die without doing anything. The 'washing hands' syndrome is rampant in our society. Be that as it may, it is evident that culpability for "letting something happen" depends on the context.

There are, of course, situations in which letting something evil happen, i.e. not preventing its happening, is commendable. The most obvious examples of commendable forebearances are those involving interference in someone else's private affairs; for instance, it is commendable not to intervene in a marital dispute but to *let* the couple say what they want to each other. The principle of nonintervention has a moral basis as well as a practical one, for it follows from the principle of respect for the liberty and moral autonomy of persons. The principle of self-determination or liberty, as it is involved here, is usually contrasted with paternalism, which permits compelling others to do what one thinks is good for them, even when they themselves do not think that it is.[9] From the principle of self-determination, or antipaternalism, it follows that even though I know that what you plan to do will be disastrous for you, other things being equal, I have no right to prevent you from doing it. Smoking is a good example: provided that Jones's smoking is not a nuisance, it follows from the principle that we ought not to prevent him from smoking. More controversially, it follows from the principle that, other things being equal (e.g. that it hurts no one else), it would be wrong to prevent someone from committing suicide. In the cases with which we are concerned here, it would be paternalistic to force someone to stay alive, even though he has an incurable disease, wants to die, and thinks that it would be the best thing for himself and for his family.

How do these considerations about the morality of letting something happen apply to letting a patient die? Is the latter merely an escape, an abdication of responsibility? Or, on the other hand, is it an expression of respect for the moral autonomy of a person, say, an incurable, suffering patient: That is, is it a case of commendable nonintervention?

Letting versus making something happen

We must now examine the notion of nonintervention more closely; in particular, we must examine the difference between letting something happen and making it happen or doing something to a person.

The first thing we need to find out in a case of letting something happen is precisely *what* it is that is being let (allowed to) happen. What is it that one could prevent by intervening? Sometimes a patient is allowed to die through termination of treatment: in that case, one is refraining from prolonging his life. As we shall see presently one could ask why that is not killing him. On the other hand, if in letting a patient die slowly one is also letting him suffer excruciating pain or letting him pass through a senile existence like a vegetable then one is refraining from preventing suffering or from saving him from a senile existence. If this is what is involved, letting him die would hardly seem commendable.

To pursue this point further, it should be noted that the notion of P's letting X happen always implies a counterfactual conditional of the type: "If P did Y, then X would not happen." Therefore, in order to understand fully what is meant by saying that P let X happen, we must be able to specify *what P could have done* but did not do (i.e., Y) that would have prevented X from happening. Besides the suffering that P could prevent, if X is the patients's death, then, *ex hypothesi* P cannot prevent X—in the long run, that is. All that P can do is to postpone X, the patient's death. So there is something delusive about the notion of letting a person die, in the medical context, because he is going to die anyway. The medical case is therefore not like Rachel's example about Jones and his cousin.[10]

The point that I want to bring out is that letting the patient die is properly contrasted logically not with killing the patient but with treating the patient or perhaps with prolonging his life. (Here I need to restrict "treatment" to life-prolonging treatment, excluding, for instance, palliation.) In a sense, therefore, killing and letting die are not mutually exclusive. As opposed to distinguishing between killing and letting die, the real issue concerns the morality of not doing something, e.g. not treating or not prolonging life. Specifically, we have to ask whether not-doings, i.e. omissions and forbearances, belong to a different ethical category from doings. This question, in turn, will lead us into a discussion of the relevance of the description of an action, i.e. the ethical relevance of describing an action as a "letting happen" or as a "killing."

Are omissions actions?

It is often held that there is a significant ethical difference between doing something and not doing something, between acts and omissions, or, in philosophical jargon, between positive and negative acts.[11] It is held, for instance, that not-doings—omissions—are not subject to the same kind of moral standards used to judge and critically evaluate positive doings. Thus, other things being equal, a person is not responsible for omissions (or their consequences) in the same way as he is responsible for his positive acts (and their consequences). In this sense, not doings are not actions in the full ethical sense.

Of course, it is necessary to qualify these assertions with the phrase "other things being equal," because sometimes people are held responsible for their failing to act; that is, for their omissions. Parents who fail to take care of their children and doctors who fail to take care of their patients are held responsible for their omissions. Legally and perhaps also morally, we hold people responsible for their omissions when they have a prior duty to do what they fail to do. This is the basic notion behind the concept of negligence. We may broaden this notion by adding that roles and expectations also define actions that one can be condemned for not performing.

With these qualifications, the view in question holds that omissions per se are not the sort of thing for which a person can be held responsible. Underlying this position regarding omissions is what may be called an "interventionist" view of human action.[12] Human action is viewed as an intervention in the normal course of nature. Not to act, then, means not to intervene; and one can be held responsible only for one's interventions. Indeed, only interventions are subject to the precepts of morality.

It is easy to see why this doctrine might appeal to a doctor who subscribes to the distinction between killing and letting die for according to it letting die (not doing anything) amounts to not intervening in the course of nature. As a nonintervention it is a nonact and therefore not something that a person can be held responsible for. Hence, except in cases of negligence, a doctor is not responsible for a person's death if he lets him die, because that is a nonact; killing him, on the other hand, would be a positive act, an intervention for which he would be responsible.

Apart from the metaphysical underpinnings of the interventionist view of action and omission, its application to the problem at hand raises new questions. What is and what is not to count as an intervention? Is the act of deliberately deciding not to intervene itself an act in the ordinary sense or an intervention? And how about the positive steps that a doctor might take to avoid doing something; for example, walking away or hanging up on the phone? It is hard to believe that leaving orders not to resuscitate is not an intervention of some kind. Can we really say that a doctor is not responsible for the act of deciding or for various measures he undertakes as part of his plan of nonintervention? It is clear that the line between intervention and nonintervention is very fuzzy, to say the least.

The other part of the interventionist doctrine is the notion of the "normal course of nature." Again, it is unclear what is and what is not to be considered "normal." How do normal human interactions, say, of helping, fit in here? Are feeding, even intravenously; giving drugs like insulin; or massaging the heart normal or not normal?

Many versions of interventionism link the theory with a causal theory of action; that is, the theory that an action consists of a "causing something to happen," a "bringing about of something." (This theory is also sometimes called "consequentialism.")[13] According to the causal analysis, a nonaction would presumably be a not-causing something to happen and, as such, would (by definition) not be an action. In other words, the causal theory of action seems to imply that one can act only positively (in the sense of *causing* something to happen), and that the omission of an act, a nonperformance, is not an action, because it is a not-causing. If we add to this a causal theory of responsibility, namely the proposition that a person is responsible only for what he causes, then it follows that we are not responsible for our nonactions or, for that matter, for states of affairs we might have prevented. (Adherents of this view would have to say that the kind of responsibility involved in negligence is conventional or legal, rather than causal.)

Two points need to be made about the causal theory I have just described. First, we might question the underlying assumption that there can only be positive causes; that is, that omissions and privations cannot be causes. It may possibly be true that this is the case in physics, but it is a strange assumption for bio-medical science and even more so for clinical science, for in these latter areas, diseases are often attributed to the absence of normal or favorable conditions, e.g. the absence of oxygen (anoxia) or an insulin insufficiency (diabetes). It is therefore not illogical to attribute someone's death causally to the failure of someone else to feed him, to provide him with drugs, or to treat him.

A second and even more important point is that a presupposition of the attribution of responsibility to an agent for something he did or did not do is that he might have acted otherwise. More generally, if we want to be able to evaluate an act morally, either a past or a future act, we must be able to compare it with other possible acts. In other words, the concept of counterfactual possibility is an essential element in the ethics of action (and omission). Thus, Bennett gives a causal, consequentialist account of the difference between killing and letting die in terms of counterfactual possibilities; that is, "would . . . if's." A positive act like killing consists of "the only set of movements which *would* have produced that upshot" and an omission like letting die consists of "movements other than the only set which *would* have produced that upshot".[14] In other words, "to kill X" means that under the circumstances, there is hardly anything else that one could do that would have the effect that X dies, and "to let X die" means that almost anything that one could do would have the effect that X dies.

There are many reasons for rejecting this kind of analysis, however. As Casey points out, for example, a causal-counterfactual analysis of this type includes many things that we would not ordinarily consider "omissions," "refraining from doing," or "letting something happen." There are limits to the kind of possible nonacts that we attribute to a person. Casey writes: "The view we take of a man's character, or of his role in a certain type of situation, sets limits not only on what we can regard him as responsible for in that situation, but also, as we have seen, on what we can properly describe him as doing or refraining from doing."[15] There must be some reason to believe that the person in question is or should be *concerned* with what is happening. In his role as doctor, a person might be expected to treat or not to treat, but not to take a thousand dollars from his private bank account to buy a drug for a patient that is needed to save her life.[16]

Consider all the things that a person might do at a certain time. Under normal circumstances, there is obviously an indefinitely large number of possibilities; he could wiggle his right middle toe, scratch his forehead, shout, jump in the air. Certainly it would be absurd to say of most of these possible actions that the person in question *failed,* refrained from or omitted to perform them, for most of them are outside the compass of meaningful consideration; we would not blame or commend a person for not doing them, we do not deliberate about them.

These examples help make our task clear: we must find some way of distinguishing between those possible actions that are irrelevant to the assessment of conduct and those that are relevant. In our previous terminology, we need a way of determining whether an omission, a negative act, is to be regarded as an action or whether it is simply a possibility which does not fall under the rubric of action at all and to which moral categories are inapplicable. There are two ways, I believe, in which this distinction can be made. The first involves the *Why?* of an action (accountability), and the second involves the *What?* and *How?* of an action (the structure of an act).

Accountability: The why of an action

First, let us begin with the concept of an action in general. Here borrowing from Anscombe, we might say that an action is distinguished from a mere bodily movement in that it is always possible to ask for a reason for the action.[17] "Why did you do that?" This logical property of actions will be called "accountability," by which I mean that it always makes sense to ask for an account of why one does or did something. (I use the term "accountability" in order to distinguish what is involved here from other senses of the term "responsibility.")[18]

Now, it should be clear that we often can and do ask a person to account for his nonactions. "Why didn't you do that?" "Why didn't you come?" "Why didn't you treat the patient?" The request for reasons of this type also arises in connection with propositions about what one ought to do: "Why shouldn't you refrain from treating?" "Why shouldn't you let the patient die?" In contrast, there are lots of things of which it would be absurd to ask, why didn't you do that? e.g. "Why didn't you wiggle your toe at 11:34 A.M. today?"

The point I want to emphasize is that many forms of nonaction, refrainings and omissions, have the ordinary logical properties of actions, i.e. doings. This is important, because the simple not doing of something does not mean that one is let off the hook; one still has to explain. A doctor who refrains from treating must be able to give a reason for not-treating; in most cases, I am sure that this is possible. Insofar as "letting a patient die" falls into this category of nontreatment, it represents an action for which one is as accountable as one would be for, say, killing.

Act-descriptions: The what and how of an action

A second way of explaining the difference between possible actions in general and those nonacts (omissions) that are also actions is to observe how the latter fit into the structure of action. Here we are concerned, on the one hand, with questions like, *What* are you doing? or *What* did he do? and, on the other hand, with questions like. *How* did he do it?

It has now become a philosophical commonplace that the structure of an action is complex. One way of putting this is to say that one and the same act can be described in many different ways. Thus, Davidson writes:

I flip the switch, turn on the light, and illuminate the room. Unbeknownst to me I also alert a prowler to the fact that I am at home. Here I do not four things, but only one, of which four descriptions have been given.[19]

Goldman prefers to say that there are four different acts which are connected by the relation of "generation" in an act-tree. This relationship may be illustrated by saying, with regard to Davidson's example, that I illuminate the room *by* turning on the light, and I turn on the light *by* flipping the switch. The higher level acts are generated by the lower level acts. The whole set of acts generated from one act constitutes what he calls an act-tree.[20]

One of the things that Goldman's analysis makes perfectly clear is that negative acts can generate positive acts; that is, it is possible to do something by *not* doing something else. A driver can run over someone by failing to stop (by not-stopping); and a doctor can let his patient die by not treating him. Or one could say that the doctor killed the patient by not treating him.

It should now be clear why it is so difficult to differentiate "killing" from "letting a patient die" in cases involving terminally ill patients. Which of the following nonacts come under one of these headings rather than the other? Not putting a patient on a respirator? Not feeding him intravenously? Not treating him with antibiotics? Not giving him insulin? Not giving him blood transfusions? Not resuscitating him? Not operating on him? Under the appropriate circumstances, any of these nonacts, as well as a host of others, could be described *either* as killing the patient *or* as letting him die. The meaning and use of these two act-descriptions obviously depends on the context.

The fallacy of simple description

The general lesson from all these theories of action is that the correctness of one description of an action does not necessarily entail the falsity of other descriptions. The conception that there is only one true answer to the question: What is he doing? (or, What did he do?) may be called the *fallacy of simple description*. It is obvious that this fallacy is often employed as a sophistic device to "get oneself off the hook"—as an alibi, so to speak. Thus a person can plead: "I was just following orders" or like Eichmann, "I was just organizing railroad schedules," or "I was just saving the baby," or "I didn't kill her, I just let her die." Such descriptions of particular acts may be perfectly correct but quite inadequate for other descriptions of the same actions (or other acts on the act-tree) might be ethically more important. It may be true that Jones pressed his finger, thereby pulled the trigger and fired the gun, but it does not follow that Jones didn't kill the man.[21] We cannot say that the bullet, not Jones, killed him. By the same token, we cannot say that a person's disease, rather than some action or nonaction of the doctor, killed him.

That the fallacy of simple description is a fallacy should be clear from the fact that many of the acts on this kind of act-tree are acts for which one is accountable. It generally makes perfectly good sense to ask of each of these acts on the act-tree: Why did you do that? One can ask of Jones, for instance, Why did you press your fingers? Why did you pull the trigger? Why did you fire the gun? Why did you kill the man? With regard to genuine actions, including forbearances, such questions can be asked meaningfully all along the line—they are not odd or absurd. On the other hand, as I have already pointed out, questions like these would be patently absurd if asked with regard to other kinds of possible actions.

The selection of an act-description

There are two further points that have to be made in connection with the structure of action just discussed. The first point is that the selection of an act-description, or the construction of an act-tree, is not an arbitrary, subjective matter. It is not capricious because, excluding metaphorical uses of language, there are built-in limits as to how an act can be described or generated. In his book, Goldman examines in detail several methods of generation. According to his account, in general, an act A generates an act A′, whenever there exists a set of generating conditions (C*) such that the conjunction of A and C* entail A′.[22] What this means, in effect, is that anyone linking two particular acts by generation must be prepared to justify his doing so; that is, to give his reasons for saying that "Dr. Jones's giving orders not to resuscitate Smith" generates "Dr. Jones let Smith die," rather than "Dr. Jones killed Smith."

Although generating conditions do not need to be linked causally, they frequently do involve a causal link. When they do, the procedure of generation usually relates to specific instances rather than act-types. Hence generalizations about causal generations are apt to be deceptive. That is why "X's terminating treatment of Y" sometimes generates "X killed Y" and sometimes not.

In sum, if anyone maintains that there is a significant difference between not starting to treat a patient and stopping the treatment of a similarly situated patient, he must be able to show that the acts generated by these two acts are significantly different ethically. Thus, under certain circumstances, failing to turn on the machine may in fact generate the same type of act as turning the machine off, namely, they are both acts of "letting the patient die." I will leave it up to the reader to apply the same line of reasoning to some of the other situations discussed in this book. The moral point should be clear: one cannot change an act (or a nonact) into something morally neutral or avoid responsibility for it simply by using one act-description of it rather than another.

The ethical significance of an act-description

The second point concerns the ethical significance of act-descriptions, act-generations and, in general, act-classifications. Some are clearly more significant ethically than others; one is tempted to say that some descriptions relate to what is ethically central and others to what is only incidental in an action. For example, whether Jones used his middle or his forefinger to press the trigger is immaterial; what is significant is that he killed the man. By the same token, whether a doctor let his patient die by giving an order to the nurse not to call him or by not giving an order to the nurse to call him may, in most cases, be immaterial. What matters ethically is that the patient died, that the doctor ended his suffering, etc.

The distinction implied here is often formulated in terms of the metaphysical concepts of essence and accident. A certain feature of an action, say, its intention, is held to be essential; other features, say, the specific bodily movements involved, are held to be accidental. The use of the essence-accident distinction represents a metaphysical doctrine known as "essentialism," which contends that there are built-in essences of things and that, as rational beings, we can identify these essences through, for example, some form of intuition. For obvious reasons, I find this doctrine quite objectionable. Instead, I adopt a pragmatic position and hold that what is to be taken as essential depends on the purposes one has in mind. Thus, what is essential for legal purposes may not coincide with what is essential for ethical or clinical purposes. In this essay we are concerned with what is essential from the point of view of ethics.

In order to avoid the absolutist metaphysical and epistemological connotations of the term "essence," I shall use the term "centrality" instead. Accordingly, we may speak of certain features of actions, or certain act-descriptions, as ethically central and of others as not central. The assumption that one particular feature or type of act-description is central reflects an ethical commitment or an ethical position of one sort or another. For this reason, act-descriptions are hardly ever likely to be ethically neutral. To pretend, as certain metaphysicians and linguistic philosophers do, that those act-descriptions that are relevant to ethics (e.g. in framing moral rules and principles) are themselves logically prior to and independent of ethical presuppositions is simply a subtle way of begging the ethical question—generally in favor of the *status quo* morality, or at least of a particular kind of moral rule such as a rule against "killing."

It is important to recognize not only that the selection of a particular act description of an action has ethical implications, but that the issue of what is to be taken as central in describing acts is basically an ethical issue and one that can be decided only on ethical grounds. For example, if one assumes that in the ultimate analysis an act is constituted by its consequences (e.g. changes in the world caused by the agent's intervention), then one has already chosen to side with a consequentialist ethic of some sort. On the other hand, if one focuses on the intention of an act as what is ethically central one has already committed oneself to some sort of absolutist ethics, probably one that lays undue stress on what Donagan calls "second-order rules"; that is, rules for judging the culpability, blameworthiness, or sinfulness of an action or of an actor.[23]

There are obviously many other conceptions of what is ethically central in an act-description besides the two mentioned. In my opinion, the most adequate conception of ethical centrality is one that relates it to human relationships of the sort that reflect the social virtues of integrity, respect, caring, understanding, helping, healing, relieving suffering, compassion, solicitude, sympathy and the corresponding vices. And so, I would argue, those acts on the act-tree (or act-descriptions) that come under these virtues and vices are the ones that should concern us in our medical decisions, as in our other practical decisions vis-a-vis others, if we want to view them morally.

Accordingly, the crucial difference between killing and letting die, if there is one, will depend on what kind of human relationship these acts represent in the act-tree, i.e. what moral acts they generate and from what moral acts they are generated. And to determine what this is obviously depends on the context. For example, if the act in question can be properly described as compassionate in the sense that it generates or is generated by that kind of act, then it would be virtuous; if, on the other hand, the act is best described as one of abandonment, then it might indeed be considered vicious. If this sort of analysis is followed through, then under certain circumstances administering a lethal drug to an incurable suffering patient might be virtuous and under other circumstances not; by the same token, terminating treatment might sometimes be virtuous and at other times vicious. We must always view the question within a particular context. This is one of the tenets of the position that I call "contextualism."

The rationale for letting a patient die

The ethical implications and consequences of adopting one particular conception of what is ethically central in an act-description rather than another will become clear if we take another look at the absolutist, intention notion of action. The absolutist believes that a distinction should be made between the intention of an act and the foreseen but unintended consequences of that act.[24] This distinction is used to explain the difference between killing and letting die; in killing, the consequence of the patient's death is what is intended, whereas in letting a patient die his death is not part of what is intended, it is merely a foreseen consequence. To some of us, this distinction seems sophistic, resting on nothing more than a verbal trick; in any event, we need a clear, acceptable criterion for determining what is and what is not part of the intention of an act.

One suggestion is that the clue to what is involved in an intention is to be found in the reasons for the action in question. Accordingly, the distinction between killing (e.g. by administering a lethal drug) and letting die (e.g. by turning off the respirator) might be reduced to a difference in rationale.[25] In the rationale for killing, humanitarian considerations are usually paramount, e.g. the pertinent reasons would be such things as the preservation of the moral integrity and the alleviation of the suffering of the patient and of his family. In the rationale for letting die (not-treating), on the other hand, the paramount consideration is the pointlessness of further treatment in view of its hopelessness and the hardship that further treatment would impose on the patient and his family, e.g. in suffering and economic burden.

It should be observed at once that when so interpreted, the rationale for killing (i.e. positive euthanasia) is, in important respects, the same as the rationale for undertaking treatment in the first place, for the aim of both is the patient's general welfare and the fulfillment of his needs. In contrast, the rationale for letting die, e.g. for ceasing or not initiating treatment, is like the rationale for not treating other sorts of incurable conditions, including many in which death is not involved at all, e.g. incurable blindness or even baldness.

When viewed in this light, the decision to "let a patient die" has the character of a purely medical decision; that is, a professional decision based on medical reasoning, rather than a decision based on more general moral considerations. It is easy to see, therefore, why physicians feel more comfortable in describing a decision that results in a patient's death as "letting him die" rather than as "killing him." By choosing this description they can subsume the decision under what might be called "the ethics of treatment," i.e. professional medical ethics, and they can thereby avoid becoming involved in wider, controversial moral issues. Of course, the professionalization of the issue in such decisions ties in very neatly with the prevailing dictum that it is the doctor's business to "preserve life" rather than to "kill."

The ethics of treatment

We must now consider how the ethics of treatment might be used to support the distinction between killing and letting die. Let me begin by giving a brief account of what I mean by the "ethics of treatment."

The ethics of treatment is a species of professional ethics; it is the professional ethics of physicians. Professional ethics, as intended here, lays out the special obligations and privileges that persons have as members of a profession, especially in their relation to their clients.[26] It is important to distinguish this kind of ethics from the ethics of a technician such as a plumber or a TV repairman, since the specific obligations of the latter are exhausted when they honestly and efficiently deliver the services or good requested by their clients. Professionals, on the other hand, are expected to do more. In particular, they are required to consider not just what their clients want, but what they themselves, in their considered and informed judgment, believe to be in their client's best interest. In this regard, their professional ethics sets limits to what they may do and what they must do for a client.

Consequently, one of the basic requirements of professional ethics in general is that the professional person be prepared to advise his client against a certain course of action if, in his professional opinion, it is not feasible or if it is undesirable because of the excessive cost or undue hardship that it would involve for the client. Just as it would be wrong for a lawyer to take a case to court that he knows he will not win, or for an engineer to draw up plans for a building that cannot be built, so it would be wrong, professionally, for a physician to undertake a course of treatment that he knows will be ineffective or too costly, e.g. in terms of suffering or finances.

Indeed, in cases where he thinks the treatment is inadvisable for some reason or other, the physician may, in his role of professional, even be under an obligation to refuse to honor the patient's request for such treatment. Not to do so would violate his professional integrity. Thus, it would be wrong for a doctor to prescribe a drug for a patient that he knows will be ineffective or will be unnecessarily painful and costly, even though the patient asks him to do so. We should not be surprised, therefore, to find that the doctor's view of what is right for him to do is often quite at variance with the patient's view of what he ought to do.[27]

Bearing this general requirement of professional ethics in mind, we can see that a physician might, for professional reasons stemming from the ethics of treatment, decide to terminate the treatment of an incurable, dying patient on the grounds that further treatment is pointless. This decision would be made on narrow professional grounds, i.e. the ethics of treatment, where only the appropriateness of further treatment is in question. In such cases, perhaps, we would not want to say that he decided to let the patient die; rather, he decided to terminate treatment and as a result the patient died.

If this analysis is correct, then it should be clear that the real point at issue between advocates and opponents of the ethical significance of the distinction between killing and letting die in the euthanasia context is an ethical one, namely, whether a decision leading to a person's death should be made on grounds taken from an ethics of treatment or on what might be called humanitarian grounds, i.e. caring, compassion and the desire to help the dying person die with dignity. The issue might be more simply described as the scope of a physician's moral responsibility towards his patient: Is his responsibility limited to questions concerning the appropriateness of treatment or does it extend further and include duties to his patient as a person?

Treatment and moral responsibility

Some comments on the moral aspects of an ethics of treatment are in order. To begin with, it is easy to be misled by the term "responsibility," for it means many different things to different people. Roughly speaking, ethical theories can be divided into theories of limited responsibility and theories of full responsibility.[28] Where responsibilities are tied to tasks, roles and offices, they tend to be viewed as limited; a person is considered to have no responsibility for the wider consequences of those acts of his that are performed in carrying out his assigned tasks, roles or offices. Thus, the ethics of treatment permits a doctor, who for professional reasons prolongs the life of a patient, to disown any responsibility for the continual hardship and suffering that his action brings to the patient or his family. Accordingly, that kind of professional ethics typically involves a theory of negative responsibility—what I have called limited responsibility.

Applied to physicians, the principle of the negative or limited responsibility of physicians implies that moral responsibility for many states of affairs involving indignity and suffering lies elsewhere or, indeed, in our society often nowhere. I have already commented on the ethical aspects of "just doing one's job" and abdicating responsibility for the consequences.

Up to this point, I have assumed that the ethics of treatment is taken as a *substitute* for the principles of common morality, for the principles of humanitarianism and of full moral responsibility for the health and welfare of others. But, of course, the ethics of treatment can be subsumed under a broader ethics, say, of humanitarianism, which recognizes everyone's positive moral responsibility for the health and welfare of others. If we do this, then the ethics of treatment will be a *supplement* to the ordinary principles of morality rather than a *substitute*. But in this case, the principle of the limited or negative responsibility of the physician for his patient has to be abandoned.

Morally speaking, then, the doctor is presented with a choice: if he accepts the ethics of treatment and an ethics of limited responsibility, then he must restrict his decision making to the purely professional sphere. In that case, however, he must abandon the role of moral entrepreneur, as Freidson calls it, and must disavow any pretense of basing his decision on moral grounds.[29] Ultimate moral decisions must be left to someone else. On the other hand, if he is willing to act on what I call an "ethics of responsibility," that is, an ethics of full and, in principle, unlimited responsibility for others, then he has to go beyond the narrow ethics of treatment as defined by his purely professional role. He must enter into decision making as a full-fledged moral agent; as such, he must be prepared to treat others as moral equals. He must be willing to consult with patient and family as equals and to permit them to participate as fully as possible in all decision making. Decisions themselves must be based on what is best for all concerned, particularly the welfare and moral integrity of the patient, and not simply on what is required by the physician's professional ethics, the ethics of treatment.[30]

If my analysis is correct, it follows that any doctor who chooses this course will be obliged to abandon the absolute distinction between killing an incurable, dying patient and letting him die. A further consequence, of course, is that he will have to relinquish his monopoly over decision making and over the supervision of the care of the terminally ill. By the same token, if the time should come when the life of a dying person ought to be terminated, there is no reason why the doctor must be the one to perform the merciful act.[31]

Notes

1. This chapter is a completely revised version of an essay entitled "Positive and Negative Euthanasia," which appeared in Michael D. Bayles and Dallas High, eds. *Medical Treatment of the Dying* (Boston: G. K. Hall, 1978).
2. For reasons already mentioned in the Introduction, I prefer to call them "positive" and "negative" euthanasia rather than "active" and "passive" euthanasia, which is the usual terminology. This chapter develops further certain points made by Rachels in Chapter 7. Rachels examines the distinction from the point of view of its ethical implications. This chapter explores some possible interpretations of the distinction and some of the presuppositions underlying the use of the distinction.

3. See John Casey, "Actions and Consequences," in John Casey, ed., *Morality and Moral Reasoning* (London: Methuen, 1971). I am indebted to Casey for many insights into this problem.

4. St. Thomas Aquinas, *Summa Theologica,* IaIae, qu. 19, art. 9 ad 3.

5. The details can be found in any textbook on Roman Catholic moral theology.

6. For a careful defense of the distinction, see Joseph Boyle, "On Killing and Letting Die," *New Scholasticism* 52 (Autumn 1978). I am greatly indebted to Boyle for letting me see an advance copy of this article. I shall discuss a modified version of this theory later in the paper.

7. For further discussion of this point, see Chapter 7. For a defense of the consequentialist position, see Jonathan Bennett, "Whatever the Consequences," *Analysis* 26.3 (1966), pp. 83–97.

8. Thus parents were found guilty of "involuntary manslaughter" and of child abuse after they stopped insulin treatments for their child and he died. *Boston Globe,* 20 July 1970.

9. There is already a considerable literature on paternalism, especially in the context of medical decision making. See, for example, Samuel Gorovitz et al, eds., *Moral Problems in Medicine* (Englewood Cliffs, N.J.: Prentice-Hall, 1976), pp. 182–241.

10. See Chapter 7.

11. For a helpful discussion of some of the issues, see Judith Jarvis Thomson, *Acts and Other Events* (Ithaca, N.Y.: Cornell University Press, 1977), chap. 15, "Omissions." See also quotations from Paul Ramsey in Chapter 7 to the effect that an omission is not an action.

12. For a description of this position and bibliographical references, see Alan Donagan, *The Theory of Morality* (Chicago: University of Chicago Press, 1977), p. 46.

13. For a critique of the causal theory of action, see Ladd, "Ethical Dimensions of the Concept of Action," *Journal of Philosophy* 62 (November 1965). Also, Irving Thalberg, *Enigmas of Agency* (New York: Humanities Press, 1972), sec. 1. (References to literature on the causal theory can be found in Thalberg's book.)

14. See Jonathan Bennett, "Whatever the Consequences."

15. Casey, *Morality and Moral Reasoning,* p. 168.

16. Casey, *Morality and Moral Reasoning,* p. 167.

17. See G.E.M. Anscombe, *Intention* (Oxford: Blackwell, 1957), pp. 9, 24–28.

18. I have tried to distinguish a number of different senses of "responsibility" in "The Ethics of Participation," in J. Roland Pennock and John Chapman, eds., *Participation in Politics* (NOMOS XVI), (New York: Atherton-Lieber, 1975), pp. 98–125.

19. Donald Davidson, "Actions, reasons, and causes," *Journal of Philosophy* 60 (1963). Reprinted in Norman S. Case and Charles Landesman, eds. *Readings in the Theory of Action* (Bloomington: Indiana University Press, 1966), p. 180. See also, Alvin I. Goldman, *A Theory of Human Action* (Englewood Cliffs, N.J.: Prentice-Hall, 1970).

20. Goldman, *Theory of Human Action,* chap. 2. It should be observed that generation need not be causal. For example, I can pay a bill by sending my creditor a check; sending the check is not a cause of paying him, it *is* paying him.

21. It is obviously quite correct to say that the shooting, the bullet, Jones, etc., etc., killed the man. One explanation does not exclude the others. Sometimes it is said that the disease killed a patient rather than a person. They are not mutually exclusive statements. Both might be true. See Goldman, *Theory of Human Action,* pp. 80ff.

22. Goldman, *Theory of Human Action,* p. 41.

23. Donagan, *Theory of Morality,* chap. 2.

24. This distinction underlies the so-called "Principle of Double Effect." For references and a useful discussion, see Donagan, *Theory of Morality,* pp. 157–64, and the article by Boyle mentioned in note 6. Needless to say, I do not accept this principle; in fact, I regard it as an immoral principle.

25. See Donagan, *Theory of Morality,* pp. 122–27; also Boyle, "On Killing and Letting Die."

26. There is a considerable literature on professionalism. For a good discussion of professionalism in medicine, see Eliot Freidson, *Profession of Medicine* (New York: Dodd, Mead, 1973), chap. 4, "The Formal Characteristics of a Profession."

27. Here it should be noted that not only do doctors sometimes continue treatment against the wishes of patients (or of their families), but they sometimes *dis*continue treatment against their wishes. There is, thus, no reason to assume that the professional ethics of treatment will be consistent either with the wishes of patients (or their representatives) or with the general principles of morality.

28. See Ladd, "The Ethics of Participation."

29. See Freidson, *Profession of Medicine,* pp. 252–55.

30. For more on the ethics of responsibility, see Ladd, "Legalism and Medical Ethics."

31. In India, it was traditionally the oldest son who was expected to set the funeral pyre ablaze.

9 Social Perspectives on Medical Decisions Relating to Life and Death

RAYMOND S. DUFF AND A.G.M. CAMPBELL

Any discussion of the ethical issues concerning life and death in the medical context rests on the biological bases of human existence. Like all living things, human beings are born from parent stocks; they grow, reproduce, age and die. They are subject to genetic and environmental hazards which may deform, incapacitate or kill at any time from conception to old age. A long history of evolution links them to living and nonliving things on the surface of the earth. The enormously complex and poorly understood processes of natural selection operate apparently without regard for man's most cherished values such as justice, kindness and love. Accordingly, human experience is replete with ironies and tragedies that are due simply to these inescapable facts of biology. It is obvious that there are many facts, for example, about death, that, realistically, we cannot expect science and technology to overcome.

It should therefore come as no surprise that modern medical technology can limit many of our ills, but cannot cure them; and that it can often delay suffering, disability and death, but cannot prevent them. Indeed, it may even prolong suffering and the process of dying. In medicine, for every "cure" there are many "half-cures."[1] For every instrument of "high technology" there are many more instruments of "half-way technology."[2] Most cures are easily applied so that little time and money are required for their use. By contrast, most of the resources of modern medicine are concerned with half-cures which may permit some people to function at a reasonably satisfactory level but which provide for others only the biologic existence of socially-dead persons. Of course, there are many situations which lie between these half-cures. Most treatments for the unconquered problems of congenital malformations, genetic disorders, heart and vascular diseases and cancer are half-cures. Treatment efforts may so alter conditions that some are enslaved by the crushing burdens of caring for the sick and disabled. Some persons may indeed prefer disease or even death to those treatments that are seen as meddlesome tinkering. The uncontrolled provision of curative medicine may preclude the development of more adequate preventive measures and may, paradoxically, result in higher overall morbidity and mortality. And, since many congenital malformations have a genetic component, if great efforts are made for survival in all instances, it is possible that future genera-; tions might be harmed. In this case, as in others, the rights of society as a whole, including future society, appear to conflict with the rights of individuals. Thus, over and over again we have to face the difficult and unavoidable question, To what extent, if any, must the strong and healthy respect the rights of the weak and unhealthy to survive and reproduce?

One answer, which was given by the stoic Spartans, seems to accord with natural selection although it violates other, human values, such as the values of justice and humanity. Another answer, given by some interpretations of the Judeo-Christian tradition, seems to respect these other values, but to disregard natural selection and the need to balance priorities. More than ever before, modern medical technology forces us to ask the question: If man is to insure maximal protection of his values as a whole, which of these answers should be adopt or what compromise between them is possible?

If, as a result of interfering with the processes of natural selection, the increasingly powerful tools of modern medicine have created new moral dilemmas for us, they have at the same time presented us with an array of new choices as far as patient care is concerned. These choices regarding patient care will be the subject of the rest of the chapter. Our particular concern will be with the following four questions: Who should decide? Whose rights should be considered? What options should society permit? When should society intervene?

As a background for considering these questions, we will first discuss the institutionalization of patient care in the twentieth century and its impact upon decision making for the care of the sick.

The institutionalization of patient care

Professionals of any occupation have more power, independence and control than their clients in their interrelationships. This is so because a knowledge differential always favors the professional.[3] In the case of the medical profession, there has been a long history of professional paternalism,[4] dominance,[5] and monopolistic tendencies.[6] In twentieth century medicine, this power imbalance has become even more marked as a result of unprecedented institutionalization of patient care, teaching and research.[7] A brief review of this development as it has taken place in the United States follows.

The fundamental reason for institutionalization was the fact that many critical advances in medicine could be achieved only by specialized research and development based on the physical and biological sciences. This division of labor required an arrangement so that persons of varied interests could work together. Specialists tended to be divided according to the classification of systems or subsystems of the body, such as circulatory, respiratory, endocrine. Supported by the reforms following the Flexner Report of 1910,[8] these specialists, also known early in the century as scientists (as distinct from clinicians), comprised a new class of physicians. As the years passed, more and more specialists and fewer and fewer generalists were trained. This was understandable because students were imitating their most impressive mentors, who were practically all specialists of increasingly narrow fields of interest. The practice of a specialty became even more appealing when students realized that the specialist, primarily taking care of paying patients, had a much better income than the generalist who couldn't be so selective.[9]

Another reason for the institutionalization of specialized medicine was that research was paying off. The successes of medical technology were exciting, perhaps heady, for the profession and for the public.

More and more researchers in the medical schools were being supported more and more by research funds from governmental and philanthropic sources, while for a variety of reasons organized medicine vigorously and successfully opposed financial support for medical education and medical care.[10]

The health lobby, which had a good start before 1940, became very effective after World War II. Known to some as "Washington's Noble Conspirators," it persuaded the government to provide the means for vast expansion of biomedical research.[11] In addition, propagandizing leaders of the voluntary health organizations pleaded for public support and lobbied for funds. As a result, the Congress often voted more funds than the federal health establishment or the administration believed could be wisely used—a most unusual situation.[12] Understandably, a good thing was exploited. Diseases, organs, cells, biochemical processes—all were studied, and good or even promising results were heralded far and wide. Efforts were made through research and clinical work to push unsolved problems into the solved or, even better, the prevented category. The propagandist's appeal often suggested, for example, that "conquering" cancer, heart disease, or even old age shouldn't be more difficult than going to the moon or creating an atom bomb.

Apart from the promise of biomedical research and development, the crusade to solve the problems of illness using the emerging technology was attractive for another reason. During and shortly after World War II, the Nazis were regarded as an almost pure and perhaps unprecedented evil, and as Vonnegut pointed out this could have had a corrupting influence on the Allies who could view themselves as better than they really were.[13] Alexander's report on the part played by the German medical profession in the atrocities set the pattern so that American medicine would never follow the Nazi example.[14] Physicians, he argued, must not participate in choosing death on any ground of what he called "Hegelian rational utility."[15] Using the moral "slippery slope" argument, he contended that every step in this direction would surely lead to evil choices for any sort of convenience or excuse. The solution to illness and disability had to be found in the emerging, promising technology. After all, it seemed, the mastery of technology, including the creation of the atom bomb, had contributed magnificently toward the defeat of our enemies, and wasn't disease also an enemy?

The focus of public and professional attention on the development of new benefits coming in rapid succession was so sharp as to obliterate, for a time, serious consideration of some unintended consequences of concentrating and institutionalizing vast professional powers. But several observers voiced concern if not alarm over what was happening to patients and to the medical profession as a whole. Even in the mid-1930s L. J. Henderson deplored the loss of the "general view" of medicine required in Hippocratic teaching.[16] He attributed the loss to the ascendancy of scientists or laboratory men who tended to serve science and the subsequent decline in prestige of clinicians who cared for patients. This situation had developed when in the early years of the twentieth century few middle- or upper-class patients would enter teaching or research insitutions because benefits for them had not been demonstrated and suitable accommodations had not been provided.[17] This left the specialists in these institutions in a position to study and treat diseases in the rather powerless poor. As late as 1950, medical students entering their clinical years at a leading university heard a professor say in a lecture that one reason for having poor people as patients was to provide "clinical material" for medical education. When he was challenged by students about inequities and undignified care, he replied that he was only reflecting a long-standing tradition in America.[18]

Hospitals and medical schools become more and more oriented toward diseases, organ systems, cells and biochemical processes.[19] Departments were organized according to the interests of specialists, who were given great power and freedom to develop their own interests. The interests of the sick were subordinated to those of the specialists, who were highly rewarded for developing their research. With money only they or their departments were able to obtain, they could and did isolate themselves from both the immediate medical school and the parent university. They could and did ignore patients, especially the poor, by delegating patient care responsibilities as much as possible to trainees in medicine. They could and did ignore practitioners from whom they were recently descended. They were then relatively free to engage in research and, with the Noble Conspirators, to promote legislation which was self-serving. As teachers and role models, they created a different profession of medicine.

For the new brand of physician, who could be called technocrats or biocrats,[20] the sick person often became "a mere case which (not who) passes through the doctor's office, his past, present and future unknown, except within the meager abstractions of etiology, diagnosis, and prognosis, and his personality and relations with other persons not even thought of."[21] The methods of scientists were analytic and reductionistic to the neglect of synthesis for the patient's benefit. Again, Henderson noted, "Somebody ought to understand and treat real men and women, not mere medical, surgical, or social cases. . . . No more than a partial division of labor is possible. You may in theory analyze a person into aspects; in practice you may not do so with impunity. Half a sheep is mutton."

In 1939, Robinson reported an elaborate study of 174 unselected patients admitted to the Johns Hopkins Hospital: "The results of this study bring us face-to-face with the problem of how to obtain as a routine practice, in the highly specialized services of our hospitals, knowledge of the patient as a whole and how to use this knowledge effectively. It is in the teaching hospitals that this problem is of particular significance as it is here that the medical profession of the future is observing for the first time the methods and standards of medical practice and where concepts and sentiments are being implanted in young and developing minds."[22]

As a result of these developments, patients began to complain of neglect when they were ignored as persons or when technology failed or abused them. A related complaint was the excessive and perhaps unnecessary utilization of technology on those who could pay the fees and underutilization on the poor who could not.[23] Studies of utilization and medical discipline have raised many questions about the absence of professional self-regulation.[24] This point is mentioned in passing only as an illustration of how other interests in medicine may compete very successfully with the interests of patient, family or the public, and how, as a result of public ignorance or bias these interests may be neglected or subordinated to professional interests of professors in advancing the state of the art or of practitioners in raising their income.[25]

The emerging system of medical education and practice focused on diseases rather than people, on the profession's interests rather than the public's. While the consequences of this change in focus were felt throughout medical practice, the most obviously neglected aspect of care in the crusade against disease was the ancient art of easing the agony of dying. Early in the century, there were relatively fewer old people to call attention to life's inevitable end; dying occurred more often at home; and there were still some family doctors around who could help the dying because these doctors, presumably, had a larger view of patient care. But to the new medicine, death was considered to mean failure, and this was offensive. It was no longer necessary nor sometimes even possible to let pneumonia, uremia, heart failure, stroke, severe prematurity, or congenital malformation bring death like a friend. To acquiesce in these inevitable processes was considered plebian if not contemptible. House staff, those youthful physicians on the "firing lines" of acute hospital care, talked of "saving lives," not of providing comfort for the dying. It was often said, "He didn't die while I was on duty." (Remember the bumbling old doctor in Sinclair Lewis's *Arrowsmith* whose elderly, ailing patient was dying of a curable infectious disease?) But many citizens had different views of what is right. They would agree with Alsop that: "A dying man needs to die, as a sleepy man needs to sleep, and there comes a time when it is wrong, as well as useless, to resist."[26]

It was presumed that generally the choices of professionals were more rational than those of patients or families. The sick and their families were expected to accept care as professionally defined. In this, Freidson charged physicians with "moral entrepreneurship."[27] For example, when doctors had managed to preserve life in a deformed infant, parents were supposed to accept this and cooperate in treatment. Considerable literature instructed professionals in the appropriate techniques of persuading patients and families to cooperate. Pinkerton advocated counseling relationships that would "foster our empathetic understanding and so make it easier to identify and subsequently correct mechanisms of nonacceptance."[28] In a similar approach, the National Association for Mental Health in Great Britain prepared a statement directing professionals "when to tell" and "how to tell" parents about their handicapped infants so as to maximize acceptance.[29] In the absence of consensus towards alternatives of care, these articles, written by lay or professional persons with an interest in providing care, were well-meaning attempts to guide professionals in helping families live with their tragedies.

Taking note of how doctors handled the passing of information to patients, Waitzkin and Stoeckle offered the proposition: "A physician's ability to preserve his own power over the patient in the doctor-patient relationship depends largely on his ability to control the patient's uncertainty."[30] In this regard, they indicated that patients (or families), being less knowledgeable about illness than doctors, were almost always more uncertain than doctors. The latter, believing that sometimes bad news is bad for the patient, tended to withhold or give misleading information (for example, about prognosis with treatment). Thus, through patients' ignorance and uncertainty, doctors could prevail over them. Since uncertainty is ever-present in medical care, it may have been used to control the patient or family without anyone's awareness of it. The "competence gap," as described by Waitzkin and Stoeckle, was probably greatest, or at least believed to be greatest, when specialists were involved.

The training of researchers rather than of clinicians in the teaching hospitals gave great influence over patient care to physicians still in training. In most clinical departments, the senior resident was the chief executive officer for patient care. He was the one who scheduled house staff, medical students, and faculty for patient care and teaching assignments. It was mainly house staff who were the immediate decision makers and actors in the care of patients. They controlled most consultations among faculty, and they directed practically all patient care in the poor person's accommodation, the wards.[31] In the semi-private and private accommodations, the house staff had to cope with the patient's private doctor with whom they often disagreed, but direct confrontation between faculty and practitioners was rarely necessary. The faculty controlled the house staff who were, in turn, in immediate control of patients. In most disputes, house staff could prevail over practitioners because the latter were rarely on the scene and, having less knowledge of rapid changes in medicine, they were less certain, more hesitant; like patients, they were relatively weak. In the hospital setting, practitioners were frequently discounted and sometimes disregarded. The profession found it embarrassing to disclose these inner political struggles to patients or families. Such a disclosure might disturb public confidence in hospitals and the profession, and that, it was argued, would be "antitherapeutic." As a result, for the management of most patients in large teaching hospitals, the wisdom of practitioners derived from years of caring for the sick and dying was not effectively present and sometimes not welcomed in teaching and decision making at the bedside. Decisions for the care of the sick reflected this fault. In the 1930s, Robinson found, for example, that social and emotional components of illness though "frequently recognized by the physicians responsible for the clinical study and care of patients . . . were almost as frequently set aside."[32] Thirty years later, Duff and Hollingshead reported similar findings, only perhaps conditions had worsened.[33]

Problems resulting from these conditions then emerged. In the Duff-Hollingshead study, for example, the management of dying was found to isolate the patient and often the family as well. Families, usually without adequate financial support from insurance or government, were required to pay the costs of care while patients commonly were coerced into fighting death to the bitter end. There was little discussion of failure or of dying or death. The right to choose the way to die or even to modify it was denied. The pleas of one dying man for help to commit suicide were met by a stern, moralizing warning from the senior physician that he (the patient) ought to fight for his life in accordance with the codes of medicine, the laws of the land, and the commandments of God; he must not risk loss of insurance for his family, disgrace himself or his family, or compromise his status in life or after death by thinking criminal thoughts or acting upon them. The doctor never discussed the plain fact that he could offer this patient very little except further suffering. Another patient who was dying of abdominal cancer asked frequently if it was "the day for me"; that is, to die. He was told repeatedly that the physicians were doing their part and that the answer to his question depended on how hard he fought for himself. He concluded that the doctors were passing the buck, but he was too weak to do anything about it and his family was confused. The doctors recognized the dilemma and were uneasy. After this patient's death, one doctor said, "Not one of us had the guts to tell him he was dying. . . . It was difficult to say whether he thought we were really doing something for him or that we were just a bunch of bastards."

By the 1960s, there were far more old and dying people in the country. Practitioners trained in the new medicine could do little for many of them, and most of the old family physicians had died.[34] The situation was further complicated by the fact that more and more people were dying in health care institutions[35] where technological imperatives tended to prevail over the interests of patients and sometimes even over common sense. Since defeat in extending life could not be accepted gracefully, dying could not be accomplished with dignity. While dying patients usually knew their end was near, sometimes wanted to talk about it, or occasionally sought relief in an earlier death, physicians usually were preoccupied with technology and tended to coerce or "program" patients into cooperating on medical terms. Medicine was oversold. Many physicians recognized the dilemmas for patients but justified their approach by arguing that the fight against disease could be won only by pressing on. They were applying the tools of a complicated technology within a complex organization which sought not only to treat patients but to advance the state of medicine and to maintain a favorable public image. These different objectives were often in conflict with each other. Talking about the management of failures was discouraged because it might neutralize the propaganda used to get support for research, teaching, or care, and so patients were left to drift. Rehabilitation, even when it would help, was neglected[36] and, for the more hopeless, merciful death was denied. Thus, many patients were tormented both by disease and by acts of omission and commission in treatment.

While these ironies had become apparent, the control of a necessarily institutionalized technology was not easy to achieve. Many lay and professional persons had come to believe the widespread propaganda or to accept it as benevolent. As Chapman has indicated, spokesmen for medicine used a lot of self-congratulatory rhetoric and provided few unbiased appraisals of the reforms that followed the Flexner report.[37]

These difficulties were vastly compounded by a coincidental alliance between the state and church on the one hand and medicine on the other concerning the issue of institutional morality in deciding about care of the dying.[38] Since almost all of medical education and increasing proportions of practice had become institutionalized, the issue of institutioned morality was especially important. Whatever had been done previously in the privacy of homes and physicians' offices could not remain secret if done in institutions where many persons witnessed the whole spectrum of care. If a decision for death had been made in home care, it could go undetected because the family was likely either not to know what had been done or to have approved; knowledgeable neighbors would tend to be discreet because they would want to be accorded similar consideration when facing their own tragedies. (Of course, such choices might be made in ignorance of modern advances which might make acceptable treatment possible.) But if a choice for death was made in a hospital, it might be reported. Persons not directly involved in a decision and not even knowing the patient, family, or physician might find out about an act or a failure to act which was morally unacceptable to them personally or might be in violation of institutional policies or customs. There was fear that such persons might complain to institutional, state, or church authorities because examples of this kind of action, some involving criminal charges, were on record.[39] Such conditions forced upon decision makers the morality of the most conservative or, as one observer noted, the "busybody conservative."[40] For good or bad reasons (and probably there were both), the resulting restrictions of freedom worked against allowing patients to die or against killing them. Since the prevailing policy also obligated most persons to fight for life, or at least to appear to do so, in effect it trapped both patients and physicians, although unequally: patients were caught in treatment which was not likely to benefit them and might do them much harm, and they were, in general, quite helpless to control the situation. Physicians were not so uncomfortable since they had captives on whom to practice and an assured income for doing so.

Another aspect of the dilemma was that "allowing to die," even if some could get away with it, didn't always solve the problem. Occasionally it resulted in greater, sometimes appalling, disability of a surviving person who even without treatment failed to die of his disease.[41] Thus both the patient and the physician were trapped because neither could confidently opt for death. This forced the profession and the public to use half-way technology to the point that the patient was wholly dependent on it. To be entitled to die, it appeared that the patient must be in a hopeless state, defined most conservatively, and otherwise heroic measures, defined most liberally, were required to sustain life. Stopping before then posed a severe threat to the physician's status in the profession, in the hospital and possibly in a court of law.

Despite educational bias and restrictions of practice, many physicians in all specialties cared for patients with exemplary humanism. They sometimes risked their careers in doing so, but as individuals they could not control the conditions that a tyrannical institutional morality imposed on them and their patients. The profession as a whole was too involved with conflicts of interest to organize against it. The prevailing policies helped hospitals and other segments of a vast medical-industrial complex to find expanded markets[42] and the state of the healing arts may have been improved. A further complicating factor is that physicians who were doing well financially often had investments in these industries and numerous segments of that complex had very active lobbies in the Congress.

Many of the foregoing difficulties are illustrated in Zuelzer's discussion of newborn intensive care units:

Conceived primarily for post-operative care and acute catastrophies, filled with gadgets, staffed by people conditioned to emergencies, shielded from the public eye more than any other hospital ward, these are the places where decisions for a lifetime are made. It is hard to conceive of a worse setting. When do we turn the machines off? When should we have turned them on in the first place? . . . The beep of the oscillograph is becoming the voice of the new barbarianism.

In the case of a severely defective infant whose life can be saved by surgery but whose defects remain, he observed,

Here it is not so much the difficulty of making a decision that must trouble us, as the fact that more often than not no true decision-making process comes into play. By a sort of collective irresponsibility the infant is brought to the operating table, often before the parents know that their child is defective, to say nothing of their having the option. The obstetrician leaves the task to the pediatrician, the latter postpones the painful duty to the last possible moment, but meanwhile identifies the bowel obstruction and refers the case to the surgeon. The surgeon has little choice but to proceed, although he may have had no contact with the parents whatsoever. The operation is a success, the child will live, and now someone will brief the family with averted eyes that they have a mongoloid on their hands. A triumph of modern medicine— or medicine at its worst?

What is the outlook for the child born with a large myelomeningocele after the neurosurgeon is through with him? Will he vegetate in some institution, paraplegic, perhaps blind, soiled and utterly helpless, until infection mercifully carries him off? Is it humane to prolong that kind of life? Are we justified in tinkering with dialysis machines, renal transplants, and immuno-suppressants in young children with renal dysplasia—trading growth failure, steroidism, infection, and above all misery for the limited survival of a human that assuredly will never become eubiotic? [Zuelzer's term designating the capacity for purposeful life.]

Considering genetic factors in congenital anomalies as well as many other conditions, Zuelzer adds that "we cannot forever circumvent the regulatory mechanisms of evolution."[43]

In summary, then, the progressive institutionalization of medicine involved an almost inevitable concentration of power in a professional elite. This elite was rewarded most for research and what they were doing was what they taught. Early in the century, they were concerned with practice as specialists; so their students tended to specialize. Later, especially after 1940, the elite did more and more research and became increasingly subspecialized. Hence, they tended to train researchers and were inclined to neglect both practice and training for practice, whether general or specialty. This arrangement gave authority over patient care in hospitals to physicians-in-training who placed technological imperatives above patient interests and who rated the wishes of professionals over those of patients. Physicians felt obligated to fight for a patient's life against all odds and could do little to help him die. Institutional morality raised may issues reflecting conflicts of interest between patients, families, physicians, and the medical- industrial complex.

Deciding care: what can be done?

The conditions in which decisions about care are made tend to limit or cripple rational thought. To begin with, they involve intense feelings. Disability, dependency, suffering, incompetence, and dying are constant fears and all too often they are oppressive realities. Those who deal with these problems at an abstract level are generally unaware of the details of illness, of secret beliefs and secret practices that may be illegal or, in the views of some, morally reprehensible. Revelation of specifics may endanger the persons involved. Even discussing the subject generally may be risky. But the importance of the issues appears to justify these risks.

Another condition that makes rational thought about these decisions difficult is that they frequently involve sharp conflicts of interest. One person's continued living may be very inconvenient for another who helps decide care. A person may prefer to die, but close relatives demand he live so that their sense of loss or guilt for a sometimes murderous wish can be minimized. In addition, physicians don't like to lose a struggle. It is acutely painful for health professionals to admit failure. Sometimes they blame themselves or one another for selected deaths because they know they have goofed. They are fearful that others may blame them or possibly sue them for failure or alleged failure. They fear loss of status or income or loss of an opportunity to advance the art of medicine. In addition, it has been shown that physicians as a group are more fearful of death than laymen, making their sensitivity about this subject understandable.[44]

In the light of these considerations, we shall now discuss and try to answer the four questions posed at the beginning of the chapter.

Who should decide? All final decisions about care should be made jointly by patients, families, and physicians. If the patient is incompetent and the family is unable or unwilling to help, a surrogate should be provided. These are the only persons who possess and can integrate the necessarily complex, intimate and detailed knowledge about people and diseases so that good moral and good medical choices can be made. Our studies[45] disclosed that in spite of conflicts of interest, these persons appear to make good choices for patients of all ages when they listen to one another and tell the truth about their views and feelings. It seems unlikely that any committee, however composed, could make better choices. Indeed, they would probably be worse. Of course, persons deciding care should seek whatever advice they need from extended family, clergy, or other lay and professional persons, but advice of this kind should be used only selectively because it may be contradictory or harmful.

These decision-makers will experience much agony, especially when they feel they must choose death; therefore, those whose advice had been sought, but not followed should give them appropriate respect and support in a spirit of humility, and otherwise mind their own business. Inappropriate intervention in the intensely private affairs of persons facing tragedies can be tyrannical. It is far too easy and very tempting to impose an inappropriate but comfortable morality upon persons deciding care who themselves may find a better morality to be acutely uncomfortable.

Regarding the role of the physician in deciding care, it appears necessary, as suggested by Fox[46] in 1965 and by Duff and Hollingshead[47] in 1968, that every patient ought to have one physician whose chief function is to safeguard his (the patient's) personal interests.[48] This physician must take into account both the rights of others and the benefits and limits of technology. He should resist the advice of specialists or others when such advice does not serve the patient's interests. (Specialists are necessarily biased toward science and often unwittingly tend to subordinate patient interests to it.) This proposal would require that the decision-making power now held by specialists be shifted to personal physicians and especially to patients and their families.

Whose rights should be considered? The rights of patients to live or die and the rights of family members and others in present and future generations must be considered. No other approach will permit justice to prevail because everyone is related biologically and socially to others in the past and present and to those yet to be born. There are many who contend that decision makers in patient care cannot take these many issues into account. However, exposure of most citizens to the biology and the sociology of the family in the usual course of their lives prepares them for such tasks. That preparation is often underrated and certainly is underutilized.

What options should society permit? This is the hardest question of all. An examination of the options often taken within or outside of the law may be instructive. These options are reflected in some private beliefs about death and dying that exist in our culture among those persons closest to the tragedies. Some of these beliefs concern the authority of the doctor. In the face of a "lost cause," such as anencephaly, hydranencephaly, trisomy 13, or conditions having a similar prognosis in infants as well as terminal conditions among adults, many believe the doctor has the authority to "let the patient die" or "put the patient to sleep," as the veterinarian would do to a suffering pet. Inquiry about these views has disclosed that some people believe that such practices have existed for an indefinite period. This was no surprise to many physicians. Allegations of not resuscitating or otherwise insuring that a hopeless patient not survive may be discussed quietly in the inner circles of the profession, and there is indirect evidence of such practices. For example, when optimism arose in the treatment of spina bifida, the stillbirth rate for this condition fell sharply in one English town.[49] Infants now being treated for spina bifida would in earlier times without doubt have been consigned to the grave. Consider the following from a letter received recently on this general subject:

A very good friend of mine from Philadelphia once told me that her mother always told the family doctor when he came to deliver one of her children, "If there's something wrong with it, don't tie the cord." She lived in a small midwestern town. I suppose, before the rise of "modern medicine," a lot of women and their doctors solved problems when they were small and I don't think God ever held it against them if the solution was made with a pure heart. Man's laws have to be loose enough to permit God to work in the hearts that make decisions.[50]

Problems of severe deformity recognizable at birth may often have been solved by immediate passive or, if necessary, active infanticide. In this regard, consider also the cloakroom comments among obstetricians about deliberately prolonging the delivery of a baby who is probably badly damaged so as to insure death and thus avoid a fate considered worse than death. While many would understand such a choice by an obstetrician, it surely gives us a chill to contemplate the possibility that the infant killed by the mode of delivery might have been perfectly normal. Whether or not to attempt resuscitating an apparently dead newborn presents a similar dilemma.

Nowadays it is a practice not to resuscitate patients in some instances. This decision is usually made by patient, physician, or family, separately or together. Naturally, special problems arise when the patient is not able to participate in choosing because of age or incompetence. There is agreement on the correctness of the choice in some situations, but not in others. That people draw their lines in different ways is illustrated by contrasts observed recently at two conferences in Connecticut. In the first, the Kennedy Foundation film *Who Should Survive?* had been shown and was being discussed at a meeting of the Connecticut League for Nursing.[51] This group in general felt that the film discounted or ignored the tragedy of mongolism for the child, the family, and society and that it propagandized blindly for survival of the infant and against the decision for death made in the film. The nurses appeared willing to accept the decision for death in the film, and they were suspicious of the motives of the film's producers. In the second conference, a meeting of the Pro-Life Council of Connecticut, several speakers referred to *Who Should Survive?* and condemned the decision for death that was made in it. The keynote speaker indicated that he had been drawn into the right-to-life crusade by the film when it was originally shown in Washington, D.C. in 1971. Another speaker, a physician, talked about his opposition to arbitrary choices for death. Then, inconsistently, he described how he himself repeatedly arbitrated decisions for death in his own hospital.[52]

In our own studies, consideration was given to the prognosis for the patient and the likely impact of the patient's living or dying on the family. There was abundant evidence that families were willing to sacrifice, but not foolishly. Others have reported similar findings. Anderson and Sheatsley noted that families and patients decided care without regard for cost.[53] This appeared to be true whether the money came directly from the family (even poor ones) or from insurance companies or government. Hunt reported great sacrifices made by families for children with meningomyelocele.[54]

In our exposure to persons making life and death choices, we observed that patients, families, and health professionals used both their heads and their hearts in search of solutions to the incredibly perplexing problems confronting them. Sometimes they felt obliged to abandon the comfortable, conventional morality of Ramsey[55] in favor of the less orthodox and less comfortable positions of Joseph Fletcher[56] and Daniel Maguire.[57] They believed that there was a time and a reason to choose death and a justification for deciding the mode of achieving it. All of this, they contended, must occasionally be within their authority if they were to be effective in caring with kindness for the sick and in adapting to life in the future.

It has always been acknowledged by professional and lay persons that choosing death is an awesome, final act and that risks of harm are involved. Those we interviewed, however, felt that the choices of involved individuals would provide not only benefits but also prudent limits of the practice, though this might not be the case if the power to decide were vested primarily in an institution such as government, hospitals, the church, or the medical profession alone. Persons serving institutions must sometimes protect their own careers by deciding against individual citizens. They may also "walk away" from the decision because it does not concern them personally. There seemed to be general accord with Ladd's contention that "certain facets of the organizational ideal are incompatible with ordinary principles of morality."[58]

These considerations indicate that our society will be less hypocritical if we acknowledge what is in fact privately said and done about choices of death. To assure less hypocrisy and greater freedom, society must allow for a full-range of choices including euthanasia and suicide, although the difficulties and dangers are clearly recognized. Many people are asking for a choice by saying that they want to live until they die or want to die while they are still living. Either way, they want more control over living and over the indignities of dying. It is generally acknowledged that the hospice movement was begun primarily because such lay controls over living and dying are denied by most doctors and hospitals.

Finally, when should society intervene? Presumably, it should intervene only if three conditions are met. First, it must show that harm is being done to someone. Second, it must prove that a better alternative is available. Third, it must demonstrate the capacity and the will to support those on whom it imposes an unwelcome choice.

Making decisions based on the foregoing terms in a contract involving informed consent, as described by Katz[59] and Veatch,[60] no doubt will require some adjustments that will not be easy. For example, to support the "principle of totality" by which a person acts in his overall best interest, patients or families with suitable medical advice must be allowed occasionally to set aside the duty to preserve life (the "sanctity of life") in order to save other important values.[61] It is evident that for free people, choosing death has now become necessary in order to control the use of modern medical technology that has given man so much more abundant life in the first place. Without this second choice, modern medicine is often necessarily oppressive. Morison summarizes these views:[62]

Squirm as we may to avoid the inevitable, it seems time to admit to ourselves that there is simply no hiding place and that we must shoulder the responsibility of deciding to act in such a way as to hasten the declining trajectories of some lives, while doing our best to slow down the decline of others. And we have to do this on the basis of some judgment on the quality of the lives in question.

In summary twentieth century concentration of decision-making power in physicians and health institutions has compromised and sometimes even imperiled the care and the freedom of persons. Some aims of hospitals and of physicians are necessarily in conflict with the aims of patients. The aims of science and of the vast medical-industrial complex and the understandable desire of all to adhere to a comfortable morality of patient care combine to limit the freedom of individual citizens. Here, we make two suggestions: First, the power of deciding patient care should be redistributed; personal physicians should have more power, specialists less. More importantly, in decision making regarding their own lives and deaths, patients and families should have more influence, hospitals and the profession as a whole, less. Second, regarding individual choices for care and death, society should not intervene except under the three conditions mentioned earlier.

All that is said here is based on a large number of studies and reports and on the authors' intimate exposure to human tragedy. No effort has been made to square the positions taken with law, custom, or the views of any particular persuasion. This was necessary in order to concentrate on the issues and to be faithful to the suffering and to those who care for them. The adoption of the suggestions given here logically will depend on two considerations. The first is the degree to which we trust ourselves or can learn to do so as we face those special choices at the end of life. The second concerns the kind of society in which we want to live and die.[63]

Notes

1. Sir Theodore Fox, "Purposes of Medicine," *The Lancet* (23 October 1965), pp. 801–5.
2. Lewis Thomas, "Reflections on the Science and Technology of Medicine," *Yale Medicine* 8 (Winter 1973), p. 1.
3. Robert K. Merton, *Sociological Ambivalence and Other Essays,* (New York: The Free Press, 1976); Leon R. Kass, "The New Biology: What Price Relieving Man's Estate?" in *Readings on Ethical and Social Issues in Biomedicine,* ed. Richard W. Wertz, (Englewood Cliffs, N.J.: Prentice-Hall, 1973).
4. "Ethical Dimensions of the Physician-Patient Relationship through History," *Ethics in Medicine,* part 1, eds. Stanley Joel Reiser, Arthur J. Dyck,

and William J. Curran (Cambridge: The Massachusetts Institute of Technology, 1977).

5. Eliot Freidson, *Professional Dominance: The Social Structure of Medical Care,* (New York: Atherton Press, 1970).

6. Jeffrey L. Berlant, *Profession and Monopoly,* (Berkeley: University of California Press, 1975).

7. Richard Harrison Shryock, *The Development of Modern Medicine: An Interpretation of the Social and Scientific Factors Involved* (New York: Hafner Publishing Co., 1969).

8. Abraham Flexner, *Medical Education in the United States and Canada,* A Report to the Carnegie Foundation for the Advancement of Teaching (New York: The Carnegie Foundation, 1910).

9. Bernard J. Stern, *American Medical Practice in the Perspectives of a Century* (New York: The Commonwealth Fund, 1945).

10. Cecil G. Sheps and Conrad Siepp, "The Medical School, Its Products and Its Problems," *The Annals of the American Academy of Political and Social Science* 399 (January 1972), pp. 38–49; James G. Burrow, *AMA Voice of American Medicine* (Baltimore: Johns Hopkins Press, 1963).

11. Elizabeth B. Drew, "The Health Syndicate: Washington's Noble Conspirators," *Atlantic Monthly* 220 (December 1967), pp. 75–81.

12. Stephen P. Strickland, *Politics, Science, and Dread Disease: A Short History of U.S. Medical Research Policy* (Cambridge, Mass.: Harvard University Press, 1972).

13. Kurt Vonnegut, Jr., "Essay for the Wheaton Library," *Wheaton College Alumni Magazine* 40 (Winter 1973), pp. 15–17.

14. Leo Alexander, "Medical Science under Dictatorship," *New England Journal of Medicine* 241 (14 July 1949), pp. 40–47.

15. Editor's note: In point of fact, as every philosopher knows, Hegel was not a utilitarian and would have found both the term and the concept of "rational utility" anathema.

16. L. J. Henderson, "Physician and Patient as a Social System," *New England Journal of Medicine* 213 (2 May 1935), pp. 819–23.

17. Rodney M. Coe, *Sociology of Medicine* (New York: McGraw-Hill, 1970).

18. Personal observation of Raymond S. Duff.

19. Raymond S. Duff and August B. Hollingshead, *Sickness and Society* (New York: Harper and Row, 1968).

20. Gerald Leach, *The Biocrats, Ethics and the New Medicine,* rev. ed. (England: Penguin Books, 1970).

21. L. J. Henderson, "The Practice of Medicine as Applied Sociology," *Transactions of the Association of American Physicians* 51 (1936), pp. 8–22.

22. G. Canby Robinson, *The Patient as a Person: A Study of the Social Aspects of Illness* (New York: The Commonwealth Fund, 1939).

23. Duff and Hollingshead, *Sickness and Society.*

24. Robert C. Derbyshire, "Medical Ethics and Discipline," *Journal of the American Medical Association* 228 (1 April 1974), pp. 59–62.

25. Rosemary Stevens, *American Medicine and the Public Interest* (New Haven, Conn.: Yale University Press, 1971); Leonard Tushnet, *The Medicine Men: The Myth of Quality Medical Care in America Today* (New York: St. Martin's Press, 1971).
26. Stewart Alsop, *Stay of Execution* (Philadelphia: J. B. Lippincott Co., 1973).
27. Eliot Freidson, *Profession of Medicine: A Study of the Sociology of Applied Knowledge* (New York: Dodd, Mead, 1970).
28. Philip Pinkerton, "Parental Acceptance of the Handicapped Child," *Developmental Medicine and Child Neurology* 12 (April 1970), pp. 207–12.
29. "The Birth of an Abnormal Child: Telling the Parents," *The Lancet* (13 November 1971), pp. 1075–77.
30. H. Waitzkin and J. K. Stoeckle, "The Communication of Information about Illness: Clinical, Sociological and Methodological Considerations," *Advances in Psychosomatic Medicine* 8 (1972), pp. 180–215.
31. Stephen J. Miller, *Prescription for Leadership: Training for the Medical Elite* (Chicago: Aldine Publishing Company, 1970).
32. Robinson, *Patient as a Person.*
33. Duff and Hollingshead, *Sickness and Society.*
34. Duncan W. Clark and Brian MacMahon, eds., *Preventive Medicine* (Boston: Little, Brown, 1967).
35. Orville G. Brim, Jr. et al., *The Dying Patient* (New York: Russell Sage Foundation, 1970).
36. Harold Willard and Stanislav V. Kasl, *Continuing Care in a Community Hospital* (Cambridge, Mass.: Harvard University Press, 1972).
37. Carleton B. Chapman, "The Flexner Report by Abraham Flexner," *Daedalus* 103 (Winter 1974), pp. 105–117.
38. Thomas W. Furlow, Jr., "A Matter of Life and Death," *The Pharos* (July 1973), pp. 84–90; Daniel C. Maguire, "Death by Chance, Death by Choice," *Atlantic Monthly* 233 (January 1974), pp. 57–65; idem, "Death, Legal and Illegal," *Atlantic Monthly* 233 (February 1974), pp. 72–85.
39. David W. Meyers, *The Human Body and the Law* (Chicago: Aldine Publishing Company, 1970).
40. Duff and Hollingshead, *Sickness and Society.*
41. John Lorber, "Selective Treatment of Myelomeningocele: To Treat or not to Treat," *Pediatrics* 53 3 (March 1974), pp. 307–8; John M. Freeman, "The Short-Sighted Treatment of Myelomeningocele: A Long-Term Case Report," *Pediatrics* 53 3 (March 1974), pp. 311–13.
42. Barbara and John Ehrenreich, *The American Health Empire: Power, Profits, and Politics* (New York: Vintage Books, 1971).
43. Wolf W. Zuelzer, "Medicine and Ethics: Part III," *News and Comment,* American Academy of Pediatrics 25 (March 1974), pp. 10–12.
44. H. Feifel, "Perception of Death," *Annals of New York Academy of Sciences,* vol. 164, art. 3 (19 December 1969), pp. 669–77.
45. Duff and Hollingshead, *Sickness and Society;* Raymond S. Duff and

A.G.M. Campbell, "Moral and Ethical Dilemmas in a Special Care Nursery," *New England Journal of Medicine* 289 (25 October 1974), pp. 890–94.

46. Fox, "Purposes of Medicine."

47. Duff and Hollingshead, *Sickness and Society.*

48. Paul B. Beeson, noting the English experience, made some suggestions along the same line. See "Some Good Features of the British National Health Service," *Journal of Medical Education* 49 (January 1974), pp. 43–49.

49. D. M. Forrest, "Modern Trends in the Treatment of Spina Bifida: Early Closure in Spina Bifida, Results and Problems," *Proceedings of the Royal Society of Medicine* 60 (April 1967), pp. 763–67.

50. Private communication.

51. Meeting of the Connecticut League for Nursing, Monhegan College, Norwich, Conn. 27 March 1974.

52. State Conference on "Issues of Life and Death," Pro-Life Council of Connecticut, Albertus Magnus College, New Haven, Conn. 30 March 1974.

53. Odin W. Anderson and Paul B. Sheatsley, "Hospital Use: A Survey of Patient and Physician Decisions," *Research Series 24* (Center for Health Administration Studies, 1967).

54. Gillian M. Hunt, "Implications of the Treatment of Myelomeningocele for the Child and his Family," *The Lancet* (8 December 1973), pp. 1308–10.

55. Paul Ramsey, *The Patient as a Person* (New Haven: Yale University Press, 1970). Ramsey believes in what he calls *only* caring for the dying. See pp. 113–44.

56. Joseph Fletcher, *Morals and Medicine* (Boston: Beacon Press, 1960). Fletcher defends the concept of euthanasia.

57. Daniel C. Maguire, *Death By Choice* (New York: Doubleday, 1974). Maguire defends the right to choose.

58. John Ladd, "Morality and the Ideal of Rationality in Formal Organization," *The Monist,* 54 (LaSalle, Ill.: Open Court Publishing Co. 1970).

59. Jay Katz, *Experimentation with Human Beings* (New York: Russell Sage Foundation, 1972).

60. Robert M. Veatch, "Models for Ethical Medicine in a Revolutionary Age: What Physician-Patient Roles Foster the Most Ethical Relationship?" *The Hastings Center Report* 2 (June 1972), pp. 5–11.

61. Pope Pius XII, "The Moral Limits of Medical Research and Treatment," *Proceedings of the First International Congress of Neuropathology, 1952,* pp. 713–25.

62. R. S. Morison, "Death: Process or Event?" *Science* 173 (20 August 1971), pp. 694–702.

63. We acknowledge with appreciation and thanks the editorial assistance of Mrs. Janet Turk and Miss Cathi Carter.

Index

R 726
E 775

174.24
~~LAD~~

Ladd, John ed.
DATE DUE
Life and Death
Ethical Issues Relating to /

DATE DUE			
APR 1 7 1980			
MAY 5 1980			
FEB 1 7 1981			
MAR 2 3 1981			
APR 3 0 1981			
APR 2 8 1982			
MAY 1 0 1982			